Winner of the Jules and Frances Landry Award for 2008

SOUTHERN LITERARY STUDIES

Fred Hobson, Series Editor

CALLS *and* RESPONSES

THE AMERICAN NOVEL OF SLAVERY SINCE *Gone with the Wind*

TIM A. RYAN

Louisiana State University Press
Baton Rouge

For three remarkable women,
Dee Anna Phares, Susan Ryan, and Octavia E. Butler

Published by Louisiana State University Press
Copyright © 2008 by Louisiana State University Press
All rights reserved
Manufactured in the United States of America
First printing

Designer: Michelle A. Neustrom
Typeface: Adobe Jenson Pro
Printer and binder: Thomson-Shore, Inc.

Chapter 1 first appeared, in somewhat different form, as "Designs against Tara: Frances Gaither's *The Red Cock Crows* and Other Counternarratives to *Gone with the Wind*," *Mississippi Quarterly* 59 (Winter/Spring 2006), and is reprinted with permission.

Library of Congress Cataloging-in-Publication Data

Ryan, Tim A., 1971–
    Calls and responses : the American novel of slavery since Gone with the wind / Tim A. Ryan.
      p. cm. — (Southern literary studies)
    Includes bibliographical references and index.
    ISBN 978-0-8071-3322-4 (alk. paper)
    1. American fiction—20th century—History and criticism. 2. Slavery in literature. I. Title.
PS374.S58R93 2008
813'.6—dc22
                                                                            2007042885

CONTENTS

APPENDIX

PREFACE

The central argument of this study of American slavery in fiction and history of the last century is that a truly scholarly approach to the subject should seek to transcend basic binary oppositions and divisive barriers, whether these are between disciplines, races, or ideologies. In these pages, I approach individual novels and historical studies as contributions to a complex, developing cultural conversation about American slavery.

Calls and Responses is one such contribution, and it does not merely respond to a long history of discourses about slavery, but is also the result of a lifetime's conversation—a continuing series of instructive, inspiring, and edifying dialogues with teachers, colleagues, friends, students, family, and even talkative strangers. This book owes its existence to the collaborative energies of all of those who have participated in many personal and professional calls and responses with me.

My heartfelt gratitude to all my friends, colleagues, and mentors in the Department of English and the Core Humanities program at the University of Nevada, Reno, for a decade of stimulating intellectual exchange, challenging work, inspiring examples, impeccable collegiality, bighearted support, and trivial gossip. Particularly deserving of mention are Daniel Anderson, Phillip Boardman, Michael Branch, Dennis Cronan, Dennis Dworkin, David Fenimore, Cheryll Glotfelty, Jimmy Guignard, Jen Hill, Paul Knox, Robert Merrill, Esra Mirze, Marc Oxoby, and Patricia Stich. I must also express my gratitude to Cami Allen, Alec Ausbrooks, Jodie Helman, Geri McVeigh, and Rachel Richardson for their sterling administrative support.

Special thanks to Bernard Schopen and Richard Abram, not only for be-ing wonderful teachers but also for providing me the opportunity to guest lecture on American slavery in their Core Humanities 203 classes, and thus to explore a few of the ideas that eventually developed into this project.

Especially honorable mention must go to three particular stars of the UNR firmament. I extend a shamefaced apology to Eric Rasmussen for my incurable Americanist tendencies and my sincerest gratitude for ev-erything he has done for a lowly non-Renaissance man. Scott Casper— at whose legendary Spring 2001 session of History 721 this project really began—gave more than magnanimously of his time and expertise. I have particularly fond memories of long lunches spent discussing *Gone with the Wind* and *The Known World*, and I am extremely eager to read the fruits of Scott's own researches into American slavery, which I know will be remark-able. Above all, I am thankful to Stacy Burton, who steered me unerringly through the many pitfalls of this project and tirelessly devoted hours of her barely existent time to provide incisive critiques of my sloppy drafts.

Beyond the doors of Frandsen Humanities, I hail my wonderful and inspiring longtime friends: Neil Humphries, Peter Mitchell, and Sherone Rogers, and salute three particularly invaluable comrades—Scott Walker, without whom my failing English would have been far from "unpossible," Ellen Penny, for all her support and care, and Christine MacLeod, for luring me into this profession in the first place. Thanks as well to Alan Marshall, John Howard, Kimberly Springer, Janet Floyd, Gail MacLeitch, Shamoon Zamir, James Miller, Stephanie Green, Rosa Torrado, and all who sailed the good ship American Studies at King's College London during my lecture-ship there. Especially warm regards are due my immediate family—to my parents, Sue and Tom Ryan, for all their sustenance and encouragement over the years, and to Garry Ryan, Paula Crawford, and their fine families. I also owe a debt of gratitude to the new members of my kinship group, particularly to the incomparable Johanna Sizemore and to Daniel Doornbos and Gillian Flato for their inexhaustible generosity as well as their photo-graphic expertise.

I am very appreciative of the professionalism of the team at Louisiana State University Press. Executive Editor John Easterly was unwavering in his enthusiasm for this project from day one, while series editor Fred Hob-son and my anonymous outside reader provided wonderfully astute, helpful, and supportive evaluations of the initial manuscript. Sincere thanks as well to LSU Press director MaryKatherine Callaway and to Derik Shelor, freelance copy editor extraordinaire. I also extend grateful thanks to Noel Polk and Laura West at *Mississippi Quarterly* for graciously providing an initial forum for my interpretations of slavery fiction.

Finally, I offer eternal loving gratitude to my most intimate collaborator: a brilliant scholar, loyal friend, astute editor, exhilarating partner, and quite awesome humorist—Dee Anna Phares, who has encouraged, inspired, redeemed, and renewed me. Without her shrewd judgment, unyielding good humor, and invaluable cheerleading, this project would never have been completed.

CALLS *and* RESPONSES

Introduction

CALLS AND RESPONSES

$\mathcal{W}$hen Toni Morrison published what would become her most renowned novel, she was worried that *Beloved*'s depiction of slavery might make it "the least read of all the books I'd written because it is about something that the characters don't want to remember, I don't want to remember, black people don't want to remember, white people won't want to remember" (quoted in Angelo 257). It is certainly true that slavery in America—so utterly at odds with the Founding Fathers' stirring rhetoric of freedom and equality— remains a national shame, an ugly, gaping crack in the mythology of the United States, a troubling subject that it is safer to avoid or, at least, to politely sanitize. Yet it is not only the benefit of hindsight that makes Morrison's trepidation regarding the reception of the novel that would cement her reputation now seem misplaced. After all, the "peculiar institution" has long been a dominant and popular theme in American fiction. Several of the country's most celebrated and widely adored—and, in some cases, thoroughly reviled—literary phenomena have vividly dramatized slavery. *Uncle Tom's Cabin, Gone with the Wind,* and *Roots* are ubiquitous American legends; even people who have never read them know about Eliza's flight across the icy Ohio, or Scarlett O'Hara's determination never to be hungry again, or Kunta Kinte's refusal to give up his cultural heritage. Numerous fictional accounts of slavery have won Pulitzer Prizes, including *Gone with the Wind, The Confessions of Nat Turner, Roots, Beloved* itself, and, more recently, Edward P. Jones's *The Known World.* To alter a phrase that should be familiar to readers of Morrison's work, slavery is the unspeakable thing that is frequently spoken in the American novel. We may indeed not want to remember it, but we cannot seem to evade the stark fact that slavery was as fundamental to the creation of the United States as the Constitution. Nor are we able to forget that the complex race relations we daily negotiate are the institution's enduring legacy. Like Sethe, the protagonist of *Beloved*, we cannot hope to forge a viable future for ourselves unless we face up to and come to terms with the traumas and burdens of the past, however much we would prefer to repress them. Slavery disturbs us profoundly, yet writers and readers alike are nonetheless irresistibly drawn to it, compelled to search for some kind of meaning in its vicious exploitation, senseless cruelty, incomprehensible suffering, and massive hypocrisy. The impossibility of thinking about slavery is matched only by the impossibility of not thinking about it.

This book is a comprehensive chronological study of how American novelists since the 1930s have imagined the institution of slavery and the experiences of those involved in it. It addresses more than a dozen significant texts, from the first major modern fiction about the institution—Margaret Mitchell's *Gone with the Wind* and Arna Bontemps's *Black Thunder* (both 1936)—to the most recent noteworthy novels on the topic—Edward P. Jones's *The Known World* and Valerie Martin's *Property* (both 2003).[1] This is also—in multiple respects—a revisionist study. It complicates existing critical assumptions about American slavery fiction, it insists upon the necessity of interpreting novels about the past directly in relation to specific historical scholarship, and it presents a substantially new narrative about the development of American slavery fiction in the last century.

My purpose in *Calls and Responses* is to conceptualize a variety of discourses about slavery as an ongoing cultural conversation that transcends both racial and disciplinary boundaries. This discursive exchange is akin to the call-and-response style of African American gospel music—a style, of course, that originated in Africa and developed in the United States during slavery. As Craig Werner describes it, "At its best, the gospel impulse helps people experience themselves *in relation to* rather than *on their own*" (28). The object of this study is to make visible the relations between the many cultural discourses about American slavery. I show how African American writers do not simply resist or present alternatives to white-authored versions of slavery but how they enter into dynamic dialogue with them, and, equally, how novelists of all races engage actively with existing historiographical debates. In sum, *Calls and Responses* emphasizes intertextuality, interdisciplinarity, and interracial exchange.

I argue that slavery novels do not challenge some nebulous discursive hegemony but are, in fact, engaged in constructive and measured dialogue with specific works of history and fiction. I advocate reading novels like *Beloved* not in opposition to a monolithic orthodoxy about slavery, but in relation to specific arguments by such diverse historians as U. B. Phillips, Stanley Elkins, and John Blassingame, and in response to particular literary works, from Frederick Douglass's famous narrative through *Gone with the Wind* to *Roots*. *Calls and Responses* does not neglect the works of white writers or approach them only as "false" versions of slavery that novels by black authors exist to correct.[2] I certainly interrogate the ideologies of *Gone with the Wind* and the problematic assumptions about slave psychology that pervade *The Confessions of Nat Turner*, but I also explore more progressive literature by white writers, such as Frances Gaither's long-neglected 1944 melodrama *The Red Cock Crows* and Valerie Martin's recent *Property*.

This study is itself a response to previous scholarly calls. Existing criticism concerning the postmodern historical novel in general and contemporary African American fiction about slavery in particular is primarily celebratory. Scholars have been concerned to illuminate and to valorize recent literature's critique of dominant ideologies as well as to commend its emphasis upon the perspectives and experiences of those whose voices have been traditionally suppressed or neglected in society. The artistic self-assertion of traditionally marginalized groups and individuals in the face of repressive forces and tyrannical discourses comprises one of the most important and salutary cultural developments since World War II, and it is crucial that scholarship continues to acclaim the emergence of alternative voices and visions in historical fiction. In order to highlight this development, however, critics often rely upon a problematic rhetoric that is organized around excessively general and overly simplistic binary oppositions. Existing studies frequently imply—and sometimes even overtly assert—a rigid dichotomy between dissenting fiction and conservative historiography, between the enlightened politics of contemporary culture and the benighted ideologies of traditional literature, between the subversive discourse of the margins and the oppressive discourse of the mainstream, and between the inherent authenticity of black writing and the intrinsic racism of white literature.

In *Calls and Responses*, I move beyond merely celebrating the expression of black voices and experiences in recent fiction about American slavery—or, at the very least, I reconfigure the terms of this celebration. My analysis complicates the common assumption that there is only a stark binary opposition between authentic, contemporary, subversive, black-authored fiction about slavery on one hand, and a traditionalist, monolithic, racist historiography created by whites on the other. Where previous studies tend to define historical discourse as singular, I emphasize its plurality. Where other criticism suggests that contemporary novels reject and transcend established discourses about the past, I show how fiction actively engages with existing historiographical debates. Where certain analyses suggest that there was a dramatic cultural rupture in the 1960s that fundamentally altered the nature of the discourse about slavery, I focus upon significant continuities in representations of the institution over time and attend to the gradual, long-term development of cultural perspectives on the topic. Where some scholars see black and white writers as essentially isolated from and entirely at odds with one another, I draw attention to the potential for productive exchange between them.

Nonetheless, the notion that writers of the last few decades have critiqued and presented compelling counternarratives to a long-lived and oppressive historical hegemony is an important one. Angelyn Mitchell—in her astute analysis of recent slavery novels by African American women, *The Freedom to Remember*—recalls her school days in a segregated southern town, where white patriarchy dominated the culture in general and the curriculum in particular. "Where," she wonders, "were the voices of my ancestors?" Mitchell's book explores how contemporary black women's fiction compensates for the absence of such voices by reimagining slavery from an African American and female perspective (xi, 7). In his valuable study of the novelistic genre he terms the "Neo-slave narrative," Ashraf Rushdy similarly explores an innovative black-authored discourse about slavery that emerged in the late 1960s as a counternarrative to an enduring and racist "dominant hegemonic discursive formation" in American culture. Rushdy identifies the key texts in this tradition as African American novels that "assume the form, adopt the conventions, and take on the first-person voice of the antebellum slave narrative" (*Neo-slave* 13, 56, 55, 54, 3). Scholarship on postmodern literature is organized around similar assumptions. Brian McHale describes the contemporary, avant-garde historical novel as a revisionist fiction that critiques and reinterprets received ideas, "demystifying or debunking the orthodox version of the past" (90). In her groundbreaking work on "historiographic metafiction," meanwhile, Linda Hutcheon observes that the "unitary, closed, evolutionary narratives" of traditional historiography have given way to new discourses: "we now get the histories (in the plural) of the losers as well as the winners, of the regional (and colonial) as well as the centrist, of the unsung many as well as the much sung few, and I might add, of women as well as men" (*Politics* 66). All of these studies, in other words, explore how contemporary counternarratives—often by women, African Americans, and other traditionally excluded individuals—challenge and present alternatives to a long-dominant white, racist, patriarchal historical metanarrative.[3] Taken as a broad summation of recent literary and cultural developments in general, this is entirely reasonable.

Such an account, however, is ultimately too generalizing to withstand very close examination. The idea that contemporary literature subverts a dominant cultural hegemony assumes the existence of a coherent orthodoxy as a given. History, however, is not—and never has been—a series of agreed-upon facts and dominant master narratives. Instead, it is a network of ongoing debates and continually contested interpretations; in short, there actually has been a long tradition of histories in the plural.

The cultural and historiographical conversation about American slavery, in particular, has always been organized around conflicting opinions and clashing narratives rather than a single predominant metanarrative. American culture of the antebellum era, for example, involved a complex variety of competing discourses about the institution, including the memoirs of escaped slaves (such as Frederick Douglass and Harriet Jacobs), the arguments advanced by advocates of slavery (most famously, George Fitzhugh), white liberal abolitionist sentiment in both fiction and nonfiction (for instance, the writings of Harriet Beecher Stowe and William Lloyd Garrison), the stirring invective of militant African Americans (famously, David Walker's subversive pamphlet), pro-slavery novels (exemplified by the works of William Gilmore Simms and Mary Eastman), and the fiction of African American writers (such as Douglass's *The Heroic Slave* and William Wells

Brown's *Clotel* [both 1853]). Nor did this complicated dialogue about slavery end with emancipation. Discourses about slavery have, as this study shows, remained diverse throughout American history.

At no point has there ever really been a coherent, single master narrative of American slavery. Certainly, some discourses have a greater cultural presence and influence than others, and individuals can indeed be subject to repressive ideologies—something that Angelyn Mitchell's account of her schooling in self-proclaimed "KKK Country" in the 1970s vividly illustrates. During her North Carolina childhood, Mitchell "had few opportunities to see myself or read the stories of people who looked like me and my folk in what I formally learned." The only available literary texts about slavery were *Uncle Tom's Cabin*, *Gone with the Wind*, and the works of William Faulkner. The antebellum South she encountered at school and in literature thus seemed purely a white construction. Only later in life would Mitchell discover the existence of black-authored texts about slavery (x–xi). She and her schoolmates received what was, to all intents and purposes, a hegemonic white discourse about slavery.

A serious theoretical problem occurs, however, when scholars extrapolate from such a situation to imply or even explicitly claim the objective existence of a monolithic, dominant cultural discourse about slavery and race—and the absence of significant alternatives—in the United States before postmodernism, the civil rights movement, and the development of contemporary African American literature. It is precisely because they wish—understandably—to distinguish the qualities of postmodern fiction and the achievements of recent black novelists that critics have tended to understate drastically the degree to which there have always been dissenting historical counternarratives.

In their attempts to clarify what constitutes a postmodernist approach to the past, theorists often have overstated what is distinctive and innovative about the "new skepticism or suspicion about the writing of history" (Hutcheon, *Poetics* 106). In her study of contemporary historical fiction, Amy Elias cites Hayden White's two categories of historical perspective. On one hand, there is the rational impulse of the traditional historian to establish and articulate "the truth" about the past, while, on the other, there is a postmodern approach that acknowledges how essentially unknowable the past is and emphasizes that any historical narrative is an entirely artificial construction. Elias asserts that it this second approach that encourages a more ethically oriented engagement with the horrors of the past (39). Hutcheon, meanwhile, notes that one of the consequences of postmodernism's denaturalizing of history is "a new self-consciousness about the distinction between the brute *events* of the past and the historical *facts* we construct out of them" (*Politics* 57). Yet historians and historical novelists have always understood that textual "facts" are distinct from reality itself. Indeed, if historians and novelists had ever approached the past as if there were no significant difference between actual events and the ways in which those events are reconstructed and assigned meaning in discourse, then there would have been little need to reinterpret history or debate its meanings—which, in fact, has been the fundamental work of historians since Herodotus challenged Homer's discourse about the Trojan War. It is not simply that these two Greek writers disagreed about the *facts* of history. If Helen really had never been present in Troy, as Herodotus argues, then the *meaning* of the Trojan War is entirely different to the meaning constructed about it by the *Iliad*. Herodotus not only challenges Homer's facts but also the romanticism of his discourse about the war. He mobilizes a radically new kind of discourse—scholarly, skeptical, empiricist— against Homer's heroic, imaginative, poetic discourse. There is, in other words, an ideological as well as a factual dimension to Herodotus's disagreement with Homer. The assumption that historians and historical novelists prior to postmodernism simply purported to "tell the truth about the past as an end in itself" neglects the clear political agendas and the ideological self-consciousness that have routinely characterized works of history and fiction (White quoted in Elias 39).

Nineteenth-century novelists who dramatized American slavery were quite aware of the ideological biases inherent in any historical narrative. Take, for example, Harriet Beecher Stowe's largely forgotten second novel, *Dred: A Tale of the Great Dismal Swamp* (1856), the story of a militant fugitive slave, based loosely upon Nat Turner. Precisely because of its abolitionist agenda, Stowe's text often approaches history not as a series of transparent facts, but as a collection of contesting discourses. Stowe's book roundly criticizes the "considerable naïveté" of those historians who had written about Denmark Vesey, a former slave who conspired to lead a rebellion in Charleston in 1822. Indeed, the novel quotes at length a Charleston magistrate's narrative of the Vesey uprising only to provide a sharply contrasting version of its own. *Dred* underlines that the "facts" of history are determined by those who are placed in a position to write them, and it suggests that Vesey's "history is just what George Washington's would have been" had the British crushed the American Revolution. Another episode in the novel dramatizes how a single evangelical camp meeting has entirely different meanings for different people. At one point, the narrator even muses, "One might almost imagine that there were no such thing as absolute truth" (269–73, 544, 322–24, 555). All of this is not so far away from the kind of postmodern historical novels which, Hutcheon says, "juxtapose what we think we know of the past . . . with an alternate representation that foregrounds the postmodern epistemological questioning of the nature of historical knowledge. What 'facts' make it into history? And *whose* facts?" (*Politics* 71). While not metafictional in formal terms, the philosophy of Stowe's abolitionist fiction is equally postmodern in Elias's sense of the term: *Uncle Tom's Cabin* and *Dred* are not concerned simply with "the truth about the past as an end in itself," but rewrite American history with the aim of prompting people "to aspire to freedom and dignity through an active response" to the "monstrous spectacle" of history (Elias 39). Stowe, furthermore, is far from being the only nineteenth-century American novelist who displayed such a conscious understanding of history as ideologically inflected discourse. One of her bitterest critics, the novelist William Gilmore Simms, claimed that his fictional portraits of an idealized plantation South "aim at something more than the story. I am really . . . revising history" (quoted in Van Deburg 174n).

Just as critics have overemphasized what is unique about the postmodern historical perspective, scholars who are concerned to celebrate contemporary African American reinterpretations and dramatizations of history have often implied that such works are largely unprecedented. Rushdy, for example, suggests that before the emergence of black writing in the 1960s, "American historians had dealt with the slaves as if they were solely property" (*Neo-slave* 26). Such a generalization neglects the broad variety of discourses and developments within slavery historiography, and it dismisses the achievements of numerous African American historians who were active between the 1860s and 1960s. Rushdy fleetingly acknowledges "a brief flurry of work produced by the Old Left in the thirties" that anticipated the concerns of the new black discourse about slavery in the late sixties, but he relegates a lengthy litany of radical 1930s historiography to his footnotes and his study ignores fiction written about slavery in that decade altogether (*Neo-slave* 32). Of course, with Toni Morrison now rightly established as a literary icon and African American Studies programs flourishing in universities, one might say that what is unprecedented about the new wave of black counternarratives is its cultural impact. Such an argument, however, still sorely undervalues the achievements of previous generations of black writers, artists, and scholars. Are the writings of African Americans since the 1960s inherently more significant than those of Martin Delany, the activist, historian, and novelist of the 1850s, or of Carter Woodson, who created the Association for the Study of Negro Life and History in 1915 and who founded the *Journal of Negro History* a year later? Indeed, did not the stories of Charles Chesnutt, the histories of William Wells Brown, the novels of Frances E. W. Harper, and, of course, W. E. B. Du Bois's *The Souls of Black Folk* constitute a subversive and important "new discursive formation" about slavery and race more than a century ago? Rushdy's assertion that "African American fiction in general has undergone a virtual renaissance since the sixties" also rather blithely dismisses a powerful body of black writing produced between 1945 and 1968—exemplified by the works of Ralph Ellison, James Baldwin, Richard Wright, Chester Himes, and Ann Petry—that did as much to lay the groundwork for subsequent black literature as any of the factors that Rushdy identifies: the "shift from the civil rights to the Black Power movement, the evolution from consensus to New Left social history in the historiography of slavery, and the development of a Black Power intellectual presence in the dialogue over Styron's *Confessions of Nat Turner*" (*Neo-slave* 55, 3, 4–5).

Existing scholarship also tends to suggest that an individual's ideas about slavery are fundamentally determined by his or her race, and that there is an immense and inevitable chasm between black and white perspectives on the subject. In his comprehensive survey of the portrayal of the institution in American culture, William Van Deburg asserts that for two centuries black discourses about slavery have remained entirely different to (predominantly racist) white ones (159, 109). While this may be accurate as a broad generalization, Van Deburg's own material consistently implies a more complex and interesting picture of the depiction of slavery and race in American culture than such a rigid racial binary opposition can contain. Van Deburg acknowledges, for example, that white historians during Reconstruction "contradicted traditional American images of enslaved blacks" in their work on the Underground Railroad. Similarly, he praises two white novelists in that era, J. T. Trowbridge and Epes Sargent, whose progressive works vividly portrayed black characters to be the equal of any Anglo-Saxon. Conversely, he concedes that several African American poets and black minstrel troupes produced the most appallingly stereotypical images of black people in that period (76, 90–91, 98, 112).[4] He is similarly critical of one of the most prominent black spokesmen of the post–Civil War era, Booker T. Washington, who dismissed Nat Turner, the famous slave-rebel, as "a dreamer . . . a fanatic" (81). Washington's attitude toward the legendary slave rebel certainly contrasts dramatically with the celebratory account of Nat Turner published by the white abolitionist Thomas Wentworth Higginson.[5] Obviously a writer's subject-position is significant: many white-authored accounts of slavery have been at best dubious and at worst utterly racist, and African American writers have tended to produce the most astute and compelling portraits of slavery. Nonetheless, it is too simplistic and essentialist to assert that an individual's attitudes toward slavery are entirely dependent upon his or her racial identity.

An equally problematic but similarly common assumption is that because contemporary fiction about the past is critical and dissenting, then the discourse of history to which it responds must—logically—be conservative and repressive. I have quoted scholars who define history as the "orthodox version of the past" and as a "dominant hegemonic discursive formation." This sweepingly simplistic assumption—that historical discourse about slavery espouses a single, coherent, unchanging, monolithic ideology—has become unfortunately commonplace in the critical literature on recent African American fiction concerning slavery.

To take but one example, numerous scholarly analyses of Sherley Anne Williams's novel *Dessa Rose* often lapse into abstractly grandiose claims about the book's rejection of and resistance to historical discourse. Indeed, Adam McKible even goes so far as to suggest that "history is the Master narrative a dominant culture tells itself," and that subversive novels such as *Dessa Rose* "shatter the confines of hegemonic historiography" (224, 234). Another scholar argues that Williams's novel prevents us from continuing to approach history "from a monologic standpoint," neglecting to consider that the sheer variety and multiplicity of existing historical (and fictional) discourses already work against such monologism (King 359). Similarly, Andrée-Anne Kekeh sees *Dessa Rose* as "a revisionist comment on slave historiography," as if the historiography of slavery were not eternally in the process of revising itself. To Kekeh's credit, however, she does tentatively question whether the character of Dessa might be seen as "the modern historiographer revising and subverting the institutional historical constructs?" (220, 226). While astutely suggesting that Williams may be pursuing an identical project to contemporary historians rather than challenging them, Kekeh's question is nonetheless still mired in the assumption that it is only recently that historians have begun to challenge entrenched, monolithic versions of the past. The fact is that in her novel's "Author's Note," Williams actually identifies a forty-year-old historical study as her chief reference source. Furthermore, Kekeh still suggests that *Dessa Rose's* racist villain is "the embodiment of law, history, and intellectual discourse" (221). Here, once more, is the assumption that history has traditionally spoken with a single voice—one that is authoritarian and racist.

In its concern to celebrate the political and ideological dimensions of contemporary African American historical fiction, scholarship even has a tendency to blur all distinctions between twentieth-century historiography about slavery and the racist historical discourse created by the antebellum white South. When McKible identifies *Dessa Rose's* racist slave-hunting villain as the representative of "the Master narrative of antebellum slavery," or asserts that Sethe, in Toni Morrison's *Beloved*, "shatters the truth value of Schoolteacher's method of historiography," he is ostensibly arguing only that Williams and Morrison offer their narratives in opposition to those constructed by antebellum slaveholders (223, 232). Novels like *Beloved* and *Dessa Rose* are, however, of rather limited interest if they are to be interpreted simply as challenging the discourses of long-dead proponents of an institution that was abolished 150 years ago. Such works are better illuminated by a critical approach that addresses their dual historical contexts: the nineteenth-century slavery that they dramatize and the late twentieth-century culture in which they were written. McKible conflates these separate dimensions when, by making sweeping generalizations about "dominant historiography," he implies that the "Master narrative of antebellum slavery" is essentially the same today as it was in 1850. When he approvingly cites, for example, Walter Benjamin's notion that "the historical account given the greatest credence always belongs to the ruling culture," he effectively erases any sense of difference between the attitudes of antebellum slaveholders and the ideas of historians in the twentieth century (223, 224). In celebrating the achievements of *Dessa Rose*, McKible implies that it speaks back to a vast and monolithic discourse of racism that spans over a century. In short, politically concerned scholars like McKible often reduce rich and complex books like *Dessa Rose* to the level of simple protest fiction because their primary aim is to establish, endorse, and celebrate the political credentials of contemporary historical fiction about slavery.

I should add that other critics are scathing about recent novels of American slavery precisely because they see them *only* as didactic protest fiction in which literary complexity is subsumed to a simplistic ideological agenda. In the 1995 introduction to his metaphysical novel about the institution, *Oxherding Tale* (1982), Charles Johnson complains that he was frequently discouraged from pursuing a project that bore "no resemblance whatsoever to other Negro books—'protest novels' in particular—presently being ballyhooed and blessed with awards and attention." He refers dismissively to "the literature of gender and racial victimization, which was beginning to ossify by the mid-1980s," and he eagerly anticipates a backlash against "political ideology in black fiction" (ix, xix). While he is deliberately vague about which black authors he considers guilty of writing mere "protest novels" (he mentions only Alice Walker by name), one can reasonably assume— especially given that *Oxherding Tale* deals with slavery—that Johnson has the likes of Sherley Anne Williams and Toni Morrison in mind. In short, despite his negative evaluation of them, Johnson appears to read such novels as *Dessa Rose* and *Beloved* in precisely the same terms as McKible—as didactic protest books.

It is, however, extremely limited and limiting to approach such texts as radical acts of resistance to a static discursive hegemony. Even a very brief survey of the historiography of American slavery over the last hundred years demonstrates the existence of numerous arguments and significant discursive shifts—thoroughly problematizing the idea that there is, or ever has been, a monolithic "master narrative" of American slavery.[6] Historians' ideas about slavery have changed significantly from generation to generation. Furthermore, while it is certainly true that racist apologists for slavery were often the most prominent cultural voices until at least the 1950s, there has never been a hegemonic consensus of opinion on the topic at any time. Since *Calls and Responses* is fundamentally concerned with the ways in which novelists engage in debate with slavery historiography, it is worth surveying the field in some detail.

The 1890s—the decade when a fully fledged academic discourse about American history first emerged—saw a conflict between James Ford Rhodes's northern neo-abolitionist interpretation of slavery and future president Woodrow Wilson's white southern idealization of the institution.[7] However, while these historians disagreed drastically about the nature of slavery, both assumed the innate biological inferiority of nonwhites. Wilson's work, for example, claims that slavery did "more for the negro in two hundred and fifty years than African freedom had done since the building of the pyramids," and that American slaves resided in comfortable slave quarters and rarely experienced harsh treatment (quoted in Smith 19–20). Rhodes, meanwhile, presents the institution of slavery as having been unremittingly harsh but simultaneously depicts African Americans as genetically inferior to whites.[8]

As the century turned, the white southern school of history triumphed with the rise of Georgia-born Ulrich B. Phillips, who thoroughly overturned the notion that slavery was brutal and exploitative. Phillips's picture of a kindly, paternalist institution devoted to the welfare of its subjects pervaded American culture for several decades.[9] It was not, however, immune from concerted criticism. In the early twentieth century, black and white historians—including W. E. B. Du Bois, Carter G. Woodson, and Frederic Bancroft—argued against Phillips's methodology, conclusions, and overt racism. This is to say nothing of the pioneer black historians of the late nineteenth century, such as George Washington Williams and William Wells Brown, who challenged the white supremacist assumptions of Rhodes and Wilson and instead emphasized the vibrant activism of slave cultures and communities.[10] Even among these African American historians, however, there was never a clear consensus of opinion. As John David Smith notes, "black thought regarding slavery was not a monolith, but rather a maze of inconsistencies and contradictions" (70). Opposition to Phillips culminated in the 1930s and 1940s, when several studies—including Herbert Aptheker's influential *American Negro Slave Revolts* (1943)—demolished the idea that slaves were content and docile, and emphasized instead the courageous and militant resistance of enslaved Americans.[11] Even as Phillips's attitudes were decisively overturned in the academy, however, the white southern viewpoint continued to infuse the larger culture's view of slavery via conservative school textbooks and *Gone with the Wind* (as both book and film).[12]

After World War II, both black and white historians—such as Kenneth Stampp and John Hope Franklin—followed the lead set by their New Deal predecessors and continued to emphasize the brutality of slavery and black resistance to it.[13] In addition, these historians tentatively explored slave communities and cultures. Stanley Elkins countered this approach in his landmark study, *Slavery: A Problem in American Institutional and Intellectual Life* (1959). Elkins was no apologist for slavery. Indeed, he took the view that slavery was cruelly oppressive to a new extreme by comparing the peculiar institution to the death camps of the Nazi Holocaust. Elkins also repudiated the racist assumption that people of color are intrinsically inferior to whites. Yet he still fully accepted the white antebellum southern stereotype of the average slave as "Sambo"—"docile but irresponsible, loyal but lazy, humble but chronically given to lying and stealing" (*Slavery* 82)—and he sought a new explanation for the existence of this personality type. Elkins argued that Sambo characteristics resulted from the oppressive nature of slavery itself: that the pervasive physical and psychological authority of the planter reduced slaves to childlike passivity. His controversial theories stimulated significant developments in historiographical discourse about slavery. Elkins's peers built upon his innovative use of psychological theory, sociological analogy, and his pioneering comparisons of slavery in the United States with manifestations of the institution elsewhere in the Americas. Yet the primary goal of these historians—whose studies began to emerge in the 1970s—was to refute and overturn Elkins's claims about the psychologies of enslaved Americans. They argued that instead of devolving into childlike Sambos, the people who were brought in chains from Africa and their descendants actually managed to forge vital, active, and often resistant cultures and communities within American slavery, even if they sometimes chose to wear masks of submissiveness before their white masters.[14]

Historians of the last thirty years have continued to develop this vivid picture of slave life, while also emphasizing significant variations and diversity within American slavery in different regions and at different times.[15] In doing so, they have illuminated previously neglected aspects of the subject, such as the slave market, family structure and relations in slavery, the experiences of both enslaved women and plantation mistresses, and the curious phenomenon of black slaveholders, as well as demonstrating a renewed interest in slave resistance and rebellion.[16] This is not to suggest, however, that historians are now largely in agreement about slavery. A whole series of arguments about such topics as the nature of the slave community, the extent of slave resistance, and the profitability of slavery continue to rage. Neither is the traditional white southern view of slavery entirely moribund—at least, not in the pages of popular history for the general reader. In *Myths and Realities of American Slavery* (2002), John C. Perry—while ostensibly eschewing Phillips's racism—makes the familiar arguments that the "vast majority" of slaves were well fed, that they worked similar hours to southern whites and received better medical care, that there were few overseers in the South, and that slave families were rarely divided by sale (112, 120, 151, 123, 143).

How can one identify an "orthodox version of the past" among such a tangled web of competing discourses? How can any work of fiction "shatter the confines of hegemonic historiography" when historical studies are so ideologically diverse? It is true that, very broadly speaking, there has been a discursive hegemony of sorts in America—that white-authored and often racist accounts of slavery were culturally prevalent before the 1960s. It is also the case that the last quarter-century has witnessed a massive outpouring of narratives that voice resistance to repressive ideologies. When, however, it comes to nuanced literary criticism, we require a more sophisticated theoretical basis than a series of simplistically generalizing binary oppositions between dissenting post-1960s texts and complicit pre-1960s texts, between subversive fictional and hegemonic historical narratives, and between racist white and authentic black perspectives on slavery.

This study conceives the development of slavery fiction—in recent decades, especially—as an ongoing quest for solutions to fundamental problems involved in representing and dramatizing the institution. The first such problem that writers encounter is how one can reasonably fictionalize something as incomprehensibly horrific as slavery without sensationalizing, trivializing, or neutralizing its impact. The second challenge is the more general question of how to address and portray history in fiction. Should one seek to present historical "truth," or should one approach history primarily as a discursive field? In contrast to other scholars, I do not suggest that either the development of postmodernism or the emergence of an African American fiction about slavery has been, in and of itself, sufficient to resolve the complexities of depicting the subject. I argue instead that the most significant innovation in American fiction has been a careful negotiation between traditional and postmodern approaches to history—between the idea of history as past reality and the notion of history as a series of discursive conventions.

Calls and Responses begins by demonstrating that complex dialogue between historical and fictional texts is not exclusive to the age of postmodernism through an exploration of how novelists and historians in the 1930s and 1940s engaged in debate over the class dimensions of slavery. Published at a moment when liberal historians were challenging the white southern viewpoint, Margaret Mitchell's *Gone with the Wind* romanticizes slavery, but also cleverly submerges its racist ideology by constructing slavery as a system organized not by race, but along class lines. I read Herbert Aptheker's study, *American Negro Slave Revolts*, as a Marxist critique of the class-oriented rhetoric and argument of *Gone with the Wind*. I also analyze two novels about slave rebellions published in this era—*Black Thunder*, by the African American leftist Arna Bontemps, and *The Red Cock Crows* by the white Mississippian Frances Gaither. Both texts seem to have the potential to serve as powerful counternarratives to *Gone with the Wind*, but while they challenge that book's racist assumptions about enslaved African Americans, their critiques founder because they fail to engage sufficiently with the class politics that Mitchell's book mobilizes so skillfully.

Succeeding chapters focus upon the development of slavery fiction since World War II, commencing with a consideration of a longstanding argument about slavery and slave psychologies in both fiction and history. One interpretation, which culminated in Stanley Elkins's study, asserts that the majority of slaves were passive and quiescent, with only unusual individuals asserting themselves and resisting the institution. Consequently, the exceptional slave—as fugitive or rebel—is a figure who recurs throughout history and fiction concerned with slavery. An opposing argument suggests instead that diverse slave subjectivities sprang from autonomous slave communities and active slave cultures. While William Styron's *The Confessions of Nat Turner* (1967) is routinely castigated as a racist dramatization of the argument that enslaved African Americans were docile and childlike, close examination actually reveals that its portrayal of slave subjectivities shares as much in common with the antebellum autobiography of that great African American Frederick Douglass as it does with Elkins's much denigrated theories. I also advocate reinterpreting Styron's novel in relation to other relevant texts and contexts—such as the much-neglected body of slavery fiction by both black and white writers published in the twenty-five years after World War II, a cultural conversation to which *The Confessions of Nat Turner* makes a valuable and productive contribution. Ultimately, however, this comparative analysis reveals the profound limitations of Styron's view of slave psychologies. There are subtle but utterly crucial distinctions between Douglass's and Styron's portrayals of slave identities. Furthermore, on those occasions when *The Confessions of Nat Turner* evades the inadequacies of the Elkins thesis, it is curiously reminiscent of *Gone with the Wind*. Several other novels published before the 1970s—including Margaret Walker's *Jubilee* (1966) and, more surprisingly, Kyle Onstott's sensationalist *Mandingo* (1957)—contain much more astute and credible portraits of African Americans under slavery than Styron's text.

The third chapter pursues these developments further in an analysis of how black novelists of the 1970s struggled to develop meaningful strategies for fictionalizing the institution of slavery and for engaging with Elkins's theories about slave personality. Ishmael Reed's formally innovative *Flight to Canada* (1976) satirizes and dismantles traditional literary conventions for representing slavery, and posits radical alternatives. In the process, however, Reed's novel necessarily sidesteps the question of actual slave subjectivities and the probable conditions of the institution in reality. Conversely, Alex Haley's *Roots* (1976) institutes what promises to be an enlightening critical dialogue with Elkins's theories, by involving a protagonist who attempts to resist the crippling psychological impact of slavery. Unfortunately, the conventions of the traditional literary genres that Haley has selected for his tale—the plantation epic and the family saga—divert *Roots* from resolving its dialogue with Elkins. In contrast, Octavia Butler's *Kindred* (1979) is a compelling model for the contemporary novel of slavery. Butler's text persuasively explores slavery both as discursive field and historical actuality, and it is simultaneously self-consciously metafictional and realistically authentic. *Kindred* engages in dialogue with both historical and fictional discourses about slavery—for example, by dramatizing and critiquing the Elkins thesis, and by replacing the masculinism of many black novels about slavery with an emphasis upon the experiences of African American women. I also argue that *Kindred* set the tone for much subsequent fiction about slavery, and I show how Toni Morrison's *Beloved* employs and modifies several of the strategies and ideas pioneered by Butler.

Chapter 4 has two central subjects. First, it explores the portrayal of interracial relationships between women in recent slavery novels and historiography. Second, it analyzes particular tensions that can emerge as a consequence of addressing slavery as historical reality and discursive tradition simultaneously in fiction. Sherley Anne Williams's *Dessa Rose* imagines an interracial alliance between women during slavery, while Valerie Martin's recent *Property* suggests that such a friendship between a black female slave and a white slaveholding woman in the antebellum South would have been quite impossible. Read carefully, *Dessa Rose*—like *Flight to Canada*—is actually more concerned with revising the discursive conventions for representing slavery in fiction than with making a persuasive argument about the institution's reality. The text's relative formal realism and its use of historical sources, however, tempt the reader to misinterpret *Dessa Rose* as a book about what slavery really might have been like. Conversely, *Property* presents itself as a carefully researched argument about the historical nature of slavery and represses its very postmodern emphasis upon modes of representation. My interpretation asserts that the novel's historical argument is partly advanced through an implicit intertextual debate with literary works such as *Dessa Rose* and Kate Chopin's *The Awakening*. Ultimately, *Property* makes a persuasive argument about the reality of slavery, but in the process also replicates a number of longstanding and rather simplistic literary stereotypes of white women slaveholders. As the first significant novel about slavery by a white writer in thirty years, however, *Property* initiates a new conversation between white and African American writers of slavery fiction.

The study concludes with an examination of Edward P. Jones's acclaimed novel about black slaveholders, *The Known World*, the latest in a series of novels since *Kindred* that strikes a balance between addressing historiographical questions about the reality of slavery and approaching slavery as a tradition of discursive conventions. Jones's text explores slavery as a discursive field by questioning the reliability of written histories and documentary sources, by dismantling traditional binary oppositions—such as slave/free and black/white—and by complicating the longstanding convention of presenting lower-class southern whites as vicious racists in fiction. Simultaneously, *The Known World* also engages with contemporary historiographical debates and reflects the overriding impulse of historiography since the 1970s to avoid depicting slavery as a monolith. Just like recent historical studies, Jones's novel seeks to examine specific manifestations and variations of slavery as a way of testing the larger claims made about the institution as a whole by the previous generation of historians and writers.

In sum, *Calls and Responses* shows that discourses about American slavery are—and have always been—defined by multiplicity rather than singularity, by complex dialogue between specific texts rather than simple opposition between racism and authenticity, by continuity rather than rupture, and by connections rather than disjunctions.

Designs against Tara

REPRESENTING SLAVERY IN AMERICAN CULTURE, 1936–1944

In 2001, Alice Randall's *The Wind Done Gone*—a parodic rejoinder to
Margaret Mitchell's perennially popular 1936 melodrama, *Gone with the
Wind*—reignited cultural debates about representations of race and slavery
in American fiction, as well as legal controversies about the acceptable limits of postmodern intertextuality. Some critics made grandiose claims for
The Wind Done Gone, one asserting that "Randall has achieved what some
might have deemed impossible: She has burst the bubble of a cherished
American myth, exposing the inherent racism and injustice of a chunk of
Americana that has loomed over the landscape of our popular fiction for
65 years" (Goss 1). The trust that owns the copyright to *Gone with the Wind*
was rather less impressed, however, and promptly brought suit against
Randall for unauthorized use of Mitchell's creations.[1] At the hearing, Judge
Charles A. Pannell Jr. refused to consider debates about unequal access to
historical discourse. "The question before the court," he proclaimed, "is not
who gets to write history, but rather whether Ms. Randall can permeate
most of her new critical work with the copyrighted characters, plot, and
scenes from *Gone with the Wind*" (quoted in Miller 1).

Both the legal wrangling and the critical praise for Randall's puncturing
of racist myths suggest that *The Wind Done Gone* stages an innovative challenge to a once-hegemonic discourse about slavery and race in American
culture. Conventional wisdom suggests that such counternarratives to the
official historical record are very much a product of contemporary culture
and postmodernism. According to such a view, there is little that is subver-

sive in the traditional historical novel. This critical orthodoxy has diverted literary scholars from a full appreciation and proper examination of dissenting historical counternarratives produced by novelists in the first half of the twentieth century.

In his comprehensive study, *Slavery and Race in American Popular Culture*, William Van Deburg provides a sharp critique of *Gone with the Wind* as both book and film, but he refers only in passing to a powerful and subversive novel about slavery by an African American writer published the very same year as Mitchell's opus—Arna Bontemps's *Black Thunder*, a dramatic recreation of the Richmond slave rebellion of 1800. Van Deburg also glosses over a striking fictional portrayal of slavery and insurrection produced by a white writer in this era: he buries in his footnotes a single passing reference to Frances Gaither's impressive tale of an 1835 slave revolution in Mississippi, *The Red Cock Crows* (1944) (104–6, 125–27, 206). While largely neglected by literary scholarship, *Black Thunder* and *The Red Cock Crows* vividly demonstrate that both black and white writers in the 1930s and 1940s challenged romanticized representations of slavery and racist constructions of slave psychologies long before the emergence of postmodernism or the modern civil rights movement.[2]

Both *Black Thunder* and *The Red Cock Crows* oppose the unashamedly white southern view of slavery presented in such works of history as Ulrich B. Phillips's *American Negro Slavery* (1918) and later popularized by Mitchell's novel. Contrary to his late-nineteenth-century New England predecessors and his African American contemporaries in the discipline of history, Phillips argues that American slaves were "by racial quality submissive rather than defiant, light-hearted instead of gloomy, amiable and ingratiating instead of sullen, and whose very defects invited paternalism rather than repression." For Phillips, the authority of the slaveholder was "benevolent in intent and on the whole beneficial in effect," and relations between masters and slaves "on both sides were felt to be based on pleasurable responsibility" (341–42, 328, 329). The fictions of Bontemps and Gaither dispute that slavery was such a harmonious system and that enslaved African Americans were loyal and content. Instead, their novels present slave populations that actively desire freedom and whose members are prepared to take daring and revolutionary steps to achieve it.

If *Black Thunder* and *The Red Cock Crows* persuasively critique the Phillips view of slavery, they are, unfortunately, insufficient as counternarratives to his famous literary successor. *Gone with the Wind*'s construction of slavery is rather more complex than the traditional white southern paternalist racism of Phillips's historical study. Bontemps's and Gaither's novels fail to rival the mythic power of *Gone with the Wind* partly because they do not adequately critique Mitchell's depiction of slavery as a system oriented around *class* rather than race. Neither do *Black Thunder* and *The Red Cock Crows* address gender roles and relations within slavery in ways that sufficiently challenge the orthodoxies of Mitchell's portrayal of antebellum southern society. There was an influential shift in slavery historiography in the 1930s and 1940s, which saw the racist platitudes of Phillips supplanted by a leftist interpretation of slavery—epitomized by the vision of militant slave resistance presented in Herbert Aptheker's *American Negro Slave Revolts* (1943). In fiction of this period, however, neither black nor white writers constructed narratives about slavery that constitute a sufficiently radical departure from the world of *Gone with the Wind*.

Conflicting Visions of Slavery and Class in *Gone with the Wind* and *American Negro Slave Revolts*

The popular success of Mitchell's fiction, both as literary bestseller and Hollywood phenomenon, provided widespread legitimization for the traditional white southern view of slavery—just as it was becoming anachronistic in historiography. *Gone with the Wind* encapsulates the moonlight-and-magnolias image of the antebellum South in its idyllic portrait of life on the Tara plantation in Georgia, with its benign slavery and contentedly loyal slaves. Mitchell's novel also provides a mournful portrait of the destruction of this society by the Civil War. Yet *Gone with the Wind* also modifies this myth in an unusual way. While the novel is often openly racist, it obfuscates the nature of slavery and consequent divisions in American society by constructing them as issues of social class rather than race. Mitchell's approach has confounded her critics and potential challengers ever since.

Mitchell's frequent white supremacist editorializations in her novel often obscure the fact that the world of *Gone with the Wind* is organized fundamentally along class lines, not racial ones. The admirable characters and primary protagonists of the novel are either members of the white southern planter aristocracy or the black house servant class. All of Mitchell's famous characters—Scarlett O'Hara, Rhett Butler, Ashley and Melanie Wilkes, Mammy, Prissy, and Uncle Peter—belong to one of these elite groups. The peripheral, largely anonymous, and often villainous masses in the book— alongside the Yankees—are disreputable poor southern whites and the disloyal lower class of slaves: the field hands.[3]

Gone with the Wind presents a slave population that is split dramatically between the exceptional class of house slaves—which is vividly dramatized in the novel—and the lowly caste of field hands—which is utterly invisible during the novel's antebellum scenes and which remains faceless and anonymous throughout the remainder of the narrative. Mitchell's book argues that slavery operated as a fair and just meritocracy for African Americans by providing a system in which the talented, responsible, and industrious earned liberal rewards: "[P]lantation mistresses throughout the South had put the pickaninnies through courses of training and elimination to select the best of them for the positions of greater responsibility. Those consigned to the fields were the ones least willing or able to learn, the least energetic, the least honest and trustworthy, the most vicious and brutish" (654). *Gone with the Wind* thus suggests that people became field hands in slavery not because of an oppressive labor system organized around race, but because they proved incapable of fulfilling higher social occupations and roles despite the opportunities supposedly given them. Mitchell's text presents those slaves who successfully passed these training courses as a monolithic group: a black upper class, whose members, without exception, utterly identify with the South's white aristocrats rather than with lower-class members of their own race. Mammy, for example, is proud that she was born in the "great house, not in the quarters, and had been raised in Ole Miss' bedroom" (454).

Lower-class blacks only assume significance (and then only as a group rather than as individuals) in *Gone with the Wind*'s second half, which is set after the Civil War. Like its portrayal of slavery, however, the novel's white southern propagandist portrayal of Reconstruction—in which "the negroes were living in leisure while their former masters struggled and starved"—is articulated specifically in terms of class rather than race. After Appomattox, the narrative claims, "[t]housands of house servants, the highest caste in the slave population, remained with their white folks. . . . [B]ut the hordes of 'trashy free issue niggers,' who were causing most of the trouble, were drawn largely from the field-hand class" (657, 654).

As the loyal black butler, Pork, points out, it is only "dem trashy niggers" that choose to follow the Yankees and assert their freedom rather than to stay behind to help their defeated masters. The novel explicitly identifies those blacks who are audacious enough to want to vote, who insolently push whites off sidewalks, and who supposedly perpetrate a "large number of outrages" against white women as being members of the lower class (407, 656). Scarlett O'Hara is shocked at reports of black "impudence" because "she had never seen an insolent negro in her life." Scarlett, of course, has known only well-bred house slaves, not the vulgar lower class that is capable of "outrages" against whites. Mammy, although black, is herself scathing toward the "impident lookin'" and "trashy" "[f]ree issue country niggers" who flood Atlanta after the war (521, 555, 598). While loyal former house slaves like Uncle Peter are "far too well bred to want to vote" (561), the "former field hands found themselves suddenly elevated" to positions of power in the Georgia state legislature: "There they conducted themselves as creatures of small intelligence might naturally be expected to do. Like monkeys or small children turned loose among treasured objects whose value is beyond their comprehension, they ran wild—either from a perverse pleasure in destruction or simply because of their ignorance" (654). While Mitchell's racial prejudices are palpable in this passage, the novel always rhetorically constructs those prejudices in terms of class: in *Gone with the Wind*, it is specifically *lower-class* blacks who are ignorant, childlike creatures of little intelligence.

Similarly, Mitchell's novel identifies black sexual assault of white women as a crime perpetrated exclusively by lower-class African Americans. In one scene, Scarlett is menaced by a black rapist from the sinister Shantytown, the population of which consists of "outcast negroes, black prostitutes and a scattering of poor whites of the lowest order" (777–78). She is saved from assault only by the sudden reappearance of Sam, the loyal Tara driver. Again and again, *Gone with the Wind* distinguishes between decent, three-dimensional, elite African Americans—who play a positive and constructive role in southern society—and brutish, anonymous, lower-class blacks, who are ill-equipped for the responsibilities of freedom and who threaten social stability.

Occasionally, the text obfuscates the degree to which it has constructed a rigid division between slave classes. When Sam rescues Scarlett from the

Shantytown rapist, he tells his former mistress of his experiences in the North. He reports being particularly shocked by the inability of Yankees to distinguish between house servants and a mere field hand like himself (780). The fact remains, however, that Sam was not an average slave but the driver at Tara. As Eugene Genovese observes, drivers "acted as foremen of the labor gangs and supervisors of the decorum of the quarters" and frequently "became the most important slaves on the place and often knew more about management than did the whites" (*Roll* 365–66). Sam may not be a house servant, but he is still as much a part of the black upper class as Mammy or Pork. In short, the one decent "field hand" in the novel is socially quite distinct from his supposed fellows. Like the house servants, Sam, too, identifies with the white aristocracy, not with members of his own race.

It is not simply that black house servants consider themselves superior to lower-class people of color in *Gone with the Wind*. In the novel's antebellum scenes, the elite slaves of Tara fervently believe that their association with the white master class places them higher in the social hierarchy than such nonslaveholding whites as the Wilkerson and Slattery families: "The house negroes of the County considered themselves superior to white trash, and their unconcealed scorn stung [Tom Slattery], while their more secure position in life stirred his envy. By contrast with his own miserable existence, they were well-fed, well-clothed and looked after in sickness and old age. They were proud . . . to belong to people who were quality, while he was despised by all" (49–50). Mammy even objects to the philanthropic devotion of Scarlett's mother, Ellen O'Hara, to the local poor whites, opining that "Dey is de shiflesses, mos' ungrateful passel of no-counts livin'. An' Miss Ellen got no bizness weahin' herseff out waitin' on folks dat did dey be wuth shootin' dey'd have niggers ter wait on dem" (65). The narrative, furthermore, validates Mammy's judgment, for it is through nursing the typhoid-ridden Slatterys that Ellen contracts the disease herself and dies.

Few lower-class white characters play a significant role in the novel, and the book's rhetoric demonizes those few to the same extent that it demonizes the black field hand class. Early in the narrative, Ellen discharges Jonas Wilkerson, the Tara plantation's Yankee overseer, for casually impregnating the unmarried lower-class Emmie Slattery. Wilkerson re-emerges during Reconstruction as a grasping carpetbagger with ambitions to extort Tara from its rightful owners. The lower-class white characters who are introduced in the novel's second half are even less appealing. An enigmatic brute named Archie, who briefly serves as Scarlett's coachman, has an irrational, obsessive hatred of all blacks, women, and northerners. Johnnie Gallegher, the foreman at Scarlett's mill, exploits its convict laborers so cruelly that even the ruthless Scarlett is shocked (750, 783–87). The only working-class white character to emerge from the novel with any integrity and decency is the Confederate veteran Will Benteen, who—like the elite blacks in the book—dedicates himself to helping Tara's struggling aristocrats after the Civil War, and who wins the hand of Scarlett's sister in marriage as a reward for his loyalty. What bestows virtue and nobility upon a lower-class person in *Gone with the Wind*, whether white or black, is dedication to the cause of the aristocracy and the social status quo. Benteen, Mammy, Uncle Peter, and their ilk become honorary members of the white upper class by committing themselves to its welfare and its status.

For all her overt racism, then, Mitchell constructs her romanticized portrait of slavery and her demeaning portrayal of African Americans in *Gone with the Wind* chiefly in terms of class. Mitchell's racial prejudices are undeniable, but the rhetoric of her novel judges particular classes, not races of people.[4] It is thus not sufficient for a critique of the novel merely to challenge its idealized portrayal of the institution of slavery and its patronizing depictions of African Americans. A true counternarrative to *Gone with the Wind* must dismantle, and provide alternatives to, the constructions of class that undergird the book's conceptualization of southern society.

One of the key historical studies of slavery published before the 1950s, Herbert Aptheker's *American Negro Slave Revolts* (1943), is just such a counternarrative. Aptheker's central purpose was to challenge the view of slavery, propounded by Phillips and his supporters, which claimed that African Americans were "easily intimidated [and] incapable of deep plots" (quoted in Aptheker, *American* 12). Indeed, the very title of Aptheker's work echoes and subverts the title of Phillips's most famous study, *American Negro Slavery*. In answer to the assertions of Phillips and his followers, *American Negro Slave Revolts* provides an extensive catalog of slave rebellions and establishes the existence of a significant tradition of collective resistance by American slaves. Furthermore, Aptheker's subsidiary theses explicitly address the class dimensions of slave insurrection: "Two additional facts of particular interest appear from the study. These are, first, that occasionally the plans or aspirations of the rebels were actually *reported* as going beyond a desire for personal freedom and envisioning, in addition, a property redistribution; and, second, that white people were frequently implicated—or believed to be implicated—with the slaves in the plans or efforts to overthrow the master class by force" (*American* 162–63). Aptheker's qualification of this second point—"believed to be implicated"—indicates a significant tension in his argument. As a card-carrying Communist, Aptheker aims to demonstrate that African American slaves and working-class whites often united across racial lines because of a sense of shared class interests. Throughout his study, Aptheker emphasizes the contributions of proletarian whites to acts of slave resistance. At the same time, however, Aptheker challenges the prevalent idea that slave rebellions were rare and that when they did occur they were usually instigated and led by white abolitionists. Consequently, then, in order to assert that slaves were autonomously militant and did not depend upon white aid and inspiration to revolt, Aptheker's text frequently disputes alleged connections between white abolitionists and slave insurrections. "It is simple," he argues, "to find any number of statements intimating or boldly affirming that the Abolitionists were responsible for slave unrest . . . but is far from simple to find substantiation for these assertions" (*American* 105). In short, Aptheker found himself in the complicated position of attempting to demonstrate, on one hand, that reports of slave revolts planned by white conspirators are erroneous, whereas, on the other hand, reports of insurrections organized by slaves themselves, but which involved white allies as equals, are genuine.

This may sound like a torturous argument, but recent historiography tends to confirm its accuracy. While even sympathetic scholars have concluded that Aptheker significantly overstated the number of slave rebellions, several contemporary historians substantiate his characterization of slave insurrections as being often class-oriented and sometimes interracial in nature—with whites involved as equal allies, not leaders. In *Gabriel's Rebellion* (1993), Douglas Egerton argues that the 1800 Richmond slave conspiracy was as much a class rebellion as it was a racial one. From his analysis of the trial testimony, Egerton concludes that Gabriel, the insurrection's leader, defined his enemy as the merchants who dominated Richmond's economy, not whites in general. In addition, Gabriel ordered that all those "friendly to liberty"—Quakers, Methodists, Frenchmen, and poor white women—

should be spared during the planned assault on Richmond, and he apparently even recruited several working-class whites to his campaign, with the hope that others would join when the revolution began. Furthermore, a white ship's captain almost transported Gabriel to safety after the failure of the plot (28, 51, 56, 49, 104–6, 177). Egerton also finds compelling evidence that two mysterious Frenchmen—Charles Quersey and Alexander Beddenhurst (who becomes Biddenhurst in Arna Bontemps's *Black Thunder*)—played a significant role in the uprising (182–85). Gabriel's insurrection is far from the only American slave rebellion that seems to have possessed a class dimension as well as a racial one. Recent studies of Denmark Vesey's 1822 conspiracy suggest that the former slave who aimed to burn Charleston to the ground also had his white sympathizers. According to Edward Pearson, in the aftermath of the abortive Vesey plot, one white man told a group of free blacks that there should be an attempt to rescue the imprisoned black conspirators (145–47). Finally, Stephen B. Oates notes that even the messianic Nat Turner spared one white household when he blazed his trail of destruction through rural Virginia, apparently "because he believed the poor white inhabitants 'thought no better of themselves than they did of negroes'" (88).

The feasibility of such active interracial sympathies and even alliances among the lower classes is something that *Gone with the Wind* essentially denies. While repeatedly asserting the common values and interests of aristocratic whites and black house servants, Mitchell's novel resolutely refuses to address the corresponding possibility that lower-class whites and blacks might have united because of a similar sense of shared class status. It is true that the white Jonas Wilkerson makes "a great to-do about being equal with the negroes, ate with them, visited in their houses, rode them around with him in his carriage, put his arms around their shoulders" (539). This occurs, however, only after the end of slavery, and is presented as an example of a northern carpetbagger's cynical attempts to manipulate black people for his own political gain, rather than as evidence of a class-oriented sense of interracial equality. As the narrative puts it, former field hands "were, as a class, childlike in mentality, easily led and from long habit accustomed to taking orders. Formerly their white masters had given the orders. Now they had a new set of masters, the [Freedmen's] Bureau and the Carpetbaggers, and their orders were 'You're just as good as any white man, so act that way. Just as soon as you can vote the Republican ticket, you are going to have the white man's property'" (654). Wilkerson does not identify his interests with those of southern blacks but simply keeps "the darkies stirred up" for his own political designs (646). It takes one of the book's elite blacks, Sam the driver, to see through such hypocritical exploitation during the short time he spends with a white family in the North. "Dey treat me lak Ah jes' as good as dey wuz," he tells Scarlett, "but in dere hearts, dey din' lak me—dey din' lak no niggers" (781). Furthermore, the portion of the novel set during slavery portrays poor whites as being more likely to envy, rather than identify with, the social position of slaves. When Tom Slattery professes to hate "rich folks' uppity niggers," he is clearly referring specifically to elite house slaves (49). Since *Gone with the Wind* barely acknowledges the field hand class of slaves, the reader never has to consider what Slattery's attitudes might be toward—or what he might share in common with—its members. Only in its brief depiction of the notorious Shantytown on the edge of postwar Atlanta does the book even vaguely suggest the existence of an interracial lower-class community, and this it demonizes as a refuge for outcasts and criminals.

Aptheker's historical study provides a striking alternative to the picture painted by *Gone with the Wind* by arguing that enslaved African Americans often consciously identified their interests as intersecting with those of lower-class whites, and that the two groups sometimes united in an equal partnership, rather than radical whites simply exhorting slaves to revolt. Aptheker, furthermore, implicitly rejects Mitchell's assertion that elite blacks and the white planter class had common interests. He emphasizes that members of the slave elite actually led many slave insurrections, including the artisan blacksmith Gabriel, the literate Nat Turner, and the onetime house slave Denmark Vesey. Aptheker's emphasis on class and interracial alliances in the antebellum South serves not only to dismantle white southern historiography of the early twentieth century but also persuasively refutes *Gone with the Wind*'s portrait of the class structure of Old Dixie. Whatever the limitations of his study, Aptheker nonetheless constructs a compelling narrative that engages with Mitchell's most fundamental assertions as well as those of the historians to whom he is directly responding.

Race, Class, and Gender in Arna Bontemps's *Black Thunder*

Arna Bontemps also addresses the class dimensions of slave insurrection in his novel about Gabriel's rebellion, *Black Thunder* (1936). Unlike Aptheker's later study, however, Bontemps's novel does not fully reconcile its exploration of interracial alliances with its simultaneous assertion of the existence of autonomous black militancy. This tension results in an ambivalent novel, which, for all its strengths, ultimately fails to provide a decisive critique or consistent alternative to the class-oriented rhetoric of *Gone with the Wind*.

In a series of often-impressionistic vignettes, *Black Thunder* shows various individuals' involvement in, or responses to, Gabriel's planned assault on Richmond in 1800. Gabriel's partner, a slave woman named Juba, demands that she be allowed to participate in the uprising. In contrast, another slave, the subservient Ben Woolfolk, is deeply troubled by the impending violence and eventually betrays the plot to his master. In Richmond, a white radical named Alexander Biddenhurst senses unrest among the slaves and eagerly anticipates an uprising. When he begins to realize, however, that he will probably be unjustly accused of instigating the insurrection, he flees to the North. Gabriel's army gathers just as a huge storm floods the bridge into town, obliging Gabriel to retreat. Before the slave forces can regroup, the treacherous Ben alerts the white authorities, and the rebels are arrested, tried, and executed.

Black Thunder powerfully refutes Phillips's assertions that enslaved African Americans were "by racial quality submissive," were characterized by "inertly obeying minds," and "made their master's interests thoroughly their own" (341–42, 339, 329). Bontemps's narrative presents a militant slave community that is "always whispering," constantly plotting. Many of the book's slave characters possess an active revolutionary consciousness. They are quite aware of the successful slave revolution in Haiti, and Gabriel is even directly influenced by the example of the Haitian rebel leader Toussaint L'Ouverture (21, 35, 34, 116, 117, 166). *Black Thunder* also provides an alternative to the idea dramatized in *Gone with the Wind* that there were rigid divisions between slave classes, as well as the notion that elite slaves were loyal to the white planter class. The conspiracy in *Black Thunder* seems to involve all classes of African Americans, from privileged slaves, like Gabriel, to free blacks, including the saddle shop owner, Mingo, to common field hands, such as Juba.

Contemporary historical studies tend to confirm the idea that there were close relations between slave classes rather than the fundamental boundaries between them suggested by *Gone with the Wind*. In the most renowned modern study of slavery, *Roll, Jordan, Roll* (1974), Eugene Genovese questions the idea that there was a strict demarcation between the field hand and house servant classes within the institution: "House slaves and field slaves did not generally constitute separate and mutually hostile groups; on the contrary, a variety of circumstances . . . bound them closely together. . . . [A]part from the status-bound great plantations . . . house servants regularly married field hands. . . . House servants and field hands often came from a single family. . . . Some house slaves lived in the quarters. . . . Enduring friendships grew between field hands and the house servants with whom they had played as children. . . . House slaves and field slaves often helped each other to run away" (338, 339, 340). Tara may be one of the exceptional "status-bound great plantations," but the vast chasm that *Gone with the Wind* constructs between the field and house slaves of this fictional estate hardly seems feasible. *Black Thunder's* portrait of a relatively united slave community is rather more compelling.

Upon close examination, however, it becomes clear that Bontemps's novel tends to simply erase class distinctions between slaves rather than explicitly dismantle the legend that such divisions were fundamental. In *Black Thunder*, slaves are a particular class in society, but often there is not a sufficiently clear sense of any hierarchical distinctions at all between members of this class. At times, the novel does not seem to be questioning the idea that slave populations were divided by class so much as it seems to be ignoring it. Bontemps's portrait of a diverse but interconnected black community is one of the most notable aspects of *Black Thunder*, but the book's blurred, inconsistent, and undeveloped treatment of slave classes works against this achievement somewhat. For the most part, it is only the privileged slaves in *Black Thunder* who are identified according to occupation: Gabriel is a coachman, Criddle a stable boy, Drucilla a cook, Ben a servant, and Ditcher a driver. One assumes that Juba, Martin, and the other slave characters are field hands, but the novel does not explicitly identify them as such. Most of the book's slave characters are simply of an indeterminate class. Indeed, the only point at which the narrative specifically identifies a character as a field hand occurs in order to emphasize, not question the distance between slave classes. When Pharoah turns up at the Sheppard kitchen, Ben, a house slave, struggles to recognize him, because he rarely sees field hands (70). Ben, furthermore, is a character who would be much happier in the pages of *Gone with the Wind* than in *Black Thunder*. This elderly, pampered house slave is persuaded to join the conspiracy, but his identification with the white planter aristocracy is so great that he soon betrays Gabriel to his master (11, 48–49, 51, 112–13). The only way that Ben differs from Mitchell's black characters is in the value judgments placed upon his behavior. Ben would be heroic in *Gone with the Wind*, but is merely a pathetic traitor in *Black Thunder*. However, since the field hand Pharoah joins Ben in his betrayal of the plot, Gabriel's rebellion is exposed by a house servant *and* a field hand. Ironically, the most explicit alliance in the novel across slave classes is one that is detrimental to the slave community as a whole.

Black Thunder is more explicit in its treatment of class issues when it explores relations between white radicals and black insurrectionists. In Bontemps's narrative, Biddenhurst (one of the "two Frenchmen" of the historical record) sees the southern system in terms of class, not race: "You had the filthy nobles in France. Here we have the planter aristocrats. We have the merchants, the poor whites, the free blacks, the slaves—classes, classes, classes." Biddenhurst is also pleased at signs of "definite foment among the masses" in Virginia and he eagerly anticipates (if in rather anachronistically Marxist terms for 1800) a "revolution of the American proletariat" resulting in a world with "no more serfs, no more planters, no more classes, no more slaves, only men." Furthermore, Biddenhurst boldly invites the enslaved Gabriel to drink with him in the local wine shop, and Gabriel ultimately decides that his forces will spare the local French population when they march on Richmond. After Gabriel's revolt fails, Biddenhurst still dreams of aiding "semi-secret groups working for the deliverance of bondsmen" (21, 76, 22, 86, 152).

As an African American Marxist, Bontemps is concerned with both black militancy and class-oriented revolution, but he does not reconcile the two in the pages of *Black Thunder*. Race ultimately triumphs over class in his novel. Although it devotes many pages to the activities and beliefs of white radicals, such as Biddenhurst, Bontemps's book does not depict these agitators as the instigators of Gabriel's rebellion—or, ultimately, as being directly involved in it at all. While the southern planter class in the novel simply assumes that white activists are behind the plot, the novel takes pains to argue that Gabriel's rebellion was, in the final analysis, solely the work of African Americans (149). Biddenhurst never does keep his assignation with Gabriel at the wine shop and he flees the South with several white compatriots as soon as he begins to suspect that "there *is* something up" with the slaves of Richmond, for which he fears he will be unfairly blamed. Later, in Philadelphia, Biddenhurst offers help to the increasing flood of fugitive slaves, but he foresees the creation of the Underground Railroad as an essentially African American achievement, musing that "these runaways would develop a regular transit line" (75, 141). His desire to aid the inevitable "revolution of the American proletariat" goes no further than simple intent. Biddenhurst is an armchair radical who fantasizes about revolution yet plays no active or concrete role in bringing it about. His militant philosophy yet rather ineffectual actions are indicative of an ambivalence that pervades *Black Thunder*. The novel moves in contradictory directions—boldly dramatizing the possibility of interracial rebellion only to dispute its feasibility and significance. The novel thus retreats from the implications of one of its central narrative strands.

Close to a fifth of *Black Thunder* concerns Biddenhurst and his radical French friends, but, despite such a presence in the novel, they ultimately do little more than impotently sympathize with slaves—and then hastily flee at the first sign of trouble. Furthermore, by focusing so much upon Biddenhurst, the narrative depicts the relationship between anti-slavery whites and blacks as one in which educated middle-class white radicals had compassion for enslaved people of color, but shared no real *class* interests with them. The character of Biddenhurst thus represents the very archetype that Aptheker was concerned to dismantle: the privileged intellectual agitator who stirs up black militancy. *Black Thunder*, like Aptheker's study, disputes the notion that black Americans in slavery only revolted when encouraged by white radicals. Unlike Aptheker, however, Bontemps does not reconcile this position with his sense of the potential for interracial class politics in the antebellum era.

Black Thunder devotes a great deal of its narrative to white characters such as Biddenhurst simply in order to present dramatic contrivances that explain away historical evidence for the involvement of white people, such as the "two Frenchmen," in the conspiracy. One of Gabriel's generals, for example, is captured with a document bearing Biddenhurst's name and address, but the text establishes that this was only because the general had earlier acted as a messenger between Biddenhurst and a mulatto prostitute (171–75, 56–58). In a parallel episode, Mingo tricks a naive white printer into giving him a gun. In short, whatever sympathies they have for slaves, the novel's white radicals are essentially hapless fall guys, who unwittingly incriminate themselves in an uprising to which they have no real connection whatsoever.

While such ineffectual would-be Jacobins are prominent in the novel, *Black Thunder* utterly ignores a very different social class of whites with which the historical Gabriel would have had considerable contact. In his recent study of the Richmond rebellion, Egerton shows that Gabriel was a skilled smith who was "hired out" by his master and thus toiled in the racially mixed workshops of Richmond: "In this casual atmosphere, black and white mechanics labored side by side and in the process often developed strong bonds that cut across racial lines. . . . Laboring together in a small city that was far more integrated than northern urban centers, artisans and unskilled day laborers of both races fell into the natural habit of retiring together to dine and drink. . . . Many grog shops were infamous, according to one Virginia authority, 'for the equality which reigned [between] the blacks and whites.' . . . Over time, a working-class subculture emerged. Apprentice boys, servant girls, bond hirelings, radical whites, free blacks . . . banded together" (*Gabriel's* 27, 29). By making *his* Gabriel a coachman rather than a smith, Bontemps deprives his protagonist of membership in this working-class subculture of Richmond and steers his narrative away from the subject of interracial class-based relations. Bontemps, of course, may simply not have known Gabriel was an urban artisan—for even Aptheker does not mention Gabriel's occupation. Neither, however, is there any historical evidence that Gabriel was a coachman. Bontemps, then, *chose* to make his fictional Gabriel an elite slave figure on the plantation, rather than a participant in the interracial urban culture of Richmond—a culture that the novel actively portrays: Mingo talks familiarly to the white printer Cruezot, while the mulatto prostitute, Melody, has a white clientele.

Bontemps's choice of occupation for Gabriel highlights the fact that his novel is ultimately more focused upon race than upon class—and is more concerned to emphasize autonomous African American militancy than the potential for interracial class action, despite the author's leftist politics. Rather than developing the "natural habit" of dining with white equals, the

Gabriel of *Black Thunder* is instead rendered speechless when Biddenhurst, a white man of higher class, proffers his "astonishing" invitation to share a drink. Indeed, Gabriel is "embarrassed by the white man's attentions" (22). In *Black Thunder*, Gabriel has no contact at all with lower-class whites. The novel flirts at great length with the idea of interracial alliance in nineteenth-century America only to undermine and to reject it as a factor in Gabriel's uprising. The book celebrates autonomous black rebellion rather than exploring interracial class solidarity. Like *Gone with the Wind, Black Thunder* ultimately refuses to bring white and black lower classes together, while establishing connections and sympathies between members of the black and white *upper* classes: Ben betrays the slave conspiracy precisely because he identifies with his white master. The novel judges Ben harshly for such treachery, of course, but *Black Thunder* provides no corresponding scene of interracial identification among the lower classes. Like *Gone with the Wind*, therefore, Bontemps's novel presents interracial cooperation only among elites.

Consequently, if *Black Thunder* provides a powerful portrayal of enslaved African Americans as militant revolutionaries, it offers no coherent alternative to the class-oriented visions of *Gone with the Wind*. Ultimately, in fact, Bontemps's novel does not even advance a fully compelling critique of Ulrich Phillips's view of slavery and slave insurrections. *Black Thunder* may counter Phillips's assertions about the benignly paternalist nature of slavery and the docile character of slaves—but it is not as if Phillips denies the existence of slave rebellions. The white southern historian addresses such insurrections in his chapter on "Slave Crime," and declares that "One errs . . . in assuming a dearth of serious infractions" on the part of slaves, since "investigation reveals crime in abundance." Phillips even acknowledges the magnitude of the Gabriel conspiracy, observing that it "eclipsed all other such events on the continent in this period" (454, 474). Furthermore, Phillips neglects to mention the alleged involvement of whites in Gabriel's uprising, so *Black Thunder*'s denial of the direct participation of Biddenhurst in the conspiracy in no way upsets Phillips's white southern view of the event. The two differ fundamentally only in their value judgments of the plot: Phillips considers it a "crime," while Bontemps sees it as a legitimate and admirable revolt against oppression.

Black Thunder is also somewhat limited in terms of its treatment of gender. Bontemps's novel simply does not transcend *Gone with the Wind*'s clichéd portrayals of African American women. Both male and female novelists may have been prone to portray antebellum black women in stereotypical terms largely because, until recently, there was no coherent or considered historical discourse about female slaves. According to Deborah Gray White, even as late as the 1980s, "African-American women were close to invisible in historical writing." White argues that being "[b]lack in a white society, slave in a free society, women in a society ruled by men" meant that female slaves constituted "the most vulnerable group of antebellum Americans" (3, 15). Until the 1980s, black women were equally vulnerable in the pages of literature. White observes that two particular stereotypes of black femininity have pervaded American culture since the age of slavery. "On the one hand," White asserts, "there was the woman obsessed with matters of the flesh, on the other there was the asexual woman. One was carnal, the other maternal. One was at heart a slut, the other deeply religious. One was a Jezebel, the other a Mammy." *Gone with the Wind*, of course, contains the most renowned instance of the latter archetype—indeed, the most famous black character in Mitchell's novel has no name other than "Mammy." *Black Thunder*, unfortunately, does little more than go to the opposite extreme by presenting Juba, its central woman of color, as what White calls "a person governed almost entirely by her libido, a Jezebel character" (46, 29).

To be fair, Bontemps's novel clearly seeks to celebrate African American women. *Black Thunder*'s subplot—in which Gabriel rejects Melody, a sophisticated light-skinned urban prostitute, for the darker-skinned slave, Juba—is a prescient 1930s assertion of the "Black is Beautiful" notion. Furthermore, while Gabriel calls the rebellion "a men-folks' job," it is Juba who ultimately leads the march on Richmond, astride her master's horse and wearing his riding boots (84, 80). Nonetheless, the text still largely characterizes Juba as a simplistic, stereotypical Jezebel. As she leads the throng into action, Juba's "fragmentary skirt curled above her waist, her naked thighs flashing above the riding boots," and she feels "the warm body of the colt straining between her clinched knees." Bontemps is quick to repeat this picture of Juba sitting "erect, feeling the pure warmth of the colt's fine muscles gnawing back and forth between her naked thighs" (80, 109). Even after the rebellion founders because a crucial bridge is flooded, *Black Thunder* presents Juba looking forward to a second attempt the following day in precisely the same eroticized language: "Juba got a sensuous pleasure out of the excitement. . . . She could hardly wait to put on Marse Prosser's stolen riding boots again. She could still feel Araby twitching and fretting between her clinched knees. Lordy, that colt. He was pure joy itself. Almost as much fun as a man, that half-wild Araby" (114). There is not a single scene in which she appears that Bontemps does not sexualize Juba. Even as she stands on the auction block at the end of the novel, he draws attention to her as "the tempestuous wench with the slim hips and the savage mop of hair. . . . [T]here was something about her figure, something about the bold rise of her exposed breasts that put gooseflesh on a man" (224). Whatever his intentions, Bontemps seems incapable of valuing African American women for anything other than a wild, exaggerated eroticism. There is nothing progressive about such a por-trait, for, as White notes, the "primary beneficiaries" of the Jezebel myth have been white males: southern slaveholders, of course, traditionally used the Jezebel stereotype as a way of justifying the sexual exploitation of female slaves (White 27).

Although it emerged in the same year as Mitchell's novel, *Black Thunder* had little chance of rivaling the phenomenal popular success of *Gone with the Wind*. Nonetheless, Bontemps's tale of an audacious slave rebellion had the potential to provide a significant counternarrative to Mitchell's romanti-cization of slavery and the South. *Black Thunder*, however, does not provide an entirely satisfactory alternative to Mitchell's strategy of conceptualizing slavery in terms of class rather than race. While Bontemps's novel compli-cates the notion of rigid divisions between slave classes, it does not reconcile inherent tensions in its treatment of the class dimensions of slave resistance, and, in addition, it fails to sufficiently revise *Gone with the Wind*'s portrayal of black women. *Black Thunder* thus falls short of being a sustained critique of the white southern ideology so skillfully reconfigured in *Gone with the Wind*.

Frances Gaither's *The Red Cock Crows*

Frances Gaither's *The Red Cock Crows* (1944) emerged the year after Her-bert Aptheker's analysis of slave militancy had challenged received ideas about slavery within the historical profession. But it also emerged into an American culture that had been hypnotized by *Gone with the Wind*'s vision of slavery for almost a decade.[5] Gaither's novel stages an encounter between Mitchell's and Aptheker's texts: it is a plantation romance about a slave uprising. *The Red Cock Crows* projects Aptheker's visions of violent slave rebellions onto the placid idyll of a Tara-esque Mississippi plantation.

In many ways, Gaither's novel is an impressively progressive dramatization of militant slave resistance for 1944, especially from the pen of a white Mississippian. It is unfortunate, therefore, that *The Red Cock Crows* has been long out of print and thoroughly neglected by modern literary scholarship. Gaither's novel nonetheless suffers from limitations similar to those that plague *Black Thunder*. In spite of its powerful portrayal of slave militancy, and despite boldly gesturing toward interracial unity among members of the lower classes, the book's examination of the relationship between class and slave resistance ultimately unravels. *The Red Cock Crows* eschews both the white southern self-justification of *Gone with the Wind* and the leftist vision of lower-class solidarity of *American Negro Slave Revolts*, but it proves unable to construct a coherent alternative to either. *The Red Cock Crows* daringly addresses the possibility of class alliances across racial boundaries only to eventually reassert a rather conservative orthodoxy of social stratification that is insufficiently distinct from the vision of southern society to be found in *Gone with the Wind*.

The portrait of slavery and rebellion in *The Red Cock Crows* is also complicated—as is Bontemps's book—by its treatment of gender. By exploring similar questions about white women's roles in southern society to those that Mitchell's novel addresses, *The Red Cock Crows* shifts the focus of its narrative away from its ostensible concern with slavery and slave resistance. Furthermore, the novel's portrayal of black women is undermined by the same reliance on the Jezebel stereotype that diminishes *Black Thunder*. *The Red Cock Crows* begins as a tale of collective revolution by enslaved blacks, but transforms into a story of the liberation of a single aristocratic white woman. While Gaither's novel powerfully portrays both black males and white females as noble rebels, it also replicates reactionary discourses about lower-class white men and black women.

The Red Cock Crows begins with the arrival of Adam Fiske, a northern schoolteacher, in the community of the Forks and Scott's Bluff, Mississippi, in the 1830s. While running a schoolhouse on the Shandy plantation belonging to Ward Dalton, Fiske falls for Fannie, the southern patriarch's daughter. Dalton, however, refuses to allow Fannie to marry a northerner, and she becomes engaged instead to a local planter named Trooper Clay.

While this sentimental plot unfolds, Scofield, the Shandy driver, begins plotting a slave insurrection. When a local white woman overhears two slaves planning violence, the community forms a Committee of Safety to investigate the conspiracy. Vigilante violence swiftly consumes the Forks, and the committee rapidly devolves into a kangaroo court, resulting in the hangings of a number of largely innocent people, both white and black. Fiske's rather vague anti-slavery sentiments are sufficient for the committee to convict him, and he is saved only when Scofield is finally arrested and testifies to Fiske's innocence—to the chagrin of the jealous Trooper Clay. The committee expels Fiske from the region, while Fannie—who is increasingly distraught at Trooper's callous attitude toward her slaves—abruptly flees her fiancé and the South in search of the exiled schoolteacher.

Rather than completely reversing *Gone with the Wind*'s portrayal of slavery, *The Red Cock Crows* undermines it from within, appearing to replicate it only to take it apart. Thus the narrative begins with a northerner's surprised discovery of the relatively benign nature of slavery. Fiske is pleasantly taken aback on his first day at Shandy to learn that slaves are not obliged to work on Saturday afternoons and that their masters throw parties for them on weekends. It also becomes apparent that several of the Dalton slaves possess considerable material wealth of their own: "Aunt Sarah . . . had by popular boast two trunks crammed full of dresses and gold trinkets given to her by her white folks. Scofield owned the horse he rode. Montgomery had large sums lent out to planters all over the Forks." Furthermore, there is no physical cruelty or corporal punishment at Shandy. "It just wasn't done. . . . Nobody struck a Negro in anger. Once an overseer had been fired for doing it. Even official whippings were rarely administered and then only as a last resort for flagrant crime such as stabbing or infidelity." In addition, the ruling white class considers the idea of dividing slave families by sale to be quite inconceivable. Two of Fannie's slaves have "most inconveniently acquired wives and children, from whom, of course, they could not be separated." The general opinion of the community is that "ain't ary one of Dalton's niggers would run, if a good-natured white man was to write out a pass and put it in his hand" (12–13, 52, 145, 307, 95).

Such assertions may seem merely to repeat the idealized picture of slavery created by such white southern writers and historians as Mitchell and Phillips, but can be explained on two counts. First, those like Mitchell and

Phillips who claim that slavery could be a benevolent institution are not entirely without historical evidence to substantiate their arguments. Even modern historians, such as Eugene Genovese, concede that that some slaves did, as *The Red Cock Crows* suggests, work only a half-day on Saturday and enjoy weekend parties thrown by their masters, and that slaves sometimes did amass relatively considerable material wealth (*Roll* 566–67, 569, 313–14). Second, with the American popular mind so in thrall to *Gone with the Wind*, had Gaither depicted slavery as merely brutish and oppressive, she would likely have alienated many potential readers. In order to critique *Gone with the Wind* persuasively, Gaither had first to construct a world somewhat akin to the one that Mitchell's novel portrays.

Gaither's astute strategy is to acknowledge that a number of slaveholders may indeed have developed principles of benevolent paternalism like those romanticized in Mitchell's novel, but her novel also vividly shows how such principles frequently could and, indeed, must be violated in practice. The assertion that slave families are never divided at Shandy is made but a few pages before Trooper Clay decides to break this tradition, claiming, "I've more women and children . . . right now than I know what to do with and, bad as I need two more good field-hands, I don't believe it would be worth my while to take on their families" (308). This scene contrasts ironically with a moment in *Gone with the Wind*. Early in Mitchell's novel, Scarlett's father spends an inordinate amount of money to purchase the wife and daughter of his loyal slave butler from another slaveholder, and jokingly declares that "never again will I let a darky on this place marry off it. It's too expensive" (31). *The Red Cock Crows* suggests that the paternal generosity of a Gerald O'Hara was much less likely in practice than the hardheaded businesslike decisions of a Trooper Clay.

Gaither's narrative additionally emphasizes the gap between paternalist principles and the actual practices of slaveholding by having Fannie's musings about the absence of physical punishment at Shandy occur just at the point that she loses her temper and strikes her maid, Sack (144). This is another moment in Gaither's text that parallels a significant episode in *Gone with the Wind*. While Mitchell's book essentially portrays slavery as kindly and lenient, it also provides a dramatic scene in which Scarlett angrily hits Prissy, her maid. This famous moment occurs in *Gone with the Wind* when Prissy fails to find a doctor in besieged Atlanta to attend Melanie, who is in labor. To compound this failure, Prissy then confesses that her earlier claim to be an experienced midwife was an outright lie. Scarlett "had never struck a slave in all her life, but now she slapped the black cheek with all the force in her tired arm" (366). The narrative encourages the reader to accept that Prissy is entirely deserving of this blow, and that Scarlett's response—if something less than proper—is nonetheless appropriate. When Prissy should have been desperately hurrying to find a doctor, Scarlett sees her "idling along as though she had the whole day before her," and even when reprimanded by Scarlett, Prissy still "saunter[s] down the walk at a snail's gait." After the slap, however, Scarlett sends Prissy on another errand and watches her "hurrying down the street, going faster than she had ever dreamed the worthless child could move" (353, 354, 369). The novel thus implies that while slavery was never needlessly cruel, firm discipline was often necessary and effective. Indeed, later in the novel, Prissy's own mother, Dilcey, beats her for similar failings. When Tara's house slaves are reduced to picking cotton after the war has devastated the South, "Prissy picked lazily, spasmodically, complaining . . . until her mother took a cotton stalk to her and whipped her until she screamed. After that she worked a little better" (456). Scarlett's slap is mild compared to Dilcey's whipping, but both are shown to be efficient ways of disciplining a difficult child and slave.

In sharp contrast, *The Red Cock Crows* has Fannie instantly and deeply regret striking Sack. Indeed, Fannie's "sense of her own guilt was so overwhelming she almost forgot Sack had been at all in the wrong" (145). She apologizes desperately to Sack for the blow, even begging her forgiveness. The difference between Scarlett and Fannie could hardly be clearer. Unlike *Gone with the Wind*, Gaither's novel does not suggest that striking a slave could ever have beneficial results. The book thus critiques the idea that any form of physical punishment can be considered reasonable, even as it suggests that slavery makes such violence inevitable. Scarlett, after all, is not an entirely sympathetic character, but if the system can drive so virtuous an individual as Fannie to strike a slave, then any slaveholder could be capable of violence.

More important, however, than Scarlett's and Fannie's very different reactions in each instance are the personalities and intentions of those whom they strike. *Gone with the Wind* presents Prissy as being lazy, incapable, and stupidly oblivious. After Melanie's delivery, Prissy opines, "We done right good, Miss Scarlett." Scarlett, however, recalls the situation somewhat differently, noting only "Prissy's offenses—her boastful assumption of experience she didn't possess, her fright, her blundering awkwardness . . . the misplacing of the scissors . . . the dropping of the new born baby" (371). The central implication of the book's portrayal of Prissy is that many African Americans required the discipline and structure of slavery—that, as Phillips, the southern historian, put it, "plantations were the best schools yet invented for the mass training of that sort of inert and backward people which the bulk of the American negroes represented" (343).

The scene in which Scarlett slaps her maid, however, also problematizes this characterization of Prissy. When Prissy reports her failure to locate a doctor for Melanie, we see her "dragging out her words pleasurably to give more weight to her message." Scarlett is enraged and reflects that "Negroes were always so proud of being the bearers of evil tidings." This suggests a rather different way of interpreting Prissy's "idling along as if she had the whole day before her" (353). Everywhere else, Mitchell's novel depicts Prissy as being merely congenitally lazy and of defective intelligence. But here, for a brief moment, there is a hint that malevolent intention lies behind Prissy's behavior rather than simple incapability. In this one scene, Prissy seems to take genuine pleasure in telling Scarlett that no doctor is available to help the pregnant Melanie, and she apparently deliberately tarries in her errand to seek such assistance. More significantly, in the heat of the moment, Scarlett herself suggests that such behavior is far from exclusive to Prissy when she muses that black people in general take pride in delivering bad news to their white masters.

On the face of it, this is a strange reflection on Scarlett's part because Prissy's conduct is utterly unlike that of the other tirelessly loyal slaves in *Gone with the Wind*. There is, however, a simple explanation for this apparent paradox: Prissy does not really belong in the house servant class. When Prissy accompanies Scarlett and her baby to Atlanta, we learn that "Prissy was not the most adequate of nurses. Her recent graduation from a skinny pickaninny with brief skirts and stiffly wrapped braids into the dignity of a long calico dress and starched white turban was an intoxicating affair. She would never have arrived at this eminence so early in life had not the exigencies of the war and the demands of the commissary department on Tara made it impossible for Ellen to spare Mammy or Dilcey or even Rosa or

Teena" (144). One suspects that had it not been for the exigencies of war, Prissy may well never have arrived at this eminence at all. Her premature graduation has probably saved her from flunking out of the house servant class altogether. Prissy may even have received special consideration denied more able slaves because both her parents—Pork the butler and Dilcey the midwife—are prominent members of Tara's slave elite. In normal circumstances, Prissy, on coming of age, would surely have been consigned to the fields alongside those others "least willing or able to learn, the least energetic, the least honest and trustworthy, the most vicious and brutish" (M. Mitchell 654).

Prissy, in other words, brings the qualities that *Gone with the Wind* repeatedly identifies with the black lower class into the ranks of the house servant elite—and thus directly into a novel in which the field hand class has otherwise been thoroughly erased. This is why Mitchell's narrative and rhetoric demonize Prissy as they demonize no other black character. Scarlett's observation that "Negroes were always so proud of being the bearers of evil tidings" simply does not mesh with the portrayal of individual African Americans elsewhere in the novel (353). It is impossible to conceive of either Mammy or Uncle Peter acting in such a fashion. What Scarlett really means is that it is black people *like* Prissy who actively enjoy delivering bad news to their masters—which is to say those supposedly vicious, dishonest, and brutish slaves who would normally be relegated to field labor.

While *Gone with the Wind* frequently asserts that the field hand class of slaves was incapable, lazy, and morally backward, the novel also continually implies that slavery successfully regimented this class. Mitchell's book argues that it was the freedom for which this class was unequipped and the cynical manipulations of Yankees that drove lower-class southern blacks to commit outrages against former masters. Such behavior, the narrative implies, was quite unknown before emancipation. By making the slave lower class entirely invisible during the novel's antebellum sequences, the book is able to avoid acknowledging the possibility that this group might have been capable of bitter resentment of—and even violence toward—white people while still in bondage. The pleasure that Prissy takes in the misfortunes of Scarlett and Melanie, however, suggests that the black lower class did not love its white rulers, either before or after slavery—and was even capable of deliberately discomforting the master class and enjoying any distress it caused.

The Red Cock Crows makes utterly explicit the resentment and potential violence of slaves that Mitchell's novel only fleetingly implies. Fannie Dalton strikes Sack for two reasons: because she has endangered—perhaps deliberately—the life of a white baby and because she seems to be threatening widespread slave violence against whites. Fannie questions Sack as to where the slave has taken a Dalton infant, and is shocked to learn that, despite a doctor's clear warnings, Sack carried the child down to the slave quarters, which are in the midst of a whooping cough epidemic. In response to Fannie's outburst about the dangers of infection, Sack, aware of the impending insurrection, makes the ominous pronouncement "Hit don't make no matter what [the baby] catch now," causing Fannie to lose her temper and hit her (144). Prissy's incompetent midwifery and Scarlett's vague inferences about her resentful resistance have become, in *The Red Cock Crows*, Sack's apparently deliberate attempt to endanger a white infant's life and an explicit threat of violent revolution.

One of the central points of *The Red Cock Crows* is that even the most benevolent form of slavery is still oppression, and that those who are enslaved deeply resent it. While Gaither's text sometimes subtly undermines the idea of benign paternalist slavery, it still largely constructs the institution as a relatively mild one. The novel's conspiracy, however, allegedly involves hundreds, perhaps even thousands of people from all classes of the slave population (205). The African American characters in the novel are not rebelling against cruel and brutal coercion but against a liberal and relatively kindly institution. They are planning to slaughter not Simon Legrees, but Gerald O'Haras.

The book underlines this point when the judge, Fannie Dalton's well-meaning but ineffectual grandfather, observes, "it's hungry people who make the revolutions. . . . Our people are too well-fed, too comfortable all around to cut our throats" (136). A quarter of a century later, William Styron's *The Confessions of Nat Turner* would echo this moment in its portrayal of lawyer Thomas Gray's bewilderment at Turner's murder of a master who, the militant slave himself concedes, was generous and benevolent. "How do you explain that?" Gray demands, "A man who you admit is kind and gentle to you and you butcher in cold blood" (34). The difference is that while Styron's novel presents this as a riddle—a perplexing and anomalous conundrum that the narrative must somehow explain—*The Red Cock Crows* is quite ironic when its complacent judge asserts as a truism that "comfortable" slaves do not rebel. After all, at the very moment that the judge makes this statement, Scofield—one of the most privileged slaves owned by the Dalton family—is planning a violent insurrection. While Styron's novel provides an elaborate psychological explanation for the militancy of a single slave, Gaither's text shows that the white ruling class was incredibly naive not to expect the people it enslaved to develop rebellious tendencies. Where Mitchell's fiction implies that such attributes were characteristic only of a lower class of slaves, the rebel leader in *The Red Cock Crows* is Shandy's elite driver.

Mitchell's novel effectively denies it and Styron's Gray fails to comprehend it, but as Aptheker shows and as Gaither's judge discovers, slave insurrections did, in fact, often begin not with the most oppressed but with the best-treated slaves. Indeed, Scofield is probably the most elite slave in the entire community of the Forks. As Scofield himself muses, "A born leader, Mas Ward called him. That's how come to make Scofield driver. A driver has more power than an overseer, if you come right down to it. Overseers are white, but they're here one year and gone the next. A driver stays on and builds up his power year after year. A driver gets to be mighty near the biggest man on the place in time" (97). Being the local black preacher gives Scofield even greater status in slave society. He proudly remembers "when niggers from all over the Forks crowded the old Arden gin-house" to hear one of his sermons. For Scofield, having slaves of the whole region depend upon his religious teachings is "like being driver to the whole Forks instead of just one plantation" (98).

That the leader of her novel's conspiracy is such a privileged slave is just one of several indications that Gaither was likely indebted to Aptheker's ideas—which had been published in various journal articles and pamphlets in the late thirties before the appearance of *American Negro Slave Revolts* in 1943. Certainly Gaither's understanding of the factors commonly underlying slave rebellions closely parallels the historian's theories.[6]

For instance, Aptheker observes that "areas of dense Negro population . . . were very frequently the centers of unrest." He notes, furthermore, that in the immediate area of the origin of the 1835 Mississippi rebellion, Livingston and Beatie's Bluff, "the Negroes outnumbered the whites by fifty to one" (*American* 114, 325n). Gaither closely follows Aptheker's lead by asserting early in her novel that "the black population" of her fictional community around the Forks and Scott's Bluff "was to the white as forty to one" (6). Aptheker also asserts that "industrialization and urbanization were phenomena that made the control of slaves more difficult. . . . The easier acquisition of knowledge, the greater possibility of association, and the greater confidence and assurance that city life and mechanical pursuits developed . . . were widely recognized as dangers" (*American* 114–15). In Gaither's novel, the seditious talk that leads to rebellion begins not on the plantation, but in town at the shop of the hired-out African American blacksmith Asa (38).[7]

Gaither's narrative, furthermore, makes white involvement in slave conspiracies a central theme. *The Red Cock Crows* dramatizes the idea that, if whites may not have been organizers of slave revolts, they could be willing participants in them. Members of the Safety Committee simply assume that radical whites must be at the root of the insurrection plot. A single slave's vague hearsay about "an unnamed, friendly, white man" helping the insurgents purchase arms is enough to confirm this assumption as fact in the eyes of the investigators. One member of the committee bluntly asks, "Where's the sense in stringin' up a lot of niggers nobody ever hear tell of whilst the white man that put them up to their meanness gets loose?" Later, two white patrollers discussing the issue observe that "Some white man would have to be at the bottom of it. For where, after all, could you find a darky capable of the organization and command such a far-reaching plot would require?" (196–97, 203, 243). This is another ironic moment in the novel, for Scofield, the very type of black rebel that these men declare an impossibility, is eavesdropping on their conversation. Scofield is far from exceptional, however. Unlike Styron's Nat Turner, Scofield does not face the challenge of converting a community of servile slaves into an army of ruthless soldiers.[8] Instead, *The Red Cock Crows* presents a slave community that is broadly inclined toward militancy. Long before Scofield has the religious visions that inspire his insurrection plot, slaves such as Asa and Tanyard Charlie thrill to the militant words of David Walker's "Appeal" when they hear it read at the blacksmith's shop (38). In short, the reader discovers early in the novel that rebellious talk is prevalent among enslaved African Americans.

While Gaither's book dismisses the idea that black revolution required white leaders, *The Red Cock Crows* does suggest, like Aptheker's study, that lower-class whites may still have been involved in slave insurrections. The narrative eventually reveals that Scofield persuaded an itinerant and unqualified local quack (or "steam doctor") named Purdy to write a fake pass for a runaway slave before convincing him to join the conspiracy. Purdy explains that his motivation was that "the whole Forks turn up their nose at steam-doctors. . . . Look like I can't make a friend on earth but niggers." But Purdy is anything but an organizing force behind the insurrection; rather, Scofield cleverly exploits him. As Purdy tells it, "I swear to God I never put notions in his head. He plan out the whole thing from A to Z. . . . Well, he give me the pass back to save my neck . . . and then he ask me about buyin' him some powder and lead soon as he can raise the money. And I say, 'Sure'" (255–56).

The novel, however, ultimately rejects the possibility of lower-class interracial solidarity that Aptheker asserts in the pages of *American Negro Slave Revolts*. *The Red Cock Crows* presents Purdy's involvement in the slave conspiracy not as an act of cross-racial class consciousness, but as motivated primarily by self-interest. Purdy eventually concedes that he was driven largely by hopes of material gain, confessing, "Well, with stores broke open and everything run wild, I figured there'd be a mess of stuff layin' around." If this were not enough, when Purdy suggests to his cellmate, Fiske, that they are blood brothers because they are both likely to be hanged by the Safety Committee, Fiske views Purdy "with more revulsion than ever." A mere twenty pages after this, however, Fiske feels "compassionate, even brotherly, toward Scofield, for surely now their lots were not unlike" (256, 277). Fiske, then, is happy to identify himself with a black slave insurrectionist, but is repelled at the thought that there is a connection between himself and a lower-class white who participated in a slave conspiracy. Given that Fiske is the novel's hero, one assumes that the reader is expected to share his respect for Scofield and his disgust at Purdy. In short, the potentially radical portrayal of slave rebellion in *The Red Cock Crows* founders on what seems to be a rather elitist attitude regarding not race but class.

This attitude, furthermore, is not only apparent in the novel's treatment of working-class whites. Gaither's novel goes to considerable lengths to absolve the white planter class of responsibility for the racist hysteria that seizes the community around the Forks. For one thing, the patriarchs of the planter class are relatively anonymous in, and conveniently absent from, much of the narrative. Ward Dalton, the owner of the Shandy plantation, is often away on business, and, even when he is in residence, rarely steps into the forefront of the action. Meanwhile, the men of the Clay family—the other prominent planters in the novel—have been killed in a family scandal before the narrative even begins. Certainly, Fannie's grandfather, the judge, is a prominent character, but as a frail retiree, he is somewhat removed from the business of slaveholding. For much of the novel, the primary inhabitants of the plantations are young women like Fannie Dalton and the Clay sisters. The narrative not only largely removes slaveholding patriarchs from the picture but also idealizes those few who are present. The aristocratic Malcolm Webb is portrayed as the nearest thing to a voice of sanity on the deadly Safety Committee. He quietly votes against the conviction of one hapless white defendant and publicly attempts to defend Fiske when the schoolteacher is accused. Finally, when the committee banishes Fiske from the Forks, Webb generously donates a fine horse to him. Of the few plantation-owning males with any real prominence in the narrative, Trooper Clay is the closest thing to a villain, and he seems determined to convict Fiske primarily because he perceives him as a rival for Fannie's affections. Given the popularity of *Gone with the Wind*, with its portrait of kindly paternalists like Gerald O'Hara, Gaither probably could not have got away with depicting slaveholders as cruel, authoritarian patriarchs. However, by largely removing male plantation owners from the novel and by organizing her narrative around their innocent and compassionate daughters, Gaither essentially replicates rather than challenges some of the stereotypes about slavery that Mitchell's novel perpetuates.

Furthermore, while largely idealizing the white upper class, the novel specifically identifies lower-class whites as the primary source of racial animosity and violence in the Forks. The so-called Safety Committee that investigates the conspiracy is not directed by the aristocratic planters, for many of them are absent in summer. Instead, small slaveholders and the local slave auctioneer dominate the committee and dictate its activities in tandem with lower-class law enforcement officials. Before the committee is created, there are brief, informal proceedings presided over by the upper-class planters at which slaves are politely questioned. This rational form of inquiry contrasts strikingly to the rabid, bloodthirsty committee, which becomes a "demoniac force" that slaves take to calling simply "the Death Board." Significantly, it is the "town loafers" and "choicest ruffians" who are responsible for lynching largely innocent slaves in the novel and aristocratic planters who protect blacks from the mob (255, 311, 176, 177, 162).

By romanticizing aristocratic slaveholders and demonizing poorer whites, *The Red Cock Crows* risks simply repeating *Gone with the Wind*'s claims about a kindly paternalist planter class and a brutish white working class. It is true that Gaither was writing in an era when the lynching of blacks by lower-class whites was horribly commonplace, but the idea that African Americans have suffered more at the hands of the lower classes of the South than the plantation elite (and its descendants) was not a particularly new idea in 1944, and, indeed, is a trope with a long history in American fiction by both white and black writers.

As far back as Harriet Beecher Stowe's *Uncle Tom's Cabin*, plantation owners in slavery fiction are largely sympathetic characters who often genuinely care for their human property, even if they may be ineffectual, like Tom's first master, Shelby, or troubled, like Augustine St. Clare. Stowe's novel explicitly argues that while individual slaveholders could be kindly, the very nature of the institution of slavery necessitates cruelty for which paternal generosity is insufficient compensation (50–51). In the case of lower-class whites, however, *Uncle Tom's Cabin* is content to blame the individual as much as the system. The villains in Stowe's book are not aristocratic southern planters but bounty hunters or slave-traders, such as the jovial Haley, who assures one guilt-ridden yet debt-plagued planter who is obliged to sell some of his slaves, "These critters ain't like white folks, you know; they gets over things" (46–47). Indeed, the only truly villainous planter in *Uncle Tom's Cabin* is not a southern patrician but the nouveau-riche northern arriviste, Simon Legree.

Published more than a century after *Uncle Tom's Cabin*, Margaret Walker's *Jubilee* (1966) also explores the idea that lower-class whites were often more virulently racist than slaveholding planters. Indeed, since Walker began writing her novel in the 1930s we might even consider it a pseudo-contemporary of *Black Thunder*, *The Red Cock Crows*, and *Gone with the Wind*. Grimes, the working-class overseer on the Dutton plantation in *Jubilee*, prefers the mistress to the master because she "ain't no nigger-loving namby-pamby like that s.o.b. pretty boy she's married to." Grimes whips one slave to death and burns down a cabin containing two slaves he considers to be shirking.

The aristocratic planter, John Dutton, is "incensed" at such atrocities, but he does not survive the Civil War, while Grimes lives to join the Ku Klux Klan, under whose auspices he violently intimidates the black Randall Ware into keeping out of politics and selling his land (26, 68–69, 134–35, 389–95).

What distinguishes *Jubilee*, however, is the idea that the same system oppresses both poor whites and enslaved blacks. One of the tragedies of Walker's novel is that its lower-class characters are unable to comprehend this fact. It is Dutton and "the richest planters" who control, "both politically and financially, a third of the state." This power, furthermore, is completely hereditary: Dutton and the other big wheels in the Georgia House of Representatives "inherited their roles," and Dutton comes "from a distinguished line of public figures and political tycoons." Meanwhile, Grimes lives "in circumstances not much better than the slaves," and works just as hard as they do. Sometimes Dutton temporarily employs poor whites to fill labor shortages on the plantation, but they develop no sense of commonality with African American slaves either: "Each group regarded the other contemptuously and felt that the other was his inferior." The whites "were always throwing taunts and filthy epithets at the black slaves who taunted them back again as 'Ignunt, and worthless, and lowdown, thievish, sickly looking trash.' This conflict always seemed to amuse the planters." As well it might: the slaves have been persuaded to identify with their aristocratic masters, while the book's lower-class white characters have accepted a sense of racial superiority rather than develop a spirit of class solidarity. As Grimes's wife puts it, "We'uns is poor, but thank God we'uns is white" (78, 60, 61, 62, 63).[9] While *Gone with the Wind* portrays resentment between lower-class whites and the slaves of aristocrats as somehow natural, *Jubilee* constructs it as a tragic irony and a form of social control.

The depiction of the limits of class-based relations between enslaved blacks and lower-class whites in Gaither's novel has no such sense of lost potential. *The Red Cock Crows* flirts with the idea of an interracial alliance among the lower classes only to make Purdy, the anomalous white character who joins the slave conspiracy, rather unsympathetic—partly intimidated by Scofield, partly motivated by greed. The *real* attitude of working-class whites toward African American slaves, Gaither's fiction suggests, is manifested in the mob's reign of terror and lynching. Where Aptheker argues for white working-class involvement in slave insurrections, Gaither's novel insists that the southern white proletariat was too intrinsically racist for meaningful alliances with slaves to be feasible. Such a conclusion is problematic because it effectively prevents *The Red Cock Crows* from complicating *Gone with the Wind*'s portrait of the class and racial structures of the antebellum South. By emphasizing the paternal generosity of planters and the racism of lower-class whites, and by rejecting the significance of class-based interracial alliances, *The Red Cock Crows*, for all its notable elements, ultimately largely accords with, rather than challenges, the vision of the South presented in *Gone with the Wind*. A moderate, white, liberal critique of Mitchell's novel turns out to be not much of a critique at all.

While *The Red Cock Crows* does not acknowledge a genuine connection between racial and class hierarchies, it does focus upon the ways in which white patriarchy oppresses people of color and white women alike. Early in the novel, in reference to the unfortunate Edna Lee Clay, we learn that "of course, a fallen woman was lower than any Negro." It is not, however, just "fallen" women who are evaluated in such a fashion. Just a few pages later, Trooper Clay opines, "I'd rather be the low-downest Negro, buck slave to some hard-driving farmer across the bottom than the richest woman at the Forks." Later, Fiske notes that on one Sunday the local minister admonishes wives to obey their husbands and the very next week commands slaves to obey their masters. This echoes a preceding scene in which Ward Dalton returns from a trip with a slave wife for Scofield, whom Scofield does not want, and then, a few pages later, commands Fannie to marry a man she does not love. Finally, as he is banished, Fiske angrily tells Fannie that the southern code of chivalry is nothing but a wall, and if white patriarchs "build the wall high enough they can keep their women pure and their faithful darkies innocent and childlike." Fannie ultimately sees that this is true, telling her southern fiancé, "I don't want to be just indulged and treated like a spoiled child! . . . You decide everything as you think best. It's as though you wanted to keep me shut up inside a high wall" (64, 75, 119, 113, 116, 298, 309).

Gaither's novel, in short, boldly argues that patriarchy makes women into slaves. Mitchell, of course, also critically assesses women's roles in antebellum society in *Gone with the Wind*. The narrative observes, for example, that "It was a man's world. . . . The man owned the property, and the woman managed it. The man took the credit for the management, and the woman praised his cleverness. The man roared like a bull when a splinter was in his finger, and the woman muffled the moans of childbirth, lest she disturb him" (58). *Gone with the Wind*, however, does not go as far as to explicitly compare the situation of women to that of slaves. At one point, Scarlett does observe that her mother "worked harder than any darky on this place," but the implication here is not that Ellen was like a slave but that she did even more than she required of her slaves (455). In *Gone with the Wind*, although the antebellum South is a harmonious and ordered world, it is also one in which women are expected to quietly shoulder all the responsibilities and burdens of everyday life yet enjoy few privileges and virtually no power. While the novel mourns the destruction of this world, it also seems to acknowledge the possibility of greater gender equality in the postbellum future. The changes in the South wrought by the Civil War save Scarlett from having to become like her mother. Instead, she develops into a successful businesswoman in postwar Atlanta. However, *Gone with the Wind* is, finally, at best ambivalent about female equality. The narrative encourages the reader to sympathize with Scarlett's frustrations at the limitations placed upon her by traditional patriarchy, and to take some pleasure in her determined rejection of conventional female roles when she becomes a shrewd entrepreneur after the war. Yet the novel also finally punishes her for her nonconformism, her overreaching, and her abnegation of traditional female duties. Scarlett is a selfish dreamer, a cold mother, and an unfaithful wife. In the moral scheme of Mitchell's universe, Rhett's desertion of Scarlett—just as she finally realizes that he is the true love of her life—is poetic justice.

By not taking its narrative beyond the antebellum era, *The Red Cock Crows* creates no such opportunities for Fannie. Instead, Gaither's novel further develops the parallels it has established between the situations of slaves and white women by positing flight as a woman's most viable form of resistance to white male power. We learn that some years before the novel's action began, Edna Lee Clay eloped with a music teacher, and that her father and brothers hunted the couple down as if they were escaped slaves. In the ensuing shootout, Edna Lee's father, one of her brothers, and the teacher were all killed. The father's final words were his demand to the teacher, "Come out, sir, and settle your account with us." This was, in short, a business issue, a dispute about property, and that property is regained at great cost and "shut up at Brick House disgraced forever," like a captured fugitive slave (73). At the end of the novel, Fannie is rather more successful when she becomes a fugitive from southern patriarchy—seeking freedom from circumscribed gender roles and an authoritarian white male through flight to the North, like so many of the writers of slave narratives. Although Fannie has previously visited the northern states, they still seem as distant to her as they did to many fugitive slaves. "Boston, from here, looked almost as far off as heaven," she observes (313). This is reminiscent of how the enslaved Frederick Douglass—who possesses the same initials as Fannie Dalton—perceived the unknown North: "away back in the dim distance, under the flickering light of the north star, behind some craggy hill or snow-covered mountain, stood a doubtful freedom" (57). Furthermore, when Fannie's servant, Montgomery, begins to comprehend her intention to flee, "he began to smile, exactly as if he understood and sympathized," and he provides money to the white female fugitive (310).

The Red Cock Crows thus constructs the North as a relative haven of gender equality, an embodiment of postbellum potential for female emancipation. The South, in contrast, is an outdated antebellum world of conservative and rigidly defined gender roles. Fannie flees the specifically southern conventions of chivalry that both mask and enable the practice of patriarchal power. For example, when southern men speak of politics and law, "Fannie and the other girls, mimicking their mother's gravity during such consideration of men's special interests, dropped their eyes and demurely sipped their sodas." Fiske, however, as a northerner, lacks the chivalry that undergirds the southern form of patriarchal power. He doesn't offer Fannie his arm when walking with her, and treats her "as indifferently as if she were another man." Neither does he indulge in romantic flattery or adopt "that air of submissive adoration" that southern gentlemen know how to affect. He even encourages Fannie to call him by his first name when this is not "the custom at the Forks even for married women addressing their own husbands" (29, 34, 67, 110). But it is specifically Fiske, as a representative of northern gender equality, to whom Fannie is running from her patriarchal fiancé Trooper Clay. There is a significant limitation here in that the only freedom from male oppression Fannie can imagine is with a man who is less patriarchal than her fiancé—but perhaps no more realistic alternative was easily available to women in antebellum America, or could be imagined by many women in the 1940s. Nonetheless, despite romanticizing the relative gender equality of the North, *The Red Cock Crows*, like *Gone with the Wind*, is entirely ambivalent about the consequences of female liberation. Fannie acknowledges, even as she flees her home, that Shandy and the South are still "paradise," and "nowhere else on earth could ever be so nice." Furthermore, Fannie has visited the North, and she knows that it is not "a land of everlasting bliss where all men were just or even or free"—to say nothing of women. Indeed, Fannie "knew what life was there and she did not expect to like it" (313).

While *The Red Cock Crows* draws striking parallels between the position of women and the situation of slaves, it is ironic that what is ostensibly a book about potential black liberation ultimately becomes a story about white female freedom. The slave rebels are crushed, but the fugitive white woman escapes. Indeed, Montgomery gives money to aid the escapee because "I've got no mortal use for it. Haven't I got everything on earth I want at Shandy?" This statement seems to confirm Purdy's earlier statement that "ain't ary one of Dalton's niggers would run, if a good-natured white man was to write out a pass and put it in his hand" (311, 95). While the planned slave insurrection temporarily violates the truth of Purdy's assessment, the tidy resumption of the status quo at the end of the narrative has apparently restored the loyalty of the Dalton slaves. The narrative purges militant blacks in order to make way for the triumph of a rebellious white aristocratic woman. White patriarchy keeps its hold over slaves, but loses its power over the white heroine. Fannie's flight, therefore, is radical in terms of gender politics by equating the oppression of women with slavery. The book is, however, reactionary in its racial politics by shifting its focus from enslaved African Americans to privileged white women.[10]

Despite the fact that the novel finally steers away from its ostensible concern with slavery, *The Red Cock Crows* is nonetheless fairly impressive in its portrayal of African American males, particularly for a white female writer in the late Jim Crow period. Gaither is not immune from racist discourse, however; at one point in the narrative, she refers, seemingly without a trace of irony, to the black race as "primitive man" (195). Nonetheless, the novel also very effectively uses Scofield as its central viewpoint character in several chapters. We see, for example, Scofield's trial—in which he skillfully manipulates his interrogators—largely from the perspective of the slave general himself (289–94, 300–303). The scene in which another rebel, Holiness Sam, takes a courageous stand against the Safety Committee is a similar instance of Gaither's vivid and sympathetic portrayal of black men: "Sam showed no fear. He was, rather, defiant. He met all questions with stony silence. . . . The threat of whipping left him unmoved." "Go ahead on and hang me, white folks," Sam goads his accusers, "You cut out my heart you can't make me name no name. . . . Hang me. Burn me. I ain't talkin'" (211).

More significantly, Gaither understands that the passive, childlike "Sambo" persona that some observers attributed to slaves—and which would be treated as genuine by postwar historian Stanley Elkins—was usually nothing more than an assumed protective mask.[11] In one powerful scene in *The Red Cock Crows*, the supposedly docile Scofield boldly reveals his rebelliousness to Fiske and shows him the fake pass forged by Purdy. "You know what they do to a white man help a nigger run like that, Mr. Fist? . . . They hangs him. White man rist his neck like that must think more of niggers than he do of his own self, don't he, Mr. Fist?" Scofield here is direct and intimidating in his attempt to discover whether Fiske might be a potential recruit for his campaign. Fiske, however, is quite taken aback by such audacity and responds by desperately rejecting both the substance of what Scofield is saying and the personality that says it. Fiske defensively adopts "a brisk, decisive voice" and asserts brusquely that either a literate slave or a slave-stealer aiming to entice a slave "into his own possession" must have written the pass (120). Fiske thus denies the possibility that whites could think of themselves as allies to slaves—or that Scofield could possibly be as militant as he suddenly sounds. Rebuffed, Scofield immediately readopts the mask and dialect of Sambo—what Scofield later calls his "white-folks manners, soft-spoken, self-depreciating" (289):

> To [Fiske's] relief, Scofield took up the paper and answered in his everyday agreeable voice.
> "Yass'r, Mr. Fist. Sho is. Folks say this country jes' crawlin' with nigger-stealers." (120)

Scenes like this constitute one of the most sophisticated depictions of the psychologies of enslaved people of color by a white writer up to this point in American fiction.

In sum, then, both African American males and white women rebel against patriarchy in *The Red Cock Crows*, Scofield by organizing an insurrection and Fannie by fleeing to the North. Both characters, furthermore, do much to enlist the sympathy of the reader. While the book ennobles black men and white females, however, its treatment of women of color is organized around the most simplistic and clichéd of racist and sexist stereotypes.

Coatney, the central black female character in *The Red Cock Crows*, is little more than an oversexed and animalistic Jezebel. When teased by men, Coatney "guffawed as loud as a man," and later she obliviously exposes a bare breast while riding a horse. She also stabs a man to death at a party for no clear cause. Furthermore, when Scofield searches Coatney for a hidden weapon, she sensually enjoys the physical contact, and then bites and fights the aroused Scofield and lets out a "bubble of laughter" as he attempts to rape her. Neither can one expect human compassion and loyalty from this irrational and psychotic nymphomaniac, for Coatney ultimately betrays Scofield to the authorities (16, 26, 21, 26–27, 287). Virtually all the stereotypes created by white slaveowning men—which were used to justify and legitimize the sexual exploitation of enslaved women—are present in Gaither's appallingly backward portrait of Coatney. Gaither's character is, in short, an even worse stereotype than Bontemps's Juba.

One of Gaither's other novels about slavery, *Double Muscadine* (1949)— the story of a quadroon woman put on trial for poisoning her white masters —is similarly appalling in its reliance on the Jezebel stereotype. In this story, a Mississippi planter, Kirk McLean, is consumed with guilt and disgust after he allows Aimee, a new acquisition, to seduce him: "Her desire—well, they were all alike, those poor creatures. Back in his own room afterward he had been filled with revulsion, self-reproach, regret." Another young black woman in the novel is so promiscuous in her relations with white men that she does not even "know whose baby it was inside her now" (238, 287). While *Double Muscadine* boldly addresses the miscegenation that *Gone with the Wind* utterly suppresses, the narrative still blithely attributes it to the carnal impulses of oversexed African American women, not to the rapaciousness of slaveholding white men.

The portrayal of African American women and slave rebellion in *The Red Cock Crows* is, however, complicated by the character of the maid, Sack. The book does not sexualize Sack in the manner of Coatney, but it does present her as grasping and greedy. At one point in the narrative, Fannie tells Fiske that Sack is "a whining darky who was always lying in wait for her, waiting to snatch the clothes off her back" (107). Later in the narrative, of course,

Sack apparently seeks to deliberately infect a white baby with whooping cough and eagerly anticipates the planned slaughter of the Daltons. However, despite Sack's veiled threats, the maid is ultimately able to evade punishment during the investigation into the conspiracy by claiming that she knew only what one of the rebels told her and that she was innocent of involvement herself. The Safety Committee fails, furthermore, to inquire into Sack's stealing of the plantation keys, which Fannie discovers earlier in the narrative (161, 145). Sack seems to be protected by her gender. The committee sentences and the mob hangs men of both races, but no women. Sack is potentially a very dangerous slave indeed, but she avoids punishment and continues in her privileged position in the Big House.

In fact, Sack does even better than that. The end of the novel reveals, almost as an afterthought, that the fleeing Fannie is obliged to take Sack north with her, and thus to freedom: "Sack—whom she had to bring along because Montgomery had stubbornly insisted 'folks wouldn't know what to make of a young lady traveling all by herself'—seemed to her a very poor shield against the certain discomforts and possible mishaps of the long, long road" (313). Given Gaither's attitudes and emphases throughout the novel, one is tempted to take this explanation at face value. Yet one cannot help but wonder about the implications of one slave's insistence that Fannie should take as a companion another slave who, earlier evidence suggests, was quite prepared to play a serious and even murderous role in the insurrection. While the novel emphasizes Fannie's liberation, the rebellious Sack is also rewarded with freedom. In *The Red Cock Crows*, loyal slaves are left in slavery, while Gaither's equivalent of Mitchell's despised Prissy gains her liberty. Like Prissy, then, Sack seems to undermine the very novel in which she appears. While the narrative elevates Fannie's emancipation over the plight of enslaved African Americans, and while it suggests that Sack is thoroughly enthused about the prospect of black-on-white violence, it nonetheless rewards her with the same freedom as it gives its white female protagonist.

The Red Cock Crows is in some ways an unusually powerful portrayal of slave insurrection for a southern white female novelist in 1944—in very stark contrast to *Gone with the Wind*. It is, however, also a novel that is characterized by ambivalence and which does not explore or fulfill the potential of its most promising insights. The narrative compellingly portrays the militant desire of black men for freedom, but rewards only an aristocratic white woman (and her black female servant) with liberty. *The Red Cock Crows* boldly acknowledges the possibility of alliances between lower-class whites and enslaved blacks, but ultimately backs away from the logical conclusion that such partnerships could result from a sense of shared oppression and class solidarity. Instead, Gaither's text portrays the white steam doctor involved in the conspiracy as merely weak and greedy. Despite its often-impressive portrayal of radicalized black men, the book consistently reduces African American women to offensive stereotypes. While *The Red Cock Crows* promises to be a compelling counternarrative to *Gone with the Wind*, in the end it simply does not challenge the assumptions about racial, class, and gender relations in the antebellum South that Mitchell's novel embodies. *The Red Cock Crows* uneasily steers a moderate path between the white southern conservatism of *Gone with the Wind* and the leftist militancy of *American Negro Slave Revolts*.

Defining the Limits of Discourse: The Traditional Rules of Representation in Twentieth-Century Slavery Fiction

For all their ostensible differences, *Gone with the Wind* and *The Red Cock Crows* share something fundamental in common. Both are dependent upon their era's conventional literary rules for representing slavery, race, and gender—conventions that Aptheker's *American Negro Slave Revolts* transcends. Nancy Bentley has analyzed the tacit "rules of representation for women and men, for black and white" in the nineteenth-century domestic novel of slavery. Bentley notes, for example, that violence and abuse are often inflicted upon female and black bodies in nineteenth-century literature, but not upon a white man (502–3). It is a simple task to outline a slightly different but equally rigid schema that applies to slavery novels of the first half of the twentieth century. These rules subsume all class issues, and Gaither's novel obeys these rules as completely as *Gone with the Wind*. Even *Black Thunder* is largely in thrall to them.

White-authored fiction before the 1960s tends to de-emphasize, stereotype, or otherwise neutralize those figures at the very top and very bottom of the system of slavery—powerful white men and powerless black women. These novels focus instead upon those figures in the middle of the hierarchy: white women (who are privileged in terms of race but not in terms of gender) and African American men (who are male in a patriarchal society, but black in a racist culture). By relegating the planter-patriarch—the very embodiment of slaveholding power—to the periphery and often making him relatively ineffectual, writers like Mitchell and Gaither soften the system of slavery. Gerald O'Hara in *Gone with the Wind* is an overgrown child who leaves the administration of Tara to his wife. Everyone on the plantation "from Ellen down to the stupidest field hand was in a tacit and kindly conspiracy to keep him believing his word was law." In addition, *Gone with the Wind* does not directly show Ashley Wilkes in the role of slaveholder and pointedly constructs him as effeminate (64, 30, 34). The central white male protagonist of *The Red Cock Crows* is, furthermore, a northerner, not a slaveowner, and Ward Dalton barely appears in the narrative. In another novel of slavery from this period, Willa Cather's *Sapphira and the Slave Girl* (1940), the meek slaveholder of the Mill House, Henry Colbert, tells his wife, "You're the master here" (50). These novels also neutralize the oppression and suffering of the most downtrodden and vulnerable figure on the plantation—the African American woman—by rendering her marginal or by demonizing her. Mitchell's Sack and Gaither's Prissy are unreliable and opportunistic, and Coatney is a full-blown Jezebel. In addition, Toni Morrison observes that Nancy, the eponymous "slave girl" of Cather's novel, is "voiceless, a cipher" (*Playing* 24). The reader simply is not encouraged to care about such women.

The real centers of these narratives are young white women. The plantation mistress is too close to the power of the slaveholder to be the perfect female lead. Ellen O'Hara, Miss Treasy (Fannie's mother), and even the eponymous Sapphira in Cather's novel play second fiddle to the true heroines, their daughters.[12] Black men can be significant figures in such fiction, but they are largely important in terms of their relations to the white female protagonist. As we have seen, Sam saves Scarlett from the would-be rapist of Shantytown, while Montgomery provides money for Fannie to escape the South. In *The Red Cock Crows*, the rebellious African American male, Scofield, must die for the white woman to triumph. Gaither's novel is at its most interesting when it pushes the boundaries of the rules of representation, such as those moments when Scofield emerges as a militant individual and leader of a community, no longer a mere tragic symbol. For the most part, however, *The Red Cock Crows* is thoroughly subject to literary convention.

Neither does an African American Marxist like Arna Bontemps entirely evade these rules of representation. While *Black Thunder* does not soften the oppression of slavery, slaveholding patriarchs play a smaller role in the novel than any other white characters. Their cruelty is barely more visible than in Gaither's and Mitchell's fictions, apart from the opening scene in which Thomas Prosser whips the hapless Old Bundy to death. Whatever Bontemps's intentions, Juba is still a Jezebel stereotype and Gabriel is no less doomed than Gaither's Scofield. The crucial difference is that white women—both plantation mistresses and their daughters—are altogether absent from *Black Thunder*. Rather than reorganizing his narrative around other figures, however, Bontemps simply seems to have left an empty space in his tale and has not developed a central protagonist to fill the vacuum. Gabriel, Juba, and Thomas Prosser are no more developed or significant characters than Scofield, Coatney, and Ward Dalton (who are merely secondary figures in Fannie's tale). *Black Thunder* provides a couple of surrogates for the absent white female character. The radical Biddenhurst and Melody, the mulatto prostitute, both survive the chaos Gabriel's plot unleashes upon Richmond and escape to the North just like Fannie in *The Red Cock Crows*. Biddenhurst and Melody are, however, minor and ineffectual characters. Ultimately, then, even *Black Thunder* does not articulate sufficiently developed alternatives to the traditional rules for representing slavery in literature.

If, however, *The Red Cock Crows* and *Black Thunder* failed to mount a sufficient assault upon the ideology of *Gone with the Wind* in the cultural Civil War of the early twentieth century, contemporary African American writers have been barely more successful. For all the furor it generated, many reviewers considered Alice Randall's *The Wind Done Gone* a failure in its efforts to dismantle the power of Mitchell's enduring melodrama. Carolyn See calls Randall's tale of Cynara—Scarlett O'Hara's mulatto half-sister—an "earnest allegory" in which "soporific solemnity prevails," and she concludes that "The *Gone with the Wind* myth, with all its undeniable treacle and creepy racism, is in no danger at all from *The Wind Done Gone*" (1).

In the light of my analysis of Mitchell's and Gaither's novels, it is clear that the limitations of Randall's critique of *Gone with the Wind* result not from her treatment of race, but from her failure to explore the issue of class. Randall claims that her "unauthorized parody" began with the question, "Where are the mulattos on Tara?" This is a crucial question, for, as Claudia Roth Pierpont points out, Mitchell explicitly describes the Tara slaves as being "shining black," apart from one who is specifically identified as part Indian (quoted in Miller 1, 3). While the Mitchell Trust continues to forbid depictions of interracial sexual relations in authorized sequels to *Gone with the Wind*, Randall locates miscegenation at the very center of Mitchell's mythological South, most notably in the form of Cynara herself (Miller 3). The novel thus overturns the traditional conventions of slavery fiction by focusing upon an African American female protagonist—but this was not a particularly innovative act by 2001. Beginning with Margaret Walker's *Jubilee* as far back as 1966, a number of contemporary black writers have organized their novels about slavery around women.[13] *The Wind Done Gone*, furthermore, still fails to give voice to a group of African Americans that is equally anonymous in *Gone with the Wind*. Randall observes: "When I was looking at critiquing *Gone with the Wind*, one of the things that occurred to me first was its marginalization of certain types. One group is African Americans. Certainly intelligent African Americans and, specifically, mulattoes are marginalized—excluded as a matter of fact. Another excluded group is gay characters" (quoted in Goss 1). Randall, however, seems quite oblivious to the particular act of marginalization that is the very foundation of Mitchell's construction of the South—the erasure of the field hand class of slaves from the novel. *The Wind Done Gone* is similarly concerned only with the house servant class of slave, like Cynara. Thus, like Frances Gaither before her, Alice Randall fails to dismantle the central ideological hierarchy of *Gone with the Wind* in her fiction.

Meanwhile, despite its significant limitations, *The Red Cock Crows* may still have something of value to contribute to the ongoing debate about slave insurrections. In 2001, the historian Michael P. Johnson contentiously argued that the Denmark Vesey insurrection conspiracy of 1822 was nothing but an empty scare blown out of proportion. In Johnson's revisionist interpretation of history, Vesey was merely a hapless fall guy, and the case against him was constructed from coerced testimony by a court that was determined to prove the existence of a conspiracy where none existed. This witch hunt, Johnson claims, was motivated by a desire to justify the hysterical fears of slave rebellion that had seized Charleston, as well as subsequent violence against local blacks (971). Johnson's essay provoked a heated debate in the pages of the *William and Mary Quarterly*, with one historian angrily responding that "Johnson's theory takes on the proportions of an Oliver Stone film, in that there appear to be more white perpetrators involved in the conspiracy—all of whom took their secret to the grave—than seemed to exist in the general population" (Egerton, "Forgetting" 149). *The Red Cock Crows* provides a way of cutting through this debate. The Charleston Court of Magistrates and Freeholders could have been every bit as dishonest and corrupt in its investigation into the Vesey conspiracy as Johnson claims, intimidating witnesses and hanging the innocent, much like Gaither's Committee of Safety. But, as *The Red Cock Crows* makes abundantly clear, that does not mean that there was not also a genuine slave conspiracy.

From Tara to Turner

SLAVERY AND SLAVE PSYCHOLOGIES IN AMERICAN FICTION
AND HISTORY, 1945–1968

In 1968—a full thirty-two years after its first appearance—Beacon Press republished *Black Thunder*. Arna Bontemps begins his introduction to this new edition of the novel with the words, "Time is not a river. Time is a pendulum." History, Bontemps suggests, is not linear and progressive, but repetitive and cyclical. More than 150 years after the Richmond conspiracy, resistance to slavery had transformed into opposition to Jim Crow, and the assassination of Martin Luther King evoked the execution of Gabriel during another, far distant election year (vii, viii). Just as the militancy of nineteenth-century slaves resounded with American Marxists during the Depression years, so, Bontemps hoped, might his long-neglected novel find an audience in the age of Black Nationalism. Ironically, the 1968 reappearance of *Black Thunder* coincided with the resurrection of another 1930s text concerning slavery: the much-ballyhooed rerelease of the film adaptation of *Gone with the Wind*. Furthermore, just as Margaret Mitchell's dubious fictionalization of slavery had won the Pulitzer Prize a generation before, so, in 1968, did another questionable white-authored novel about the peculiar institution garner the very same accolade.

William Styron's *The Confessions of Nat Turner* is a fictional account of the insurrection that took place in Southampton, Virginia, in 1831, told from the perspective of its famous leader. Despite its focus upon the black experience in slavery and its portrayal of militant rebellion against the institution, Styron's novel has generated considerable antagonism. Many have been inclined to see *The Confessions of Nat Turner* not as a thoughtful dramatization of resistance to slavery, but as a racist appropriation and diminution of an African American hero. At the time of its publication, a number of readers objected strenuously to the glowing tributes that the novel received from some quarters. One journalist even published a column entitled "I Spit on the Pulitzer Prize." African American critics referred to the novel as "an outright fake" and "a typical Southern white man's cliché" (Stone 105; Meyer quoted in Stone 121; Walker quoted in Stone 125). Contemporary scholars characterize the novel in similar terms—as "yet another example of white America's determination to misrepresent the Afro-American past," and as one more instance of "the reductive images and ridiculing representations of African Americans in American literature and culture of the nineteenth and twentieth centuries" (Van Deburg 140; A. Mitchell 67).

The fundamental problem for many is that Styron's ideas about slavery derive primarily from Stanley Elkins's landmark—but controversial—historical study *Slavery: A Problem in American Institutional and Intellectual Life* (1959). Elkins argues that there is extensive documentary evidence in support of the antebellum southern white opinion that the average African American slave was a "perpetual child incapable of maturity" (84). Rejecting the bigoted explanations of Anglo-Saxon racial superiority that pervade the work of earlier historians such as Ulrich B. Phillips, Elkins suggests that slavery itself produced the "Sambo" persona: that an oppressive institution and the psychological influence of the master created a docile and retarded personality. Elkins acknowledges that a few exceptional individuals were able "to escape the full impact of the system and its coercions upon personality" (85, 137). In Styron's novel, Nat Turner is just such an individual, and he sees his fellow slaves as precisely the perpetual children that Elkins describes: "a lower order of people—a ragtag mob, coarse, raucous, clownish, uncouth . . . faceless and nameless toilers," for whom Nat holds a "lifelong contempt" (135–36, 201). Such a view of enslaved African Americans has not endeared *The Confessions of Nat Turner* to some readers, who criticize its use of the "fraudulent and untenable" ideas of Elkins, and who deplore Styron's "vile racist imagination" (Kaiser 54, 57).

To many critics, both past and present, Elkins's study and Styron's novel epitomize a white-authored "hegemonic discourse on slavery" that dominated American culture before the 1970s (Rushdy, *Neo-slave* 54). In this view, Styron's *Confessions* and Elkins's *Slavery* are simply the heirs of *Gone* with the Wind and Phillips's *American Negro Slavery*—and are largely indistinguishable from them as far as their ideological assumptions about slavery and enslaved Americans are concerned. One critic thus accuses Styron of "trying to prove that U.B. Phillips, the classic apologist for slavery, and Stanley Elkins, the sophisticated modern apologist, were right when they projected Sambo—the bootlicking, head-scratching child-man—as a dominant plantation type" (Bennett 7). Another writer even describes Styron's novel as a "throwback to the racist writing of the 1930's and 1940's" (quoted in Van Deburg 140).

What distinguishes the cultural conversation about slavery in 1968 from that of 1936, however, is precisely that Styron's novel generated a critical backlash the extent of which would hardly have been conceivable in Mitchell's time. Within months of the publication of *Confessions*, John Henrik Clarke had assembled a team of African American authors to critique the novel in a volume entitled *William Styron's Nat Turner: Ten Black Writers Respond*. Styron was also dogged by a persistent African American inquisitor at speaking engagements and would later accuse his vigorous black critics of derailing a planned film adaptation of his novel (Stone 12–13, 14).[1] Ashraf Rushdy even claims that the African American critical response to Styron's novel achieved nothing less than the dismantling of the existing cultural hegemony about slavery and the creation of a new discourse about the institution characterized by "a renewed respect for the truth and value of slave testimony, the significance of slave cultures, and the importance of slave resistance." In this view, the Ten Black Writers set the agenda for subsequent fictional portrayals of slavery and ushered in a post-1960s renaissance of African American fiction (Rushdy, *Neo-slave* 4, 54, 83, 3).

The context, in other words, in which scholars most frequently place *The Confessions of Nat Turner* is that of the emergence of African American cultural, intellectual, and literary movements in the postwar period. Within this narrative, Styron's novel is the culmination—and, indeed, last significant gasp—of a long-dominant, historically false, and intrinsically racist white-authored representation of the slave experience that black writers and scholars resisted, critiqued, and overcame, thus paving the way for powerful and authentic African American accounts of slavery after the 1960s—which would include Alex Haley's phenomenally popular *Roots* and Toni Morrison's critically revered *Beloved*.

While this is a very salutary general narrative about recent literary history, it is severely reductive to read Styron's book as merely the culmination of a racist white discourse that was subsequently overturned by a more informed black one. Indeed, such a narrative is founded upon a rather crudely revolutionary conception of cultural history, in which one epoch dramatically supersedes another. Bontemps's notion of history as a pendulum is equally simplistic in its bipolarism. While the author of *Black Thunder* is right to question the popular idea of history as an evolutionary river that flows inexorably toward an enlightened destination, neither is time an unvaryingly repetitive pendulum that is fated to swing with predictable regularity between epochs or dominant ideologies. While historical patterns may recur, they do not recur in identical contexts or with identical results. We are not inevitably fated to replicate the discourses and the actions of our ancestors—and Scarlett O'Hara is not merely retreating into empty optimism when she tells herself at her moment of calamity that "tomorrow is another day" (M. Mitchell 1037). While history may not be unproblematically evolutionary, genuine human progress is clearly possible—as the abolition of slavery itself testifies. Yet historical change, however spectacular, is rarely truly revolutionary. *Gone with the Wind* records how the Civil War violently eradicated the social order of the slaveholding South—but its narrative conceals the degree to which the white power structure of the region subsequently restored its traditional plantation system and all but reinstituted slavery through an exploitative feudal agricultural system and racist Jim Crow legislation.

In this study, I do not view the history of slavery literature since the 1930s in terms of fundamental discursive revolutions, or essentially repetitive cycles, or in terms of inevitable progress, but, instead, as an ongoing cultural conversation—a vibrant series of exchanges and dialogues about America's peculiar institution. It is a complicated conversation that involves genuine evolution in conjunction with inescapable regression, and startling innovation in tandem with inevitable repetition.

Individual novels about slavery are themselves characterized by internal dialogue, as they incorporate complex discursive tensions and conflicting cultural impulses. *Gone with the Wind* was strikingly original in its time because of its emphasis upon the class dimensions of slavery, but also appallingly reactionary in its insidious whitewashing of slavery and race relations in nineteenth-century America. *The Red Cock Crows* simultaneously critiques *and* re-inscribes *Gone with the Wind*'s representations of the slaveholding South. *Black Thunder* provides powerful portraits of rebellious male slaves alongside dubious, sexualized stereotypes of African American women.

The Confessions of Nat Turner is another work that embodies multiple and paradoxical discourses. Styron's novel certainly reflects the conventions and ideologies of previous slavery literature, yet it is not indebted only to such reviled white-authored texts as Elkins's study and Mitchell's plantation novel but also to that widely lionized African American literary genre, the antebellum fugitive slave narrative—as well as a whole body of postwar slavery fiction by both black and white writers. Simultaneously, however, *The Confessions of Nat Turner* also stands as an extremely innovative work in the history of slavery fiction in terms of its narrative perspective and emphases.

While scholars have classified many contemporary novels about the peculiar institution as "neoslave narratives," they have resolutely refused to characterize *The Confessions of Nat Turner* as such. In conventional critical discourse, Styron's text is not a novelistic recreation of the fugitive slave narrative of the nineteenth century, but a distorted and racist white exploitation of the form. Indeed, one of the Ten Black Writers castigates the novel as nothing less than "*a deliberate attempt to steal the meaning of a man's life,*" while contemporary scholarship critiques *Confessions* for its "representation of a nonheroic slave rebel, its presumption of assuming the voice of a slave, its uninformed appropriation of African American culture, [and] its deep, almost conservative allegiance to the traditional historiographical portrait of slavery" (Bennett 5; Rushdy, *Neo-slave* 4). Given, however, that Styron has explicitly identified the archetypal fugitive slave narrative of Frederick Douglass as one of the central sources for his novel, it is important to consider seriously the formal and thematic similarities of *Confessions* to the nineteenth-century fugitive slave autobiography (Greenberg 220). A close reading of Styron's novel in relation to Douglass's book actually reveals surprising and substantial similarities in the portrayals of slave subjectivities in the two texts, thus complicating the common notion that *The Confessions of Nat Turner* is merely racist and ignorant about the African American experience.

Furthermore, for all its echoes of existing discourses and for all its problematic elements, Styron's book also played a crucial and innovative role in the development of postwar slavery fiction. The twenty years after World

War II witnessed a rich—but now almost entirely ignored—cultural dialogue about slavery in fiction, in which both white and black novelists depicted slaveholders and slaves in an impressive variety of ways. The most
notable general trend in this era was the gradual reorientation of the slavery
novel away from an emphasis upon the white master class and toward the
experiences of bondspeople. As the first twentieth-century novel told from a
slave's perspective—and not just any slave, but the leader of America's most
significant slave rebellion—*Confessions* stands as a genuinely original and
influential text in the canon of slavery fiction.

By conceiving Styron essentially as a disciple of Elkins's ideas, by char-
acterizing *The Confessions of Nat Turner* as simply one more racist white-
authored fiction in the tradition of *Gone with the Wind*, and by attacking
Styron's tale as merely a late manifestation of a "decaying discourse on slavery," scholars are telling only part of the story (Rushdy, *Neo-slave* 62). In this
chapter, I consider how *Confessions* reiterates, engages with, builds upon,
and departs from some of its sources and antecedents.

Ultimately, however, this reassessment of *The Confessions of Nat Turner*
does not constitute a revisionist defense of a much-maligned novel. Whatever its unacknowledged contributions to the cultural conversation about
slavery, my analysis shows that Styron's novel nonetheless takes a simplistic
approach to historiography, fundamentally misreads nineteenth-century African American literature, and occasionally lapses into the hackneyed and
discredited discourses of the traditional plantation novel. Other pre-1970s
novels actually provide much more complex portrayals of slavery and slaves
than *The Confessions of Nat Turner*—and this applies not only to works by
African American authors, such as Margaret Walker's *Jubilee*, but even to
such crudely sensationalist and seemingly racist fictions as Kyle Onstott's
Mandingo.

All the same, critics have been too quick to dismiss Styron's text. *The
Confessions of Nat Turner* is not just another articulation of white racism,
but a flawed attempt to renovate the American novel of slavery. For all its
limitations and its intrinsic (if unconscious) racism, and for all the arguments about racial credentialism that continue to circulate around a white
author's use of an African American narrative voice, *Confessions* is nonetheless a crucial transitional text, marking an important stage in the development of slavery literature in the twentieth century.

The Confessions of Nat Turner is, in short, characterized by multiplicity and contradiction. It is a text in which conflicting discourses collide. The novel is radical in its subject matter and its narrative perspective, but somewhat reactionary in its treatment of slave psychologies. It rejects the plantation melodrama formula for an extended, first-person exploration of the slave experience, yet it is also guilty of using facile racial stereotypes. It takes a boldly radical approach to the genre of the historical novel and is organized around cutting-edge historiography, yet it is also curiously simplistic in its use of scholarly theories about slavery. The paradoxical multiplicity of the discourses in Styron's novel serves as evidence that the cultural conversation about slavery is not inevitably evolutionary, revolutionary, or repetitive. Instead, it is a complex dialogue that can be progressive, conservative, clichéd, and innovative all at once.

Slavery Fiction: From *Gone with the Wind* to *The Confessions of Nat Turner*

There have always been several distinct traditions in slavery literature. Some texts, for example, are primarily concerned with the system of slavery and with plantation life as they were experienced by the ruling class, while others focus upon slavery as it was endured and resisted by African American slaves. Many white-authored historical studies from the late nineteenth century to the 1930s—regardless of their ideological positions—deal with slavery primarily as a political phenomenon in the history of white Americans. Southern plantation fiction—dating from the early nineteenth century and culminating in *Gone with the Wind*—is equally organized around the perspectives and values of the slaveholders. Such texts have traditionally tended to marginalize the black subjects of slavery and—when they do address slave life at all—are apt to lapse into simplistic stereotypes of docile and even happy slaves. Conversely, there has always been a significant literary tradition concerned with the black experience in slavery. Beginning with the fugitive slave narratives as well as works of fiction in the late antebellum period (including novels by William Wells Brown, Frederick Douglass, and Martin Delany), this tradition continued throughout the nineteenth century and into the twentieth in stories by Frances E. W. Harper, Charles Chesnutt, and Arna Bontemps, and in historical texts by George Washington Williams, Carter Woodson, Joseph C. Carroll, and, of course, Herbert Aptheker.[2] While these two traditions in slavery discourse are distinct, they are not independent of each other. Phillips's *American Negro Slavery* is essentially a white southern narrative of the institution, yet it cannot help but acknowledge slave collectivism and resistance in its chapter on insurrections. In fiction, meanwhile, *Uncle Tom's Cabin* comprehensively portrays the effects of slavery on the lives of blacks and whites alike, and Euro-American radicals are almost as prominent in the pages of *Black Thunder* as African American rebels. *The Red Cock Crows* is especially notable for entwining a tale of slave militancy with a white-oriented plantation melodrama.

It is therefore problematic to assume that the late 1960s witnessed a simple shift from white-centered to black-oriented portrayals of slavery in history and fiction, or that the discourse about slavery prior to 1968 entirely "denied the truth value and purposely excluded the testimony of former slaves" (Rushdy, *Neo-slave* 26). Texts emphasizing the African American experience under the institution have always existed, even if visions of slavery centered upon the masters of the plantation may often have been the pre-eminent ones, certainly in terms of cultural visibility.

Gone with the Wind was a landmark text precisely because it so thoroughly cemented a white-oriented version of slavery in the American mind. If the culturally predominant slavery text of the nineteenth century was *Uncle Tom's Cabin*—with its abolitionist attitudes and equal focus upon white and black characters of varied natures (however stereotypical some of the latter may be)—then Mitchell's idealization of antebellum plantation life was the discursive colossus for much of the twentieth. Through sheer phenomenal popularity, *Gone with the Wind* threatened to drown out alternative voices in the cultural conversation about slavery—to negate dialogue in favor of a white southern monologue. For millions who would never hear of, let alone read, *Black Thunder*, *Absalom, Absalom!* or Joseph Carroll's *Slave Insurrections in the United States, 1800–1865*, the Tara plantation served as the defining image of American slavery. If there was ever anything approaching a "hegemonic discourse" about slavery in twentieth-century America, its name was *Gone with the Wind*.

No cultural discourse is ever truly monologic, however. Mitchell's novel had numerous and outspoken critics. The NAACP and other groups even successfully demanded excisions from the film adaptation of *Gone with the Wind*, and black organizations protested the movie in some cities.[3] However, while Mitchell expressed her irritation at some "trouble-making Professional Negroes" who deplored her book and its Hollywood adaptation, she certainly did not have to endure a concerted critical assault from "Ten Negro Writers," and *Gone with the Wind* remained—and continues to remain—phenomenally and enduringly popular as both book and film (quoted in Van Deburg 106).

Just as Faulkner's Yoknapatawpha cast a giant shadow across serious southern literature for a generation or more, so was Tara the fundamental reference point for literary depictions of slavery for three decades—however radically some of those depictions departed from *Gone with the Wind*'s conventions and ideologies. Indeed, surprisingly few novels published in this period—especially of any cultural or literary significance—unquestioningly replicate either the form or philosophies of Mitchell's book. Most slavery fiction in the forties, fifties, and sixties was not so much influenced by *Gone with the Wind* as written in active and critical response to it. By engaging with Mitchell's famous text, novelists re-invigorated the cultural dialogue about slavery, bringing white-oriented and black-oriented visions of the institution together into a promising synthesis, and giving increasing prominence to the African American experience under slavery that *Gone with the Wind* so thoroughly sanitizes and glosses over. For all its limitations, *The Red Cock Crows* is the first major text in this sequence, and *The Confessions of Nat Turner* a later watershed. A brief survey of notable slavery fiction published between 1945 and 1967 demonstrates that the cultural discourse about slavery before the 1970s was not a repressive white hegemony, but a critical multiracial dialogue that challenged the ideologies of *Gone with the Wind* while exploring alternative ways of representing slavery.

The first significant postwar novel about slavery is a curious hybrid: a black-authored, white-oriented plantation romance. In Frank Yerby's *The Foxes of Harrow* (1946), a roguish, impulsive, and charismatic Irish gambler named Stephen Fox rapidly rises from poverty to become the patriarch of a Louisiana plantation in the 1820s. He marries the aristocratic Odalie, but, alienated by her lack of passion, engages in an affair with Desiree, a free woman of color. After Odalie's death in childbirth, the narrative follows Stephen's fortunes to the end of the Civil War as he struggles with both private and public dramas, from the Union conquest of New Orleans to the romantic complications of his headstrong children. Fox is a curious combination of Scarlett O'Hara and Rhett Butler, and the style and tone of Yerby's book is highly reminiscent of Mitchell's saga—although the author smuggles a rather more progressive attitude toward racial politics into the text than is to be found in *Gone with the Wind*.

Initially, African Americans are entirely peripheral and rather stereotypically portrayed in *The Foxes of Harrow*, but they achieve gradual prominence and greater complexity as the narrative unfolds. In an early scene, we find two slave valets who "had almost come to blows in a quarrel over the merits of their respective masters"—as dubious a portrayal of the childish devotion of slaves as any moment in *Gone with the Wind* (42). Yet, from the very beginning, Yerby's novel gestures toward alternative notions about slave psychology— although readers might be diverted from the implications of these gestures by the grand, sweeping melodrama of the main plot concerning Stephen and his family. In the very first chapter, we encounter a series of oak trees along the Mississippi from which twenty-three slave insurrectionists have been hanged. The equivalent of Scarlett's noble and dedicated Mammy in Yerby's novel, furthermore, is Caleen, a Voodoo witch who is reputed to have fomented this rebellion and who is said to despise all white people. In a sequence that anticipates *Beloved*, Caleen's daughter-in-law tries to kill her own baby to prevent his becoming a slave (105–6, 137, 178–79). Little Inch, however, survives and grows up to become highly educated before fleeing to the North, where he befriends Frederick Douglass. The novel ends during Reconstruction, with Inch—now named Cyrus Inchcliff—installed as the Commissioner of Police in New Orleans, married to Stephen's former mulatto mistress, and acting as the stepfather of the son that Stephen had with her. What has seemed for several hundred pages like a very close relation to *Gone with the Wind* reaches a quite unexpected destination, with militant ex-slaves and former slaveholders caught up in complicated social and familial relations. Inchcliff foresees the restoration of white rule, yet is also confident that—in words which anticipate Martin Luther King's most famous speech—all races in America will "browse peacefully in the meadow . . . together." While Stephen's racist son, Etienne, responds to this suggestion with a vociferous "Never!" two of the book's most sympathetic characters stand as evidence of the validity of such a vision (444): Stephen develops from a complacent slaveholder, who is at first repelled by people of color, to a sage advocate of abolition and moderation, while Caleen overcomes her hatred of whites to sacrifice her life in the process of ministering to both black and white patients during a Yellow Fever epidemic. Even more than *The Red Cock Crows*, Yerby's novel invokes the structure and conventions of *Gone with the Wind* only to problematize and challenge its ideologies.[4]

Kyle Onstott's sensationalist *Mandingo* (1957) turns the myth of Tara on its head with unashamed vulgarity. Where *Gone with the Wind* resolutely rejects the idea that miscegenation commonly occurred in the antebellum South—and dismisses the notion that white masters might ever have exploited their slaves sexually—the slaveholders of Onstott's fiction have largely abandoned cotton for the more profitable business of slave breeding. The Falconhurst plantation is, in fact, a huge stud farm—and the father of many of its mulatto "suckers" is the young master of the estate. *Mandingo*, in short, exposes and crudely revels in the interracial sexuality and casual brutality that *Gone with the Wind* denies.[5]

In a very different manner to Onstott's book, *Jubilee* (1966), by the black novelist Margaret Walker, also upturns the conventions of Mitchell's text. Like *Gone with the Wind*, Walker's novel is an epoch-spanning family saga concerning slavery, the Civil War, and its aftermath—but it dramatizes the experiences of the slave woman rather than the plantation belle. *Jubilee* reverses the emphases and the moral hierarchies of *Gone with the Wind*, rendering slaveholding whites secondary and portraying most of them as callously exploitative, while focusing upon black characters and often foregrounding their Christian decency. Like Scarlett O'Hara, *Jubilee*'s Vyry is caught between two very different potential lovers. Yet, unlike the heroine of *Gone with the Wind*, Vyry stays loyal to the man she chooses to marry, and ends the narrative happily ensconced with her family—in stark contrast to Scarlett's apocalyptic domestic breakdown. Furthermore, the cruel plantation mistress of Walker's text is the antithesis of the virtuous Ellen O'Hara, while the book's equivalent of Mammy is sold for fear that she will poison her white masters!

While responding to *Gone with the Wind* and including prominent white characters, *Jubilee* is also a key moment in the process by which novelists— partly in reaction to Mitchell's text—increasingly reorganized the slavery novel around the experiences of slaves. *Jubilee*, then, represents a bridge between two different traditions of slavery fiction: it is a black-authored and black-centered novel, but it is also a plantation/Civil War melodrama that resembles *Gone with the Wind* in terms of its narrative structure and generic conventions.

Yet *Jubilee* was not the first work of postwar fiction to focus primarily upon African American characters. In 1962—four years before the appearance of Walker's novel—came the publication of a very popular tale about a young African male who is sold into slavery on the eve of his manhood ceremony. The narrative follows this man through the rigors of the Middle Passage and his acculturation to slavery in an alien New World, and it dramatizes the experiences of several of his descendants in slavery. What may sound a great deal like Alex Haley's *Roots* in outline—and which sometimes even resembles it in its details—is, in fact, the second installment in Onstott's Falconhurst series, *Drum* (1962). Where it is possible to read *Mandingo* as a crass but devastating evisceration of the sentimental hypocrisies of the plantation melodrama, its successor—for all its emphasis upon African American lives in slavery—is little more than a pornographic potboiler, its plot merely furnishing the backdrop for an endless series of interracial sexual couplings interspersed with lashings of graphic violence. Furthermore, while *Drum* climaxes in a slave rebellion, it is one in which the African American hero nobly sacrifices his life to save his white master from villainous militant blacks!

For all its offenses, however, the popular success of *Drum* provided the clearest demonstration to date—more than a decade before *Roots*—that twentieth-century slavery fiction did not have to be confined to the exploits of charming slaveholding rogues or petulant plantation belles. Despite its sensationalist perversity and racism, Onstott's novel carries echoes of literary traditions other than the white plantation melodrama exemplified by *Gone with the Wind*. Indeed, where *Mandingo* both exploits and satirizes the conventions and values of Mitchell's novel, so does *Drum* reinstall and simultaneously abuse the generic features of nineteenth-century black-centered slavery literature, while also anticipating the Africanist narratives of the 1970s. If *Drum*'s black protagonists have literary ancestors, they are the titular protagonists of Stowe's *Uncle Tom's Cabin* (1852) and *Dred* (1856), as well as Martin Delany's *Blake* (1857), not to mention Frederick Douglass's rebellious Madison Washington in *The Heroic Slave* (1853)—and, of course, the protagonists of the fugitive slave narratives.

The revival of the black-centered slavery novel spearheaded by the dubious *Drum* found a more salutary expression in *Jubilee* and culminated in 1967 with the appearance of no fewer than three books concerned with the lives and experiences of militant slaves. Black novelist Harold Courlander produced *The African*, while two white authors published fictional reconstructions of the life of the famous historical slave insurrectionist Nat Turner: Daniel Panger, with *Ol' Prophet Nat*, and William Styron with *The Confessions of Nat Turner*.

Courlander's novel is an Africanist revision of *Drum*, in which a Fon tribesman named Hwesuhunu (or Wes) is enslaved in Africa, endures the Middle Passage, and joins a band of fugitive slaves on St. Lucia that launches regular raids upon local plantations. Wes is captured and transported to the United States, but escapes from a Georgia plantation to the black outlaw community of Liberty Island before heading west alone. Wes is the very antithesis of Elkins's Sambo: he steals a book so that he might learn how to read, maintains aspects of his African culture, beats a rapacious overseer to death, and refuses to rest until he is free. *The African* thus radicalizes the slave-oriented novel, transforming *Jubilee*'s liberal, nonviolent Christian integrationism into militant Black Nationalism.

The two Nat Turner novels, although written by whites, marked an equally significant moment in the development of slavery fiction. *Ol' Prophet Nat* and *The Confessions of Nat Turner* are not merely about the famous slave rebel but are essentially told from his perspective. In Panger's novel, an unnamed white narrator discovers Nat Turner's secret diary etched in the margins of an old Bible. Styron's novel goes a stage further by dispensing with a mediating white voice altogether and presenting its entire story from the perspective of Turner. By dint of their first-person voices and emphasis upon slave experience and resistance, *Ol' Prophet Nat* and *The Confessions of Nat Turner* are technically the first "neoslave narratives"—but they are never categorized as such by advocates of the term.[6] They tend to be discounted precisely because they are the works of white writers—and because black scholars have found little to admire in Styron's portrait of the celebrated slave rebel. Critics tend to see *The Confessions of Nat Turner* as a successor to *Gone with the Wind* (and equally objectionable in terms of its assumptions about African Americans), but, within the context of postwar slavery fiction, Styron's novel is clearly part of an ongoing cultural quest to develop viable alternatives to Mitchell's representation of American slavery and to reorient slavery discourse toward the black experience. Styron's focus upon the psychology of a single militant slave could hardly be further from the emphases of *Gone with the Wind*. The next step in this process would be the appearance in the 1970s of numerous black-authored novels about the slave experience.

Whether we like it or not, *The Confessions of Nat Turner* is thus as significant an ancestor of the contemporary novel of slavery as the fugitive slave narratives, *Black Thunder*, or *Jubilee*. Styron's novel made an important contribution to postwar efforts to re-establish interracial dialogue on the subject of slavery after *Gone with the Wind* had all but squashed such a cultural exchange. Just as *The Foxes of Harrow* is an African American author's interrogation of the white plantation romance genre, so is *The Confessions of Nat Turner* a white writer's engagement with the black experience, black perspectives, black militancy, and black literary traditions. James Baldwin may not, therefore, have been so very misguided when he hailed Styron's novel as "the beginning of our common history" (quoted in Killens, "Confessions" 32).

Ironically, however, *The Confessions of Nat Turner* struck many black readers as just another white appropriation and distortion of American slavery. As one of the Ten Black Writers, the novelist John A. Williams, puts it, "Once more the history of black and white, already managed beyond belief, gets another shot of Whitey-Serum" (47). From this perspective, a white engagement with the black experience in slavery is inevitably made from a position of cultural supremacy and necessarily incorporates—regardless of an individual author's well-meaning intentions—the racist assumptions that pervade the wider culture. In the words of John Oliver Killens, another of the Ten Black Writers, Styron's novel simply "cut yet another great American black man down to the size of a boy" ("Confessions" 34). Certainly, for all its significance in the process of refocusing the postwar slavery novel upon the African American experience, Styron's novel is indeed rooted in questionable notions about slave identities—many of them derived from Elkins's study. Just like Elkins, Styron provides a chilling portrait of the oppressive nature of slavery—and a rather simplistically reductive depiction of the profound psychological impact that the institution had upon its subjects.

Exceptional Slaves and Active Slave Communities

Elkins's study of slavery is hampered by an insensitivity to crucial distinctions between different discourses concerning the subject of slavery. Any text that addresses the peculiar institution necessarily participates in multiple discourses, which—although inextricably connected—are ultimately quite independent. These include a discourse about the institution of slavery, a discourse about the culture and identities of those who were enslaved, a discourse about their enslavers, and—because the system of bondage that developed in the New World was organized around ethnicity—a discourse about race. Scholars have often tended to conflate such issues, but it is one of the projects of this study to unravel these interwoven threads. Elkins entirely overlooks the fact that the institution of slavery is a separate subject from the psychologies and cultures of those who were enslaved, and he thus neglects to consider that an individual's notions about one topic may not be necessarily matched by those concerning the other. Some writers, for example, have been profoundly critical of the inhumanity of American slavery while simultaneously harboring unshakeable assumptions of white supremacy.

Elkins argues that the cultural and historiographical conversation about slavery has always—from the antebellum era to the present day—been predominantly moralist in nature, an ongoing stand-off between those, on one hand, who believe in the fundamental inhumanity of slavery and those, on the other, who defend the institution's essential benevolence as a social system for genetically inferior peoples (*Slavery* 1). Elkins's narrative resembles Bontemps's notion of time in that it constructs historiography as a pendulum swinging back and forth between different ideological positions. Thus the arguments between abolitionists and the defenders of slavery were succeeded by James Ford Rhodes's condemnation of an exploitative institution in the 1890s, which gave way to Ulrich B. Phillips's vindication of slavery as beneficial paternalism in the early twentieth century, that was, in turn, superseded by *The Peculiar Institution* (1956), in which Kenneth Stampp, "like his abolitionist forebears," aims "to prove slavery an abomination and to prove master and slave equal" (*Slavery* 23).

This last statement implies a necessary correspondence between the denunciation of slavery and a belief in racial equality. Yet even Harriet Beecher Stowe acknowledges in *Uncle Tom's Cabin* that a virtuous white abolitionist, such as the pious Ophelia, can be utterly racist. The black child, Topsy, is all too aware that Ophelia "can't bar me, 'cause I'm a nigger!—she'd's soon have a toad touch her!" Ophelia herself finally concedes, "I've always had a prejudice against negroes" (409, 410). Indeed, for all of Stowe's consciousness of northern abolitionist racial hypocrisy, *Uncle Tom's Cabin* is itself hardly guiltless of racist stereotyping. In Stowe's novel, African Americans constitute a "susceptible race," characterized by "eager docility" and "a passion for all that is splendid, rich, and fanciful . . . rudely indulged by an untrained taste" (419, 559, 253). Northern historians after the Civil War—the ideological and sometimes literal heirs of the abolitionists—tended toward still worse bigotry. In James Ford Rhodes's *History of the United States* (1893), an impassioned indictment of slavery as a system goes hand-in-hand with white supremacist condescension toward its black subjects. "No one," Rhodes claims, "can wonder that it was a painful sight to see negroes at work. The besotted and generally repulsive expression of the field hands; their brute-like countenances, on which were painted stupidity, indolence, duplicity, and sensuality; their listlessness; their dogged action; the stupid, plodding, machine-like manner in which they labored, made a sorrowful picture of man's inhumanity to man" (309–10). Whilst almost seeming to anticipate Elkins's ideas by implying in this passage that the psychological degradation of the slave is the end result of slavery's inhumanity, Rhodes nonetheless portrays African Americans as subhuman automatons, and he later confidently states that the racial inferiority of people of color is nothing less than "scientific truth" (370).

For Elkins, the "view of American Negro slavery presented by James Ford Rhodes in 1893 has acquired a new legitimacy" more than half a century later in Stampp's *The Peculiar Institution* (*Slavery* 21). Rhodes's and Stampp's portrayals of slavery as an institution are indeed—as Elkins suggests—fundamentally similar, but their depictions of slave identities are completely at odds with one another. Both denounce the cruelty of the institution, but Rhodes is an unregenerate racist who believes that African American slaves were characterized by "stupidity, indolence, duplicity, and sensuality," while Stampp, in contrast, emphasizes that there is "no convincing evidence that there are any significant differences between the innate emotional traits and intellectual capacities of Negroes and whites" (Rhodes 309; Stampp ix). Stampp also argues that if slave rebels and runaways may have been exceptional, then they also "voiced the feelings and aspirations of the more timid and less articulate masses," and he devotes chapters to both slave resistance and the slave community (92). Ironically, if anyone provides "new legitimacy" for Rhodes's interpretation of slave *psychology*, it is, in fact, Elkins.

In his eagerness to argue that historiography has done little more than rehash pro- and anti-slavery arguments, Elkins neglects the degree to which writers and historians have also long analyzed and debated the nature of slave subjectivities. For all his claims to be transcending a debate that had reached a "stalemate," Elkins's study actually participates in an argument about the nature of slave psychologies and communities that—like the moral deliberations about slavery—began in the antebellum era (*Slavery* 24). The debate about slavery and the debate about the psychologies of those who were enslaved have run parallel to one another, but they are not the same debate. The question of the nature of slave psychologies is not, for example, primarily a moral one, but is more closely connected to racial politics. While some writers and historians have argued that the majority of slaves were quiescent subjects of an efficiently oppressive institution and that only a few exceptional slaves asserted themselves as individuals, others have claimed the existence of vibrant, active, and often militant slave communities.

Up until the middle of the twentieth century, numerous histories and novels suggested that figures like Nat Turner, Harriet Tubman, and Frederick Douglass were entirely exceptional individuals who transcended the docility of most enslaved Americans. Such arguments were, of course, usually predicated on the assumption by whites that people of color are genetically inferior. Phillips claims that planters saw the "sluggishness of the bulk of their slaves . . . as a racial trait to be conquered by discipline, even though their ineptitude was not to be eradicated; the talents and vigor of their exceptional negroes and mulattoes, on the other hand, they sought to foster by special training and rewards." Phillips, furthermore, unfailingly identifies the possession of exceptional traits by African Americans with white ancestry (339, 304, 429–30, 437, 439). While rejecting Phillips's racism, Elkins's theories resurrected the argument that self-assertive and resistant individuals in slavery were "exceptional" by attributing the passivity of the majority of slaves to the psychological impact of the institution that kept them in bondage (*Slavery* 139).

When discussing the development of slavery discourse in America before the 1960s, scholars usually emphasize the dominance of the argument that there existed a docile majority and an exceptional minority. Consequently, critics have often neglected a counterargument that has also had an enduring and significant cultural presence. According to some writers, there were vital and vigorous communities and a broad spectrum of identities and subject positions within antebellum slavery. In this interpretation of history, figures like Turner, Tubman, and Douglass are seen as emerging out of their respective communities, rather than being exceptional to them. This viewpoint became particularly visible in historiography of the 1970s, but has as long a tradition as the docile majority/exceptional minority argument. Indeed, while critics frequently dismiss the intrinsic racism of *Uncle Tom's Cabin*, Stowe's novel is very much organized around the notion of active and diverse slave communities. William Van Deburg leavens his complaints about Stowe's often-patronizing portrayal of individual black people in *Uncle Tom's Cabin* by acknowledging that the author has, at least, "created a variety of slave personalities" (34). Between the rebellious George and the passive Tom, there is indeed an impressive spectrum of slave characters in Stowe's famous fiction. On the Legree plantation alone, we find cruel black slave drivers in the form of Sambo and Quimbo, as well as the complex portrait of the educated and disturbed, yet rebellious Cassy, whose unrepentant infanticide to save her child from slavery anticipates by six years the true-life case of Margaret Garner that would ultimately inspire Toni Morrison's *Beloved*.

Any depiction of enslaved Americans—in history or fiction—can be easily located somewhere along a continuum between the two poles of the debate outlined here: the active slave community on one side and passive slave psychologies on the other. Of the texts discussed in chapter 1, *Gone with the Wind* modifies the exceptional slave argument by asserting that there was an outstanding *class* of loyal and able slaves that transcended the undifferentiated mass of field hands. After *Gone with the Wind*, however, twentieth-century discourses about slavery in both imaginative literature and historical studies became increasingly focused upon visions of active slave communities. Aptheker does not make an explicit argument about the nature of slave identities in his analysis of slave rebellions, but his very emphasis upon the frequency of collective resistance clearly reveals a belief that the likes of Turner, Tubman, and Douglass were not exceptional individuals but representatives of dynamic communities. *Black Thunder* portrays a diverse slave population, including some slaves who are militant and rebellious, such as Gabriel, and some who are docile and loyal to the white master class, including the treacherous Ben Woolfolk. Similarly, the black population of the Forks in *The Red Cock Crows* includes mutinous rebels, loyal servants who inform on their fellows, and the complex Montgomery— ostensibly an obsequious tool of the master class, but who nonetheless turns a blind eye to Fannie's flight and who subtly arranges Sack's freedom.

Elkins is so concerned to assert that his theories are innovative and so intent upon arguing that the majority of slaves were submissive that he tends to gloss over pre-existing literature and studies focused upon African American experiences, communities, and rebellions within slavery. He blithely dismisses the evidence for Aptheker's claims about slave militancy as merely "unsubstantiated rumors in ante-bellum rural newspapers," and his survey of the historiography of American slavery entirely ignores the work of both nineteenth- and twentieth-century black historians, including George Washington Williams, Carter Woodson, Joseph C. Carroll, and John Hope Franklin (*Slavery* 222n). Elkins thus implicitly rejects the idea suggested to different degrees by texts as varied as *Uncle Tom's Cabin*, *Black Thunder*, and *American Negro Slave Revolts* that there were vibrant slave communities composed of diverse individuals that were often quite capable of dramatic resistance.

Critics have unsurprisingly disparaged Elkins as a "sophisticated modern apologist" for slavery, but close examination shows that the historian's conception of slave psychologies actually carries significant echoes of the fugitive slave narratives (Bennett 7). As Bernard Bell observes, the autobiographies of escaped slaves—the key form of African American literature about slavery before the Civil War—are largely concerned with the "heroism of men and women of unusual ability and integrity" (29). In consequence, fugitive slave narratives often seem to suggest the existence of submissive slave populations in contrast to the uncommon activism of the rare escapee. Although it has been dismissed as an "uninformed appropriation of African American culture," the representations of slave psychologies in *The Confessions of Nat Turner* reiterate specific elements of the fugitive slave narratives, most notably those of the famous autobiography of Frederick Douglass (Rushdy, *Neo-slave* 4).

The Confessions of Nat Turner and Narrative
of the Life of Frederick Douglass

The Confessions of Nat Turner is organized around Styron's quest for a rational explanation for the emergence of an unusual slave who was capable of resisting the profoundly debilitating pressures of bondage. In short, Styron exploits the familiar figure of the exceptional slave, and devotes his fiction to a specific psychological explanation of one such slave's exceptionalism. Critics have tended to focus almost exclusively upon Styron's debt to Elkins when considering the sources of the novelist's ideas about slavery. After all, Styron himself acknowledged just prior to the publication of his novel that he owed to Elkins his understanding that "American Negro slavery, unique in its psychological oppressiveness . . . was simply so despotic and emasculating as to render organized revolt next to impossible" ("Quiet" 14). In Rushdy's terms, The Confessions of Nat Turner does nothing less than "employ the Elkins thesis as an explanation for the most famous slave rebellion in the history of the United States" (Rushdy, Neo-slave 40). In the Ten Black Writers collection, Lerone Bennett censures Styron for having the sheer effrontery to place Elkins's "Sambo thesis in Nat Turner's mouth" (7). Certainly, once he has transcended the mental chains of slavery, Styron's Nat Turner is deeply contemptuous toward his fellows, observing that "my black shit-eating people were surely like flies, God's mindless outcasts" (27).

However, Styron has also explicitly identified the Narrative of the Life of Frederick Douglass, An American Slave as one of his key sources, yet critics have not been inclined to examine parallels between the reviled work of an apparently racist twentieth-century white novelist and the heartfelt nineteenth-century autobiography of a bold champion of African American rights (Greenberg 220). The Ten Black Writers compare Styron's novel to the historical studies of Phillips and Elkins, the fiction of William Faulkner, Shakespeare's Hamlet, Daniel Patrick Moynihan's notorious government report The Negro Family: A Case for National Action (1965), D. W. Griffith's The Birth of a Nation, and even Lawrence Olivier's performance of Othello, but none of them so much as mentions the relationship of Confessions to Frederick Douglass's narrative. In critical studies, Styron's text is, at best, merely "a pastiche of the slave narrative genre"; more commonly, it is dismissed as a thoroughly distorted appropriation of the slave experience, "an exercise in domestication, assimilation, and finally destruction" (Joyner, "Styron's" 181; Harding, "You've" 25).[7]

Whatever their differences, however, Styron's novel and Douglass's memoir—like Elkins's historical study—are founded upon the notion that there were exceptional slaves whose extraordinary qualities of character and uncommon achievements fundamentally distinguished them from their fellows. A comparative reading of Styron's novel and Douglass's narrative shows how the portrayal of slavery and slave subjectivities in *The Confessions of Nat Turner* owes as much to the descriptions of a former bondsman as it does to the theories of Elkins. Styron's Nat Turner and Frederick Douglass both escape the mental chains of slavery through literacy, and both construct themselves rhetorically as "white." Consequently, both become isolated from the more submissive slave majority. Both Douglass and Styron's Turner, furthermore, take great efforts to guide other slaves to thoughts and acts of resistance. There are, however, crucial nuances in Douglass's narrative with which both Styron's fiction and Elkins's history fail to engage. While *Narrative of the Life of Frederick Douglass* is focused upon the figure of the exceptional slave, detailed analysis of the implications of key passages and careful consideration of the polemical purpose and intended audience of Douglass's autobiography reveal that, in comparison, Elkins's study and Styron's novel advance simplistic and reductive arguments about slave psychologies and communities.

Douglass's *Narrative* is one of the most eloquent and influential antebellum testaments to the cruelty of slavery and the determination of an extraordinary individual to emancipate himself from its bonds. Douglass describes his experiences under several masters in Maryland. One mistress, Sophia Auld, began to teach him to read until discouraged by her husband. Douglass, however, completed the lessons for himself, eliciting tuition from white children on the streets of Baltimore. Transferred to a rural plantation, Douglass asserted his independence in a fight with a brutal slavebreaker and led an abortive attempt by several slaves to escape. Restored to the Aulds, Douglass was hired out as a ship's caulker and eventually made his escape to New Bedford—where he became involved in the abolitionist movement and published his memoirs.

For all his narrative's emphasis upon resistance to slavery, however, the way in which Douglass's text depicts the workings of the institution and its effects upon enslaved Americans also seems quite consistent with Elkins's claim that the pervasive influence of the master often reduced slaves to docile submission. Most of the slaves in Douglass's narrative are seemingly incapable of asserting their individuality or humanity. Elkins's study and Styron's novel essentially agree with their African American predecessor that the conditions of slavery reduced its subjects to a childlike dependence upon the slaveholder, and that the institution thoroughly erased all family relations and feelings among slaves. Deborah McDowell argues that Douglass's assertion of a dynamic masculine identity in his autobiography is dependent upon his portrayal of black women as merely passive victims ("In the First Place" 172–77, 182). In fact, Douglass not only distinguishes himself in such a manner from enslaved women but also from virtually *all* other slaves.

Throughout his narrative, Douglass paints shocking images of "the dehumanizing character" and "the brutalizing effects of slavery" (19, 36). In one particularly memorable scene, Douglass provides a chilling depiction of a system that treats human beings as if they are merely livestock: "We were all ranked together at the valuation. Men and women, old and young, married and single, were ranked with horses, sheep, and swine. There were horses and men, cattle and women, pigs and children, all holding the same rank in the scale of being, and were all subject to the same narrow examination" (35–36). By deploying such rhetoric, Douglass seeks to demonstrate two things to the reader: that slavery was unremittingly dehumanizing and that the very nature of the institution accounts for the psychologies of enslaved Americans. Douglass's point is—contrary to the white southern orthodoxy of the time—that African Americans are not genetically inferior to whites; it is rather the debasing nature of the system of slavery that is responsible for their lowly state.

Douglass, in fact, confirms the dehumanizing effects of slavery by conceding that he was dehumanized himself. He describes spending his paltry leisure hours in a "beast-like stupor." He also vividly shows how slavery utterly destroyed African American families, observing that the policy of separating children from their mothers was entirely successful in destroying "the natural affection of the mother for the child." He reports having no sense of connection to his sisters and brothers, and he confesses to receiving the news of his mother's death "with much the same emotions I should have probably felt at the death of a stranger" (45, 13, 26).

Like Elkins, Douglass attributes the power of slavery to the physical and especially the psychological authority of the slaveholder. He tells of how one master "advised me to complete thoughtlessness of the future and taught me to depend solely upon him for happiness" (67). He concludes that "to make a contented slave, it is necessary to make a thoughtless one. It is necessary to darken his moral and mental vision, and, as far as possible, to annihilate the power of reason. He must be able to detect no inconsistencies in slavery; he must be made to feel that slavery is right; and he can be brought to that only when he ceases to be a man" (64–65). Douglass is exceptional because he eventually escapes this moral and mental darkness, a process that begins with literacy and is fulfilled by his physical rebellion against Covey, the slavebreaker—an episode that Douglass prefaces with the legendary declaration, "You have seen how a man was made a slave; you shall see how a slave was made a man" (47).

Douglass's narrative explicitly asserts that literacy (and the information he was thus able to acquire about the world) made him an exceptional figure—an abnormality even—in the African American community. It is striking, for example, that Douglass commences his description of the slave valuation with the communal assertion, "We were all ranked together," but ends it with the specifically individual statement, "I saw more clearly than ever the brutalizing effects of slavery" (35, 36 [emphases added]). In short, while ranked alongside his fellow slaves, the newly literate Douglass possesses a comprehension of the process that they do not. He is with them but no longer of them.

Later in his narrative, Douglass teaches several of his fellow slaves to read, rescuing them, he says, from "mental darkness." It is hard not to notice that Douglass's strong professions of love for fellow slaves are reserved in the narrative only for those he has taught to read. He calls his students "my dear fellow-slaves," and declares, "They were noble souls; they not only possessed loving hearts, but brave ones. . . . I loved them with a love stronger than any thing I have experienced since" (55, 56). Douglass makes no such statements of devotion anywhere in his tale about slaves who are not literate. In Douglass's narrative, literacy seems to mark the difference between dehumanized beasts of burden and ennobled African Americans. In other words, Douglass's view of the psychological effects of slavery is generally very similar to that of Elkins. Van Deburg criticizes Harriet Beecher Stowe's *Uncle Tom's*

Cabin for depicting slavery as "so cruel and debasing that human personality was either perverted or destroyed" (35). As a close reading of Douglass's narrative shows, however, white writers like Stowe were not the only ones who portrayed slavery in this manner during the antebellum period.

There are, of course, particular reasons why Douglass constructed his tale in such a way that it often seems to reflect negatively upon his fellow slaves. First, there is the question of his audience. Douglass's purpose was to convert ambivalent—even potentially racist—white northerners to the anti-slavery crusade. The narrative thus emphasizes the degradation of slavery and the vast potential of an African American individual when liberated from the physical and psychological chains that impeded him. Douglass aims to persuade his largely white northern readership that, given freedom and education, all enslaved people could become as sophisticated, eloquent, and proudly self-assertive—as American, in short—as Frederick Douglass. Under the physically and psychologically crippling yoke of slavery, the narrative argues, people of color are instead fated to be rendered inert and stuporous. Had Douglass portrayed an active slave community, one with a culture somewhat alien to mainstream white America and with the potential to explode into rebellion, it may have alarmed his audience and diminished its sympathy for the victims of human bondage.

Douglass also takes care to represent himself as an individual whose eloquent rhetoric and elegant prose would mark him as culturally "white" for an antebellum audience. Douglass, after all, compares himself not to Nat Turner or Toussaint L'Ouverture but to Patrick Henry (57). Nancy Bentley's analysis of Douglass's fight with Covey the slavebreaker vividly demonstrates the "whiteness" of Douglass's discourse: "The battle effects a change in Douglass's ascribed race identity, and the change is recognized by both men. The proof: both ignore the legal distinction that dictated that a black man could not strike a white one. While the men were fighting, Douglass was temporarily a 'white' man—that is, they were 'equals before the law.' Douglass does not deny an African identity, but he does claim white manhood" (518). William Andrews, meanwhile, argues that the climax of the narrative is not Douglass's escape—which the text does not even describe— but the former slave's "assumption of a new identity as a free man and his integration into the [white] American mainstream" (129). Deborah McDowell analyzes the relationship between Douglass's narrative and the "authenticating documents" by white abolitionists that introduce his text, and she questions whether "Douglass's 'defeat' of competing white male voices enable[s] him to find a voice distinct from theirs" ("In the First Place" 181). At the very least, in his efforts to distinguish himself from his white sponsors, Douglass cannot help but assert himself over his former fellows in slavery as well.

Another reason why Douglass's narrative gives rather short shrift to the slave community is that the writer is working within genres of literature organized around the individual. It is not just that the fugitive slave narrative must necessarily portray the "heroism of men and women of unusual ability and integrity" because only an exceptional few were able to escape from slavery (Bell 29). Douglass's *Narrative* is at its very root an instance of that most individualistic literary genre: the autobiography—whether we read it as a shadow text to Benjamin Franklin's famous memoir, as John Seelye does, or as a tale "drawn up along structural and metaphorical lines familiar to readers of spiritual autobiographies," as Andrews suggests (127, 125).

Andrews claims that Douglass's text is a specifically "American jeremiad," a genre in which "the rebellion of a fractious individual against instituted authority is translated into a heroic act of self-reliance," and whose central protagonists are "prophets crying in the wilderness of their own alienation from prevailing error and perversity." Furthermore, the kind of jeremiad Douglass has written emphasizes his problematic relationship with mainstream white society, not his connection to the black community. Andrews points out that Wilson Moses has described a specifically black jeremiad as being "preoccupied with America's impending doom because of its racial injustices." In contrast, Douglass's story is essentially a *white* jeremiad, Andrews avers, because it "affirms and sustains a middle-class consensus about America" while "excoriating lapses from it." Douglass's mission, in short, is to be "a black Jeremiah to a corrupt white Israel" (124, 123, 126). The slave population thus becomes insignificant on its own terms in the *Narrative* and important only insofar as its suffering reveals the corruption of the "white Israel" that Douglass addresses.

None of this is to diminish the brilliance and power of Frederick Douglass's work. My point is that Douglass constructed a particular narrative about slavery in a particular time for a particular audience and with a specific purpose in mind: to persuade northern whites to embrace abolitionism. In the process of so very vividly and compellingly making his case, however,

Douglass painted a relatively negative picture of the character of the average enslaved American—locked up in an emotional and intellectual darkness, reduced to the level of livestock. In the antebellum era, Douglass's narrative eloquently challenged white southern orthodoxies about the conditions of the peculiar institution and entrenched assumptions about inherent racial inferiority. In our own time, however, while many scholars would concur with Douglass's picture of the conditions of slavery, historians and novelists alike reject the idea that illiterate, enslaved African Americans existed in a bestial darkness. In short, Douglass very skillfully employs the figure of the exceptional slave as a strategy in his critique of the brutality of slavery, but his use of this figure also seems to lend credence to Elkins's view that the psychological damage wrought by slavery may have been so great that the majority of slaves were reduced to docility and a childlike reliance upon their masters (Elkins, *Slavery* 82).

The Confessions of Nat Turner is based upon similar assumptions. Styron—like Elkins—rejected or seemed oblivious to literature emphasizing activist slave communities that fostered collective resistance to the institution. Styron, for example, wrote a dismissive review of the 1963 edition of Aptheker's *American Negro Slave Revolts*, which he compared unfavorably to Elkins's work. In Styron's opinion, Aptheker "underestimated slavery's suffocating might," and his study, "badly skewed by [Communist] party dogma," fails to "hold up under scrutiny" ("Revisited" 71). Dispensing with alternative theories entirely, Styron's novel doggedly pursues the "passive majority/exceptional minority" thesis—of which Elkins's study was just the most contemporary and fully developed articulation. Furthermore, Styron's use of the formal features of the fugitive slave narrative do not divert *The Confessions of Nat Turner* from the notion of the "exceptional slave," since the classic literary explanation for the development of a rebellious individual within the psychologically crippling atmosphere of American slavery is the narrative of Frederick Douglass.

Styron's novel is set in Virginia in 1831 and is narrated by Nat Turner in the aftermath of his abortive rebellion, as he awaits execution and mourns his apparent abandonment by God. Interrogated by a lawyer named Thomas Gray, Nat recalls his childhood and youth as a pampered house servant of the Turner family. In these scenes from Nat's past, Samuel Turner teaches Nat to read and even promises to apprentice him to an architect and eventually free him. The privileged Nat develops utter contempt for most other slaves, especially field hands. Hard economic times, however, force Samuel Turner to sell many of his slaves—including Nat's friend, Willis—and, ultimately, to depart for Alabama, leaving Nat at the mercy of a succession of less paternalistic masters. While hired out to work for various white families, Nat becomes sexually fixated upon a young white woman named Margaret Whitehead. Driven by religious visions, Nat also begins to plot insurrection and seeks to turn some of his fellow slaves from passive servants into violent revolutionaries. The rebellion, however, is a clumsy mess from the beginning. Nat finds that he is incapable of slaughter and is challenged for leadership by a psychopathic slave named Will. Nat reasserts his credentials at the Whitehead farm by killing Margaret, but the rebellion is defeated soon after, when slaves loyal to their masters repel an assault by Nat's forces upon the Ridley farm. Nat is tried, captured, and executed, but, just before his death, is reconciled to God by repenting his murder of Margaret.

While Nat Turner led a violent collective revolt instead of simply fleeing slavery alone, the parallels between *The Confessions of Nat Turner* and Douglass's autobiography are nonetheless legion. Indeed, Andrews's description of Douglass's narrative as being formed "along structural and metaphorical lines familiar to readers of spiritual autobiographies" is highly applicable to *The Confessions of Nat Turner* as well. Andrews observes that the spiritual autobiography begins with initiation into knowledge of the depravity of man but also a promise of deliverance by special interposition of the divine. This is threatened, however, by the temptation to despair, but is resolved by a glorious moment of resurrection and the revival of faith (125). In Styron's novel, Nat Turner discovers the depravity of man when Samuel Turner betrays him, but receives religious visions that promise special interposition of the divine. In Andrews's analysis of Douglass's narrative, the fight with Covey is the occasion for the slave's resurrection, but in Styron's novel, revolutionary violence, though it seems to promise apotheosis, actually brings Nat Turner to despair. Turner, however, achieves resurrection and a revival of faith on the gallows by repenting his murder of Margaret.

More significant than these broad structural parallels is that in both works it is primarily literacy that serves to isolate the heroes from their respective black communities. Indeed, the term that Styron's Nat Turner uses to describe one slave—"stuporous"—is identical to that used by Douglass when describing his own pre-literate "beast-like stupor" (Styron 46; Douglass, *Narrative* 45). Like Douglass, Turner's professions of love in the novel for fellow slaves are reserved for those with the potential to become as exceptional as he is. In his youth, Styron's Nat is devoted to Willis, an uncommonly intelligent slave whom he baptizes and intends to teach to read and write—until Willis is sold (201–8). Later, Nat becomes equally dedicated to a slave named Hark, whom he converts from a timid servant to a ruthless revolutionary.

The literacy and diction of both Styron's Turner and Douglass possess racial connotations that further separate them from their respective slave communities. While Douglass constructs himself as culturally "white" in order to appeal to a white audience, critics tend to read the "white" diction of Styron's narrator-protagonist as a profound flaw—as evidence of the novel's lack of racial authenticity rather than an echo of the "whiteness" of Douglass's narrative. Killens protests that Styron frequently depicts Nat "thinking and speaking in biblical or Victorian English," while Loyle Hairston similarly criticizes the protagonist-narrator's "impeccable Victorian prose" and "eloquent abstractions" (Killens, "Confessions" 43; Hairston 67). Douglass's prose, of course, is every bit as impeccable and eloquent as that of Styron's Nat Turner, and is also peppered with biblical allusion (14, 41, 73, 76–77). Lerone Bennett dismisses Styron's Nat Turner as "a neurasthenic, Hamlet-like white intellectual in blackface," yet—when describing his fears of what escape might entail—Douglass himself quotes *Hamlet* in acknowledgment that he was often tempted to "rather bear those ills we had, Than fly to others, that we knew not of" (Bennett 5; Douglass, *Narrative* 57).

There are, however, significant distinctions between Douglass's literary "whiteness" and that of Styron's Nat Turner. Several of the Ten Black Writers are annoyed that Turner "is taught to read in Styron's fantasy not by his father and mother [as in the historical *Confessions* recorded by Thomas Gray] but by the good white folks" (Bennett 9; see also Harding, "You've" 26). Douglass, on the other hand, while receiving initial lessons from his mistress, Sophia Auld, is ultimately obliged to painstakingly teach himself to read and write (32). Furthermore, while Douglass seems aloof from other slaves in his narrative, he does not express the contempt for enslaved African Americans that Styron's Nat Turner displays, nor does he identify with his white masters and their culture as the narrator-protagonist of

Confessions does. Douglass never fantasizes about actually being white, unlike Styron's Nat (Styron, *Confessions* 232). In addition, Douglass constructs himself as white for a particular ideological purpose, while Styron simply seems to assume a white readership. Nonetheless, the literacy and "whiteness" of these two figures has the same result in each case—isolating the narrator-protagonist from the slave community.

One of the most revealing relationships between Douglass's *Narrative* and Styron's novel is each text's portrayal of the leisure activities of the majority of slaves being characterized by indolence and drunkenness. Douglass claims that the masters' object in declaring holidays on the plantation "seems to be, to disgust their slaves with freedom, by plunging them into the lowest depths of dissipation." While exceptional slaves like Douglass might exploit their leisure hours industriously, "by far the larger part engaged in such sports and merriments as playing ball, wrestling, running foot-races, fiddling, dancing, and drinking whisky" (52, 51). Styron's Nat Turner similarly muses how the average slave in his leisure hours might go "off in the woods by himself or with a friend, scratch his balls and relax and roast a stolen chicken over an open fire and brood upon women and the joys of the belly or the possibility of getting hold of a jug of brandy" (267).

It is important, however, to note the differences between these two pictures as well as their parallels. The activities Douglass describes are largely communal, while Styron's are essentially solitary. Douglass's slaves are playing, dancing, and drinking together, whereas Styron's slave has retreated, either alone or with a single friend, to the woods where he merely imagines the company of women. Where Styron's slave would like to get drunk, Douglass explicitly tells us how slaveholders actively encouraged their human property to become inebriated in a deliberate strategy of social control (51).

Close comparison of these particular passages suggests that—for all their similarities—there are, ultimately, crucial distinctions between Frederick Douglass's and William Styron's depictions of slavery and slave identities. Styron's portrait, for example, implicitly asserts the isolation of individual slaves, while Douglass's at least hints at the existence of a slave community. More significantly, while Douglass suggests that the system of slavery successfully dehumanized its subjects, he also emphasizes the degree to which the institution's dehumanizing strategies were utterly and constantly necessary to keep enslaved people suppressed. In his description of the dissipation of the Christmas holidays, Douglass makes the crucial observation that, were "the slaveholders at once to abandon this practice [of encouraging slaves to drunkenness], I have not the slightest doubt it would lead to immediate insurrection" (51). In contrast, Styron's portrayal of the personalities of enslaved Americans suggests, like Elkins's argument, that the majority of slaves were rendered so passive and docile by the everyday processes of slavery that one whisky-soaked holiday more or less hardly matters. As far as Styron's Nat Turner is concerned, the average slave speaks in "a hopeless garble, his mind a tangle of baby-thoughts. . . . Like animals [slaves] relinquished the past with as much dumb composure as they accepted the present" (142, 224). It will clearly take much more than the cancellation of a single drunken holiday to rouse such a people to revolution.

In *The Confessions of Nat Turner*, Styron's protagonist begins his recruiting campaign for his planned rebellion with the docile Hark. Nat laments that, "as with most young slaves brought up as field hands—ignorant, demoralized, cowed by overseers and black drivers, occasionally whipped—the plantation system had leached out of his great and noble body so much native courage, so much spirit and dignity, that he was left as humble as a spaniel in the face of a white man's presence." Turner believes, however, that Hark "contained deep within him the smoldering fire of independence," and he is determined "to fan it into a terrible blaze" (276). This requires considerable effort on Turner's part. Fortunately, as far as his goals are concerned, "there was the fact. . . . that [Hark's] wife and child had been sold south, and this I used as an instrument to break down his docility and his resistance, to undermine his childish fear of white people and his cowardly awe of their mere presence. It was not easy to make of Hark a potential killer, to generate true hatred in that large-hearted breast. Without causing him, as I did, to brood on the sale of his wife and child, I might have failed. But of all the Negroes, Hark was the most surely and firmly under my domination" (287). So severe is slavery's impact on character that even the cruel loss of a wife and child is not sufficient to make Hark hate his enslavers. Turner has to carefully manipulate Hark's thoughts and feelings to turn him into a potential rebel. "I have battered down Hark's defenses," Styron's Nat reports, "playing incessantly, almost daily, upon his sorrow and loss, coaxing and wheedling him" (99). In effect, Turner must replace the white master as Hark's patriarchal significant other and thoroughly dominate him psychologically in order to convert him into a killer. Styron's Nat does not so much liberate Hark as control him. He does not rescue Hark from passive dependence, but presents himself as a black master in place of Hark's white one.

Douglass, too, describes how he sought to influence the minds of the slaves on the ironically named Freeland plantation, encouraging them to desire literacy and even escape. He reports that "I succeeded in creating in them a strong desire to learn how to read" and sought "to imbue their minds with thoughts of freedom" (54, 56). Douglass does not, however, psychologically manipulate his fellow slaves in the same manner as, or to the same degree that, Styron's Turner manipulates Hark. Douglass does not become their patriarch. His individual goals are almost instantly met with collective engagement: "This desire [to read] soon sprang up in the others also. They very soon mustered up some old spelling-books, and nothing would do but that I must keep a Sabbath school. I agreed to do so" (54). It is the other slaves, not Douglass, who procure spelling books, and they petition Douglass to be their teacher, not vice versa. In contrast, the protagonist-narrator of *The Confessions of Nat Turner* does not share his literacy and he simply dictates his plan for rebellion to his recruits. The first collective escape attempt in Douglass's *Narrative* is entirely collaborative. Douglass says that "we never undertook to do any thing of any importance, without a mutual consultation," and he refers to the "plan *we* finally concluded upon" (56, 57 [emphasis added]). For a few pages in Douglass's narrative we clearly see an active, egalitarian, and resistant slave community. The failure of the escape attempt, however, leads to Douglass's being sent back to the Aulds in Baltimore.

Douglass's eventual getaway is a largely individualistic endeavor, but his description of the failed group escape from the Freeland plantation provides a vision of slave psychologies and communities that is quite distinct from the pictures painted by Elkins and Styron. Douglass suggests that the average slave is only a week of sobriety away from "the wildest desperation" and "the spirit of insurrection" (51). Elkins and Styron, on the other hand, assert that only rare and exceptional slaves could *ever* be capable of such a response. Styron, in short, establishes a much greater distance between Nat Turner and the average field hand than Douglass does between himself and the typical slave. For Styron, literacy and sobriety alone are not sufficient to explain an anomaly like Nat Turner, a slave who is so utterly distinct from the "coarse, raucous, clownish, uncouth" majority (136).

While it superficially seems to support the Elkins thesis, a close reading of Douglass's narrative reveals an institution that struggled constantly to maintain even a semblance of the mental control that Elkins and Styron assume to be thoroughly established. Douglass's slavery is not a rigid, unbending "closed system," but an inconsistent institution, however oppressive its fundamental nature (Elkins, *Slavery* 113). American slaveholders continually struggled to minimize opportunities for slave self-assertion, resistance, and communal bonding. The narrative of Frederick Douglass ultimately implies that American slavery was simply not as consistently or as effectively totalitarian as Styron and Elkins suggest.

Styron claims that in preparation for writing *The Confessions of Nat Turner* he "had to read Frederick Douglass and lot of the oral history of slavery. This was essential" (quoted in Greenberg 220). My analysis suggests, however, that Styron *mis*read Douglass's narrative, taking its portrayal of apparently passive slave psychologies at face value, neglecting its hints of more active slave subjectivities and vibrant communities, and failing to give sufficient consideration to the purpose of Douglass's rhetoric or the former slave's astute understanding of his white audience. Styron also tends to assume a monolithic slavery: if Aptheker's portrait of an eternally militant and activist community is wrong, then Elkins's depiction of a rigorously authoritarian institution that reduced its subject to passive children apparently must be right. Although it concerns an individual who resisted the psychological impact of slavery and recruited many of his fellow slaves to join in armed revolt, *The Confessions of Nat Turner*, like Elkins's study, is insufficiently sensitive to the multiple possibilities inherent in American slavery and the probable diversity of slave subjectivities.

The Confessions of Nat Turner is thus simultaneously highly sophisticated and extremely simplistic in its treatment of the past. It is not, Styron claims, a mere historical novel but "a meditation on history," or, as one critic puts it, it is "'metahistorical'—a work that is deliberately, even self-consciously concerned with concepts of history, of history as history" (Styron, *Confessions* ix; Mellard 527). A recurring theme in Styron's statements about his fiction is the freedom of the novelist from the historical record. In the original "Author's Note" to *The Confessions of Nat Turner*, he asserts that "in those areas where there is little knowledge in regard to Nat . . . I have allowed myself the utmost freedom of imagination in reconstructing events" (ix). Styron later criticized historical fiction that is "overwhelmed by an avalanche of data. . . . A bad historical novel often leaves the impression of a hopelessly overfurnished house, cluttered with facts the author wishes to show off as fruits of his diligent research" ("Revisited" 68). At the 1968 Southern Historical Association meeting, Styron even declared that "a novelist dealing with history has to be able to say that such and such a fact is totally irrelevant, and to Hell with the person who insists that it has any real, utmost relevance" (quoted in Stone 8–9). This is a bold and radical attitude for a historical novelist to possess toward primary documentary evidence—one that would become common in the 1970s—but it is not matched by Styron's approach to secondary historiographical scholarship.

The fundamental problem with Styron's novel—and one of the central reasons why it continues to generate so much antagonism—is that it advocated the "docile majority/exceptional minority" thesis in an era in which the scholarly consensus had already moved decisively toward asserting the existence of dynamic slave communities. Most historians of slavery since the 1930s—including Aptheker, Carroll, Stampp, and Franklin—had made putative, if limited, attempts to address slave resistance, culture, and character in their studies, a scholarly trend that would fully flourish in the slave-community histories of the 1970s. Rather than being the final gasp of a corrupt discursive hegemony, Elkins's study was actually a prominent exception in its time, and its assertion of the existence of populations of passive, stuporous slaves only helped to energize further discourses about activist slave subjectivities. By the time Styron's novel appeared, historians were thoroughly engaged in the process of challenging and complicating Elkins's ideas. A series of articles published in academic journals between 1962 and 1967 rendered the Elkins thesis thoroughly anachronistic before *The Confessions of Nat Turner* had even won its Pulitzer Prize.[8]

Styron continued to the end of his life, however, to insist upon the validity of the notion that American slavery was "almost uniquely despotic, a closed system so powerful and totalitarian that organized insurrection was almost entirely precluded" ("Revisited" 71). He continued as well to endorse Elkins, the most prominent post-war scholar to advance this interpretation (and the term "closed system" even derives from Elkins's study [*Slavery* 113]). Styron blithely asserts, furthermore, that Elkins's view of the institution is "shared by many other students of the history of slavery" ("Revisited" 71). In fact, Elkins's ideas have found very few adherents in the discipline of history. In a rather more honest 1982 footnote to his 1965 essay, "This Quiet Dust," Styron—while still plaintively asserting the legitimacy of Elkins's insights— also acknowledges that the historian's "work has undergone such severe revision by other historians as to make my own responses to his theories appear perhaps a bit simplistic" (14n).

The problem is not so much that Styron backed the wrong historian as that his fiction simplistically endorses *any* single historical theory. The novelist did not engage sufficiently with the theories of other historians, nor approach Elkins with sufficient skepticism. Elkins's study was crucially important for the responses and developments it inspired, but its theories were rapidly superseded. Thus Styron's novel was swiftly revealed, by his own admission, to be "simplistic" in its portrayal of slavery. Instead of developing a complex vision of the institution and its subjects that was capable of incorporating both the communal militancy of Aptheker's slaves and the prevalent passivity of Elkins's theories—both of which Douglass's narrative gestures toward—Styron simply hitched his star to a single historiographical wagon. When accused in 1968 of ignoring the work of black historians, Styron responded with the question, "When were writers of historical novels obligated in any way to acknowledge the work of historians?" (quoted in Stone 346). In fact, the central limitation of *The Confessions of Nat Turner* is precisely that it is entirely obligated to theories that are now inextricably linked with a single postwar historian. While *The Confessions of a Nat Turner* "meditates" on history, it merely replicates Elkins's historiography. Styron's novel ultimately treats Elkins's text not as a discourse that must be critically interpreted but as an essentially infallible source of historical fact.

The Confessions of Nat Turner and the Long Shadow of *Gone with the Wind*

There are, however, a few occasions on which *The Confessions of Nat Turner* briefly transcends its dependence upon Elkins and its distortion of Douglass, and promises to complicate the idea that slavery was simply a closed system that rendered the majority of its subjects entirely passive. Indeed, some of the novel's most intriguing moments altogether transcend the historiographical thesis that Styron is avowedly dramatizing, promising a more complex picture of slavery than Elkins's paradigm can contain. Ironically, however, many of these moments—instead of constituting a radically innovative portrayal of slavery and anticipating 1970s developments in slavery fiction—actually look back to the conventions and even the ideologies of *Gone with the Wind*. In superficial, formal terms, of course, *The Confessions of Nat Turner* shares very little in common with Mitchell's novel: one assumes the form of the slave autobiography, while the other is a traditional, white-oriented plantation melodrama. If, however, Styron's book does not engage in direct intertextual dialogue with *Gone with the Wind*, it nonetheless echoes its assumptions at several notable junctures. In truth, despite *The Confessions of Nat Turner*'s playing a key role in the revitalization and development of fiction organized around slave experience, it contains one of the least sophisticated postwar portrayals of slave subjectivities. In contrast, Margaret Walker's *Jubilee* engages in complex dialogue with the ideas of Elkins and the traditional stereotype of the exceptional slave. More surprisingly, Kyle Onstott's dubious *Mandingo* contains a more astute portrayal of the workings of slavery and its effects upon slave psychology than is to be found in Styron's book. Critics have, in fact, commonly disparaged *The Confessions of Nat Turner* as being evocative of earlier twentieth-century literature. Ernest Kaiser argues that "Styron has lived through twelve years of the Negro social revolution and struggle in the U.S., but this upheaval has not touched him as a novelist. He wrote *The Confessions* just as he would have written it in 1948" (65). Another reader simply dismisses the novel as "a throwback to the racist writing of the 1930's and 1940's" (quoted in Van Deburg 140).[9]

Such comments assume the outdatedness of Styron's view of slavery and, somewhat unfairly, imply a fundamental kinship between *The Confessions of Nat Turner* and *Gone with the Wind*.[10] It is true that several moments in Styron's fiction are indeed suggestive of Mitchell's novel, but what has been less readily acknowledged and what is most important is that the moments in *The Confessions of Nat Turner* which are most reminiscent of *Gone with the Wind* are those that depart significantly from the Elkins thesis. On those rare occasions when Styron's novel transcends the idea that slavery was an efficiently totalitarian system, it tends to lapse into even more anachronistic conventions for representing the institution.

At one point in Styron's novel, Nat Turner reflects upon the horrors of slavery in the Deep South, which he has learned about "by way of scary tales shuddering up through the vast black grapevine which spread throughout the South" (267–68). It is striking that the narrative identifies other slaves as the source of Nat's information. After all, the inveterate house slave might reasonably have acquired such knowledge from his master, either directly or through eavesdropping. The reader cannot help but wonder how a slave who is so contemptuous toward and isolated from his fellows that he hardly seems to converse with them at all has managed to glean such information from them. Here, if only for a moment, is a vivid suggestion of an active regional slave communications network, one in which even Styron's aloof Nat Turner seems to participate. If, as Elkins argues, only rare, exceptional individuals were able to escape the debilitating psychological effects of slavery— if the average slave really was, as Styron suggests, as "humble as a spaniel" with a mind that was "a tangle of baby thoughts"—such a network is quite inconceivable (Elkins, "Slavery" 240; Styron 131). One recalls, however, that there is an equally incongruous moment in *Gone with the Wind* referring to "that black grapevine telegraph system which defies white understanding" (813). Mitchell's novel simply defines this communications network as an inexplicable mystery since nothing in the book's portrayal of slave identities can account for it. *The Confessions of Nat Turner* is hardly any more illuminating on the topic.

There is, furthermore, at least one other moment in Styron's novel that simultaneously complicates the Elkins thesis while being strangely reminiscent of a passage in *Gone with the Wind*. Nat observes that "a white man's discomfiture, observed on the sly, has always been a Negro's richest delight." If most slaves have, as Styron asserts elsewhere in the story, a "childish fear of white people" and "cowardly awe of their mere presence," their taking active pleasure in white misfortune seems unlikely (49, 334). Nat's statement thus departs from the Elkins thesis, yet is also reminiscent of Scarlett's observation in *Gone with the Wind* that "Negroes were always so proud of being the bearers of evil tidings" to whites—when most of the individual black characters who appear in the novel, such as Mammy and Uncle Peter, would surely not be capable of any such thing (353).

I have suggested that the "Negroes" to whom Mitchell specifically refers in this instance are the disgruntled lower-class field hands, the group she otherwise erases from the novel along with any evidence of slave unrest and resistance. Styron's general commitment to Elkins's ideas encourages his use of Mitchell's outdated and dubious notion of a rigid separation between slave classes. Styron's Nat is a pampered house servant who feels no connection to the field hands at all (169). This characterization is entirely the author's invention, for there is no historical evidence to suggest that Nat Turner was a house servant. It is, however, crucial to Styron's Elkins-derived understanding of slavery that Nat be an elite slave. Elkins asserts that "the revolts that actually did occur were in no instance planned by plantation laborers but rather by Negroes whose qualities of leadership were developed well outside the full coercions of the plantation authority system," and he names Gabriel, Denmark Vesey, and Turner as instance of such figures (*Slavery* 138). Styron's Nat Turner is so exempt from the forces of the institution that oppress his fellows that he is "filled with disdain for the black riffraff which dwells beyond the close perimeter of the big house—the faceless and nameless toilers." He claims to have inherited this attitude from his mother, who was given to declaring (in words that sound like they could have come out of Mammy's mouth in *Gone with the Wind*), "Us folks in de house is *quality*" (136). Recalling his occupation as a plantation carpenter, Nat admits that he "despised with a passion that part of my job which required me to work on repairs to the [slave] cabins. For one thing . . . there was the odor—the stink of sweat and grease and piss and nigger offal, of rancid pork and crotch and armpit and black toil and straw ticks stained with babies' vomit" (184). One recalls a parallel scene in Mitchell's novel in which Scarlett visits the abandoned remains of the Twelve Oaks plantation immediately after the war and is repelled by the "faint niggery smell which crept from the [slave] cabin [and] increased her nausea" (427). For a moment, then, Styron's slave rebel does not just sound like one of Tara's elite house servants but like Scarlett O'Hara herself!

Styron's treatment of slave classes bounces between Elkins's and Mitchell's notions. Just like *Gone with the Wind*, Styron's novel simultaneously sidesteps and demonizes the lower class of slaves—who are represented in both texts by unpleasant odors in empty cabins. But where Mitchell's novel castigates the field hands for their disloyal aggression toward the white master class after the Civil War, *The Confessions of Nat Turner* attributes the failure of the Southampton uprising to the passivity of lower-class slaves, à la Elkins. Styron's Nat believes that in order for a slave to learn to really hate a master, he must "live to some degree of intimacy with the white man" so that he can come to "know the object of his hatred, and that he become knowledgeable about the white man's wiles, his duplicity, his greediness, and his ultimate depravity." Nat argues that field hands, who know "no white man other than the overseer whose presence is a mean distant voice and a lash and whose face is a nameless and changing white blob against the sky," can only muster "sullenness and impotent resentment" at best, not a true hatred that might lead to active resistance (257–58). Such a theory implies that the potential for rebellion is to be found only in the upper class of slaves and essentially rules out any active or meaningful resistance by field hands—just as Elkins suggests. This is, however, little more than abstract speculation on Nat's part: he is not a field hand and he is isolated from the slave community in general and its lower class in particular. The reader also must wonder if white overseers were really such abstractly distant figures to the majority of slaves. Nat's unsubstantiated theory about lower-class slaves' inability to hate their masters, however, stands as the novel's explanation as to why fewer than a hundred slaves join Nat's rebellion—why, as Nat's white interrogator crudely puts it, "nine out of ten of your fellow burrheads just wasn't buyin' any such durn fool ideas" (399, 397).

The portrayal of house slaves in *The Confessions of Nat Turner* is indebted both to Elkins and Mitchell. If the passive failure of the field hands to join the uprising dooms Nat's rebellion, the active response of house servants seals its fate. Elkins identifies rare cases of rebelliousness with the elite class of slaves, but also suggests that those who worked in the plantation house were in closer contact with the slaveholder, the significant other of slavery, than the field hands. Thus the majority of house slaves could be more subject to the psychological coercion of the institution and more likely to identify strongly with whites than their lower-class counterparts—just as Mitchell's elite black characters do. In *The Confessions of Nat Turner*, during the crucial assault on the Ridley house, the rebel forces are repulsed by an army of "Negroes owned by the white gentry near town . . . coachmen, cooks, some field hands maybe but . . . mostly gardeners and house nigger flunkies, even a clutch of bandana'd yellow kitchen girls passing ammunition" (399). One can easily imagine the faces of Mitchell's unfailingly loyal house slaves among this group, defending the plantation against "impident" and "trashy niggers" (Mitchell 407, 555). At least, one can picture Mammy, Sam the driver, Dilcey, and Uncle Peter—if not the problematic Prissy!

FROM TARA TO TURNER

Kyle Onstott's *Mandingo*

Twenty-five years after the publication of *The Confessions of Nat Turner*, Styron complained that his work has been unfairly "lodged in a kind of black Index Expurgatorius . . . along with such overtly racist novels as *The Clansman* and *Mandingo*" ("Revisited" 72). The treatment of African American characters in Kyle Onstott's notorious plantation potboiler certainly seems—superficially at least—reminiscent of Rhodes's despairing but intrinsically racist account of listless, stupid, machine-like slaves, and simultaneously anticipatory of Elkins's notion that the rigors of slavery and the influence of the slaveholder dehumanized slaves. Close textual analysis, however, reveals that—for all its apparent reveling in crude sensationalism—*Mandingo*'s representation of slave subjectivities is actually fairly sophisticated, and is, in fact, very close to Frederick Douglass's observations about a diverse slave population that must be constantly monitored and repressed to stave off insurrection.

Mandingo (1957) concerns life on the Falconhurst plantation run by Hammond Maxwell and his aging father, Warren. The younger Maxwell blithely fathers children by several slave women, but it is only after he has found himself a white bride in Blanche, his distant cousin, that he purchases Ellen—a slave to whom he rapidly develops a deep emotional attachment. Hammond also becomes a local celebrity through the exploits of his champion Mandingo slave, Mede, who triumphs in a series of slave-fight contests. Driven to jealousy by Hammond's relationship with Ellen, Blanche compels Mede to sleep with her. Armed with knowledge of this affair, Meg, Hammond's manservant, coldly blackmails his master's wife into sleeping with him in turn. When Blanche gives birth to a mixed-race baby, her own mother savagely destroys the child while an outraged Hammond poisons his wife and brutally kills his once-beloved Mede with a pitchfork.

The slaves of the Falconhurst plantation constitute a diverse community, from the devoted Ellen and the ostensibly obsequious but devious Meg, to the silently arrogant Mede and the imposing Lucretia Borgia, the cook and (uncredited) manager of the plantation. All, however, seem to utterly worship their white masters. The female Mandingo on Falconhurst, Big Pearl, is "docile as a kitten, biddable as putty. She delighted in being stripped and paraded and handled and bargained for" (32). Every young black woman on the plantation, furthermore, aspires to her master's bed and is prepared to accept rape uncomplainingly and even proudly—in a manner that is reminiscent of Rhodes's dismal nineteenth-century conclusions about slave sexual behavior: "The lack of chaste sentiment among the female slaves is exemplified by their yielding without objection, except in isolated cases, to the passion of their master. Indeed, the idea of the superiority of the white race was so universally admitted that the negress felt only pride at bearing offspring that had an admixture of blood of the ruling class. . . . So loose was the tie of marriage among the slaves, that the negro husband felt little or no displeasure when the fancy of the master chanced to light upon his wife" (335).

While *Mandingo*'s depiction of compliant slaves who happily debase themselves at the bidding of their masters seems to recall the racism of Rhodes's historical study, the novel's emphasis upon the way in which the oppressive nature of slavery shaped such slave psychologies is closer to Elkins's thesis. Onstott's novel goes much further than Elkins's notion of slaveholder as "significant other," however. At Falconhurst, the white master is finally nothing less than a deity, most explicitly in the scene in which Meg nervously serves Hammond a drink that the slaveholder has not asked for: "he grew diffident as he approached his young master. He bit his lip as he extended the unordered libation to his god, uncertain as to how his ministration would be received" (54).

Discipline and control, in fact, operate in a variety of ways in *Mandingo*. Most obviously, there are crude physical penalties. "We don't flog much on Falconhurst," Warren Maxwell claims—in an ironic echo of the denials of corporal punishment that are common in plantation literature—before adding that "when we flogs we flogs good. . . . [N]o nigger don't want a second dose like it." If any reader might be inclined to doubt Warren's assertion that taking "the skin offn a nigger's rump" results in "a good servant . . . from then on," the narrative provides a graphic illustration in the protracted description of Agamemnon's whipping, which is threatened for several chapters before being brutally and humiliatingly enacted, leaving Hammond in guilty tears and Meg dramatically "sobered . . . resolved to evade the chastisement which he had before invited" from his beloved master (29, 88–92).

While Lucretia Borgia may observe that the "[o]n'y way to tame a young nigger" is "to smash him," the forms of control at Falconhurst are often much more subtle than this, being largely organized around literacy, access to information, and surveillance. The Maxwells are aware that newspapers carry dangerous ideas that might influence their slaves, and they opine that the "law agin learnin' niggers to read" is the "[b]est law ever passed." "No nigger readin', no nigger risin'," Warren concludes confidently. Hammond further explains that "[w]e don't have nigger church at Falconhurst. Papa think it keeps the hands all stirred up." In short, reading and religion might give the slaves "ideas they were safer, and, for that matter, happier without." The Maxwells also find that their power is more easily rationalized and enacted without divine endorsement: "At Falconhurst, no Biblical justification of the institution of slavery was required. . . . No admonition of servants to obey masters was needed. Why suggest to them that there exists an alternative? . . . Why introduce into plantation economy a being superior to the white master?" Finally, slavery in *Mandingo* is almost an antebellum southern version of Foucault's famous Panopticon, in which a slave comes to think of constant "surveillance as a master's right, if not duty, to control his every act" (171, 37, 97, 80, 324).

Despite its emphasis upon the powerful psychological influence of the slaveholder and its portraits of submissive slaves, however, *Mandingo* is, in the final analysis, closer to Frederick Douglass's depiction of slavery than that of Stanley Elkins. Onstott's novel makes it very clear that surveillance, physical discipline, and psychological manipulation are constantly necessary in order to be effective. Passive slaves are not merely created; they must be continually repressed and controlled in order to maintain their docility. As one slave-trader in the novel acknowledges, "you cain't tell whut goes on in a nigger's haid" (10).

Significantly, whippings, illiteracy, absence of religion, and constant supervision are finally revealed to be insufficient forms of control at Falconhurst. The Maxwells may have set themselves up as deities to their slaves, but their power is far from omnipresent or omniscient. There are constant rumblings of slave discontent and resistance in *Mandingo*. Hammond is annoyed that his slaves are incapable of chopping weeds without ruining cotton plants as well. The narrative, however, suggests a different interpretation of such apparent carelessness: "He did not credit them with the foresight that the more plants they destroyed the less cotton they would have to pick" (201). Although the Maxwells teach their slaves to take pride in being sold,

Lucretia Borgia is livid when she learns that she has been put on the market and purchased. She soon runs away from her new master in order to stubbornly resume her duties at Falconhurst—to the impotent embarrassment of the Maxwells, whose power to reduce a human being to a commodity has been seriously compromised. Meanwhile, although Meg looks upon his master as a god, this does not prevent him from blackmailing Hammond's wife into sleeping with him. Furthermore, in *Drum*, the book's sequel, a single resentful slave is swiftly able to persuade his fellows to participate in a violent revolution at Falconhurst. The Maxwell slaves are thus not the "docile but irresponsible, loyal but lazy" children described by Elkins, and nor are they Styron's "coarse, raucous, clownish, uncouth . . . black riffraff" (Elkins, *Slavery* 82; Styron 136). Instead, as Douglass observes of his fellows, the slaves of Falconhurst must be carefully controlled and monitored to repress "the rebellious spirit of enslaved humanity" (51).

Onstott's novel shows an institution that—in accordance with Elkins's theories—aimed to turn human beings into tame beasts of burden through elaborate psychological manipulation. Unlike Elkins, however, *Mandingo* acknowledges that the power of the slaveholders—however ruthlessly and brutally exercised—had profound limits and that, within the interstices of the institution, slaves may have developed a variety of ways in which to assert themselves and to resist control. Unfortunately, however, literary criticism has entirely dismissed *Mandingo* and neglected the implications of its depiction of slavery and slave psychology. Van Deburg asserts that African American characters in the Falconhurst novels are merely "savage and subhuman," while even Styron rejects *Mandingo* as simply "racist" (Van Deburg 149; Styron "Revisited" 72).

Margaret Walker's *Jubilee*

More surprising than the critical disregard of *Mandingo* is the scholarly neglect of even notable works of slavery fiction published by black authors in the quarter-century after World War II. The most complex and astute treatment of slavery and slave subjectivities in fiction before the 1970s appears in Margaret Walker's *Jubilee* (1966). In contrast to *The Confessions of Nat Turner*, Walker's novel engages with and synthesizes a complicated range of historiographical ideas and positions. *Jubilee* presents a portrait not of rare, exceptional slaves, but of a rich, active, and diverse slave community. In Walker's narrative, there are unusually militant slaves, like the figures described in Aptheker's *American Negro Slave Revolts*, exceptionally passive slaves, like the personalities depicted by Elkins, and numerous characters along a continuum between these two poles. *Jubilee* thus exploits the central achievement of *Uncle Tom's Cabin*—its sense of a diverse slave community—and develops it to its full potential, free from the limitations of Stowe's racial purview. Walker's novel provides an unprecedentedly complex and comprehensive portrait of the everyday lives, experiences, culture, and communities of enslaved Americans.

Jubilee concerns the life of Vyry, from her birth as a slave on the Dutton plantation in Georgia in the 1830s to her experiences as a freewoman in Alabama in the 1870s. She is the daughter of John Dutton, the master of the plantation, and Hetta, an African slave. As a house servant, Vyry escapes the brutality of the overseer, but endures the cruelty of the plantation mistress, Salina Dutton, who resents Vyry's parentage. Walker provides a vivid picture of everyday life on the plantation: white fear of slave rebellions, secret meetings of the black underground church, and the often brutal punishment of intransigent slaves that punctuate Christmas, weddings, picnics, and other daily events. Vyry becomes involved with a militant free black named Randall Ware, but Dutton forbids her marrying him. During the Civil War, the Duttons die off and Ware disappears to help the Union army. After emancipation, Vyry decides to marry a kind stranger named Innis Brown and moves to Alabama with him. Suffering frequently at the hands of racists during this odyssey, Vyry is relieved when the white citizens of Greenville accept her as a midwife. When Ware finally reappears, Vyry cannot agree with his radical separatist politics and elects to remain with Brown, who, like her, is a moderate Christian integrationist.

Walker's narrative reflects Aptheker's belief that many enslaved Americans were dedicated to resistance and liberty: a scene early in *Jubilee* involves the execution of two slaves for poisoning their master. The underground church, meanwhile, proves to be the central site of slave resistance, as its preacher declares to his people that a Moses-like deliverer will come to liberate black Americans from slavery—before heading out himself to help more fugitive slaves along the Underground Railroad. Furthermore, the young Johnny Dutton's apparently obsequious body servant, Jim, works as a Union spy during the Civil War (83, 45, 56, 219–20). Walker's novel, however, also presents a character, the mentally disturbed Willie, who conforms closely to Elkins's sense of the brutalizing effects of slavery: "to Vyry there was no mystery. This child was just another slave who had been kicked around like a dog all his life . . . until now he acted more like a dumb, driven animal than a human being" (108–9). But where Elkins considers resistant and rebellious slaves exceptions that prove the rule, Walker's novel reverses his idea, and sees those reduced to numb passivity by the horrors of slavery as the uncommon ones (Elkins, *Slavery* 137–38). Beyond extreme cases like Willie, *Jubilee* also acknowledges that there were slaves who were passive and subservient, like the eternally grinning Lucy, whom even the moderate Vyry considers despicable for her submissive toadying. The narrative also concedes that there were "trusted slaves" who could be relied upon to expose planned acts of resistance (131, 82–83).

Jubilee thus absorbs the Elkins thesis as well as quite opposite notions about the militant, revolutionary character of enslaved African Americans into a compelling portrait of a multifaceted slave community. Through the character of her everywoman, Vyry, Walker asserts that most enslaved Americans stood somewhere in between these two extremes. Vyry is a determinedly apolitical moderate, and this quality of her character is emphasized by her ultimate choice of the placid Innis Brown for a husband rather than the novel's most exceptional black figure, the dynamic, militant, and educated Randall Ware. Here, Walker satirizes the convention of the exceptional slave by making her heroine utterly commonplace and by rendering the unusually able Ware somewhat marginal in the scheme of the novel.

In essence, *Jubilee* anticipates John Blassingame's critical response to the Elkins thesis in his crucial study, *The Slave Community* (1972). Blassingame observes that "Sambo" was not the only stereotype of slave personality to appear in antebellum white southern literature. He argues that conceptions of slaves as "Jack" (sullen but largely cooperative) and "Nat" (violent, rebellious, and prone to run away) are as commonplace in white antebellum documents as the references to Sambo to which Elkins paid so much attention. "Perhaps the only thing that the white man's stereotypes of the slave as Sambo, Jack, and Nat does," Blassingame concludes, "is to indicate the range of personality types in the quarters" (238). Similarly, *Jubilee* demonstrates significant distinctions between the passive Willie, the militant Ware, the moderate Vyry, and slaves such as Grandpa Tom who are, for the most part, reluctantly obedient but will sometimes actively resist their masters. Walker once acknowledged that her great-grandmother, upon whom Vyry is based, "was shaped by the forces that dominated her life. In the Big House and the Quarters, she could not react any other way" (quoted in Condé 214). Responding to this claim, Mary Condé argues that "Vyry's attitude is partly a result of the brainwashing . . . which Stanley Elkins has identified as one of the crucial elements in slavery" (214). This is an oversimplification of Vyry's character—and of Walker's statement. Walker specifically notes that the forces that shaped her great-grandmother were present in *both* the Big House *and* the slave quarters. In other words, Vyry is not subject only to the influence of the slaveholder but also to that of the slave community. Walker thus disputes Elkins's claim that the slaveholder was the *only* significant influence upon the psychology of the slave.

The sophistication of *Jubilee's* portrayal of slave psychologies is fully matched by the complexity of its depiction of slavery as an institution. Walker's novel rejects both the Phillips view of slavery as a benign institution and the Elkins conception of it as totalitarian Holocaust. *Jubilee* asserts that the truth involves both extremes and a whole spectrum in between. The slave community in the novel enjoys relative autonomy and privacy, and is not always under the surveillance of master and overseer. The enslaved people in *Jubilee* are permitted to cease field work when it rains, and they have their own gardens in which to grow produce for themselves (60, 62, 83). The slaves possess sufficient cultural and communal space for a life of their own, and the Dutton plantation in the novel is anything but a "closed system," yet neither is it the idealized institution that Phillips portrays. Violence and cruelty occur with considerable frequency. What, in fact, is shocking about the violence in the novel is that it occurs so matter-of-factly within the conventional routine of what otherwise seems a relatively liberal slaveholding regime. On the wedding day of Lillian Dutton, for example, the slave community participates in the festivities, singing spirituals to the guests and working hard in the kitchen. During these celebrations, however, the overseer casually brands a slave for running away (110–17). According to *Jubilee,* slaveholders could be lenient and even generous in their treatment of their human property—but their control was ultimately dependent on violence, a violence that could rupture the polite façade of plantation life at any moment.

Walker's novel actively participates in existing debates and discourses about the nature of slavery. *Jubilee* negotiates its way between the assertions of predecessors as varied as Stowe, Phillips, Aptheker, Gaither, and Elkins, locating partial truths in all of them, while suggesting that slavery is too complex an institution to be reduced to any single ideological definition. For all the sophistication of its engagement with historiographical debates, however, *Jubilee* has inspired little attention from literary critics.

One reason for this is that, while *Jubilee* engages with the historiography of slavery in informed and incisive ways, its use of primary historical data is a little simplistic. At times, Walker's work resembles the kind of historical novel that Styron criticizes for being "overwhelmed by an avalanche of data," and "cluttered with facts the author wishes to show off as fruits of his diligent research" ("Revisited" 68). Even so sympathetic a reader as Barbara Christian opines that Walker "often intrudes upon this drama with historical facts about the period" (quoted in Carmichael 57). "I had a superstructure of facts assembled from word-of-mouth accounts, slave narratives, history books, documents, newspapers," Walker reports in her essay "How I Wrote *Jubilee*," "and now I had only to give my material the feel of a fabric of life" (58). On occasion, however, this "superstructure of facts" stifles the fiction. Walker's emphasis on specific articulations of slave culture—songs, prayers, sermons, children's games, cuisine, herbal remedies, etc.—is sometimes excessive and clumsily integrated (e.g., 12–13, 17, 45–46, 52–53, 57, 71, 137–39, 147). When Vyry takes to the road, for example, the story pauses for a lengthy paragraph enumerating all of Vyry's (presumably exhaustively researched) personal effects (316). Bernard Bell comments that the novel's second section "sags under the weight of the facts about the Civil War years, often introduced by Walker through a catalog of excerpts from speeches, letters, and newspaper articles" (287). Walker brilliantly dramatizes historiographical debates, but her novel is somewhat hobbled by its awkward display of the fruits of her years of primary research. This is precisely the opposite of Styron, who asserts imaginative license over documented detail but remains in thrall to a single historiographical argument.

Another reason for the scholarly neglect of *Jubilee* is that Walker's novel predated by a decade or more the body of African American slavery fiction with which recent scholars have been most concerned—epitomized by such works as *Flight to Canada, Dessa Rose,* and *Beloved.* Contemporary

critics tend to emphasize slavery novels that are informed by postmodernism and which self-consciously draw attention to the processes by which
historical narratives are constructed. *Jubilee*, in contrast, is characterized by
straightforward social realism. There is, of course, nothing wrong with traditional realism per se, but Walker's formal conservatism means that she is
often unable to transcend popular clichés and tired conventions of slavery
fiction in *Jubilee*. Minrose Gwin admits that many of the novel's characters
are "stereotypes based on southern myth" (153). Hortense Spillers likewise
acknowledges that Walker's characters are "one dimensional, either good or
bad, speaking in a public rhetoric that assumes the heroic or its opposite"
(quoted in Carby 135). Bell concedes that the "white characters, particularly
the Dutton family, are stock representatives of the planter class," while the
"minor black characters are types clearly derived from the oral tradition"
(288). The well-meaning but troubled aristocratic slaveholder, the hysterical, racist plantation mistress, the coarse and brutal lower-class overseers—
these are stereotypes that date back at least to *Uncle Tom's Cabin*. Walker's
portrayal of black characters is better, but figures like Innis Brown and Randall Ware are symbols, not complex individuals—the Christian integrationist and the radical militant.

Despite its sophisticated engagement with historiographical theories and
debates about American slavery, then, critics tend to approach *Jubilee* as an
intriguing, if limited, precursor of the contemporary novel of slavery instead
of as a significant work in its own right. This suggests that the challenges
and traditional limitations of slavery fiction were not resolved either by African American authorship or by a revisionist historiographical viewpoint.[11]
In the next chapter, I trace the quest of black novelists in the 1970s to create
a new literary approach to slavery that would transcend the shortcomings
of *Jubilee* while also building upon its achievements.

Too many critics have been content to write off *The Confessions of Nat
Turner* as simply the climax of a long-dominant racist discourse about slavery, just as they have tended to neglect the canon of slavery fiction published
between World War II and the 1970s. In the conventional view, Styron's
novel is merely a false, white-authored portrayal of slavery that black critics
boldly challenged and African American authors ultimately replaced. My
analysis suggests ways of illuminating the significant contribution to slavery

discourse made by *The Confessions of Nat Turner* in addition to exposing its fundamental limitations. Styron's novel is a text characterized by conflicting and contradictory impulses. It is based upon Elkins's cutting-edge historical theories, but its conception of slavery also reiterates the historian's clichéd and discredited ideas about the nature of slave subjectivities. *Confessions* is a crucial step in the postwar trend that—in reaction to *Gone with the Wind*—gradually refocused slavery fiction upon the experiences of slaves rather than masters. Styron's novel is, in fact, highly significant and undeniably influential as the first twentieth-century novel entirely narrated from a slave's perspective, yet critics have often accused Styron's text of replicating the racist ideologies of Mitchell's fiction. Certainly, *Confessions* sometimes resurrects assumptions and conventions that are familiar from *Gone with the Wind*, and Styron's fiction is actually less sophisticated in its presentation of the effects of slavery upon human psychology than many of its contemporaries, from the sensationalist *Mandingo* to the astute *Jubilee*.

It is imperative to reconfigure our conception of *The Confessions of Nat Turner* because the terms of the cultural conversation about the novel since its publication almost forty years ago have too frequently been simplistic, racially divisive, and unproductive.[12] The hostile stalemate in which the initial debates concerning *The Confessions of Nat Turner* terminated is perfectly encapsulated in Styron's petulant response to an adversarial audience member at the 1968 Southern Historical Association meeting in New Orleans: "Well, then, we're at an impasse, my friend, because you say it's one way, and I say it's another" (quoted in Stone 14).

The aggressive tone of several of the essays in the *Ten Black Writers* collection actually provided Styron the luxury of being able to duck behind a shield of aggrieved self-righteousness, allowing him to decry the "malignant totalitarianism" of his detractors. Indeed, Styron confidently claimed that "responsible critics, black and white, have refuted" the criticisms of the *Ten Black Writers* (quoted in Stone 168, 169). Styron asserted that he was "subjected not even to discussible criticism but to the most intractable kind of hysteria.... [W]hile in my own mind I was guiltless of the atrocities it was claimed I committed, I knew that the general public could easily be bamboozled into thinking that the black writers had a valid case against me" ("South" 5, 6).

In the face of such condescending criticism, contemporary scholars have been too often tempted to overcompensate and celebrate the Ten Black Writers as flawlessly heroic champions of a new emergent subaltern discourse. While Rushdy lionizes the efforts and the influence of "those brave critics of 1968," the *Ten Black Writers* volume now seems in many respects a rather dated period piece, a slice of late-sixties polemic that is rather narrow in its emphases and which lacks the kind of nuanced analysis of Styron's novel that should be possible today (Rushdy, *Neo-slave* 83, 91). *Ten Black Writers* is, after all, a book that stridently demonizes Styron as a "psychologically sick" individual, notable for his "moral senility" and "vile racist imagination," and which groundlessly suggests that he "seems to relish the horrible details of the whites' bestiality toward Negroes" (Kaiser 54, 57, 65; Hairston 72). The responses of ten African American males to Styron's attempt to "cut yet another black man down to the size of a boy" may have been a worthy effort in the climate of 1968, but the discourse of the Ten Black Writers now seems quite relentless in its single-minded outrage, excessive masculinism, and even occasional homophobia (Killens, "Confessions" 34).[13]

It is important to move beyond such an aggressively adversarial discourse, just as it is crucial to transcend the reductive assumption that the debate over Styron's novel has been purely and simply a conflict between authentic black interpretations of slavery, on one hand, and dishonest and racist white representations, on the other.[14] A sense of simplistic racial divisions and the strident hostilities between Styron and his vociferous critics impeded the development of a productive interracial dialogue about slavery in the field of fiction—certainly when compared to the powerful interracial discourse about slavery that the discipline of history produced after the 1950s. Indeed, the most palpable result of the reaction to Styron's novel is that it effectively discouraged white novelists from exploring the subject of slavery for thirty years. Stephen E. Henderson, a black critic, noted approvingly in 1969 that "the next white writer will think twice before presuming to interpret the Black Experience" (quoted in Gross and Bender 488). While a few white novelists continued to produce populist plantation soap operas, serious fiction by white authors about slavery in the United States would remain a dead letter from 1968 until the publication of Valerie Martin's *Property* in 2003.[15]

For all its limitations and its dubious assumptions about slave psychology, it is, however, quite conceivable that Styron's text could have stimulated a highly constructive interracial dialogue about slavery, involving novelists and critics of various races (if not necessarily Styron himself), instead of the destructive and divisive conflict it actually engendered. James Baldwin's suggestion that *Confessions* might mark "the beginning of our common history" was soon forgotten amid the heated exchanges about the novel (quoted in Killens, "Confessions" 32).

The 1960s and 1970s witnessed a much more constructive dialogue about slavery within the discipline of history than in the realm of fiction, for the responses of historians to Elkins's famous study was of a very different character than the reaction of literary critics to Styron's book. The essays written by thirteen historians—both black and white, male and female—that Ann J. Lane collected in *The Debate over Slavery: Stanley Elkins and His Critics* (1971) provide a case in point. While virtually all the essays in the Lane volume disagree fundamentally with Elkins's conclusions, they do not angrily eviscerate his ideas or accuse him of being a racist or an apologist for slavery. Instead, they engage respectfully and constructively with Elkins's theories, and they build upon his insights to suggest alternative interpretations of history. Lane, for instance, begins the collection with "Special thanks to Stanley Elkins for having written such a provocative essay that it elicited years of lively criticism," and she notes in her introduction that "[w]hatever the limitations of [Elkins's] book . . . it has without doubt extended the examination of slavery . . . in permanent and profound ways" (3). Later in the volume, Charles A. Pinderhughes, an African American social activist and scholar—as well as a member of the Black Panther party—reports that "Professor Elkins invited me to think in a new direction. . . . His volume contributed significantly to my earliest understandings of American racism" (103). At the end of the volume, Elkins is even provided a forum in which to respond to his critics; Styron, in contrast, was able to complain that the publishers of the Clarke volume lacked the decency to offer him the right of reply (Stone 169). Here, Elkins concedes that "certain of the criticisms" of his work are quite "correct," and that he has amended aspects of his argument in response to his critics ("Slavery and Ideology" 327, 332). In the 1976 edition of *Slavery*, furthermore, Elkins "acknowledged freely the weakness of his own awareness in 1959 of the extent and significance of slave folklore, music, religion, and Negro night life" (Stone 269). Elkins's scholarly humility and his willingness to modify his beliefs and develop his ideas could hardly be more different from Styron's arrogant rejection of his critics—but then, the professional and scholarly tone of Elkins's critics is quite distinct from that of Styron's detractors.

The years immediately following the appearance of the Lane collection saw the emergence of several landmark works by both black and white historians, including John Blassingame's *The Slave Community* (1972), George P. Rawick's *From Sundown to Sunup: The Making of the Black Community* (1972), and Eugene Genovese's *Roll, Jordan, Roll: The World the Slaves Made* (1974). Such texts superseded Elkins's study, but they were to a considerable extent—no matter how different their conclusions—built upon his work. As Peter Parish puts it, Elkins "set the agenda for the next generation of historians of slavery. His influence is to be measured not in the band of disciples and converts he inspired, for their numbers were few, but in the army of critics he goaded into fresh thinking about a whole range of different questions" (7).[16]

Unlike many critics of *The Confessions of Nat Turner*, historians rejected simplistic ideological binaries or a paradigm of black-white opposition and instead sought to explore how scholars might engage with and use Elkins's sometimes questionable theories to develop new and progressive ways of understanding American slavery. While the relationship between Styron and the Ten Black Writers was one of unproductive conflict, the relationship between Elkins and his respondents was a constructive dialogue, one that pointed the way forward to a more illuminating historiographical discourse about slavery. It is no coincidence that the most enlightening slavery fiction of the 1970s and 1980s would be written not in opposition to *The Confessions of Nat Turner*, but as a thoughtful engagement with the theories of Stanley Elkins.

You Shall See How a Slave Was Made a *Woman*

THE DEVELOPMENT OF THE CONTEMPORARY NOVEL
OF SLAVERY, 1976–1987

*W*ithin a decade of the appearance of *The Confessions of Nat Turner*, Styron's representation of slavery had been thoroughly eclipsed in the popular mind by the massive cultural phenomenon of Alex Haley's *Roots*—both as a Pulitzer Prize–winning bestseller and as a TV miniseries.[1] For the first time, historical fiction about the African American experience had become, at least temporarily, the exclusive preserve of black writers. It would not be, however, until a writer of color engaged in complex dialogue with a variety of influences and discourses—history and fiction, reality and representation, slaveholders and slaves, black and white ancestors—that the African American novel of slavery would truly emerge from beneath the shadow of *Gone with the Wind*.

Black-authored fiction about slavery that was published in the 1970s is characterized by two primary impulses. First, there is the desire to interrogate the very theories of Elkins that Styron relied so heavily upon in his portrayal of slavery. Black writers of the 1970s engaged with, explored, tested, complicated, and critiqued Elkins's arguments in their fiction. The second characteristic of African American novels about slavery in this period is the quest for new formal and narrative strategies for representing the experience of the institution. Some black writers sought to appropriate traditional white literary conventions, while others used innovative postmodern strategies to explode traditional fictional discourses about slavery.

America's bicentennial year, 1976, saw the emergence of two very different, yet equally significant works about slavery by black writers: Ishmael

Reed's parodic, metafictional *Flight to Canada*, and Alex Haley's realistic family saga, *Roots*. For all its achievements, the limitations of Haley's book confirm the inadequacies of the kind of conventional narrative strategies that encumber *Jubilee*. In contrast, Reed's novel reveals both the potentialities and the restrictions of a postmodern engagement with history not as reality but as pure discourse. At the end of the decade, however, one black novelist would provide a new literary template for resolving the challenges of dramatizing slavery. Barely acknowledged in its day, Octavia E. Butler's work of science fiction, *Kindred* (1979), forges an extremely effective third way between self-conscious literary intertextuality and a more traditional, emotionally involving realism. Furthermore, Butler's novel develops an astute and informed dialogue with contemporary slavery historiography and with standard conventions for representing slavery in imaginative literature. *Kindred* is also significant for its subversion of the pervasive masculinism of black literary discourses about slavery in the 1960s and 1970s. Butler's novel provides a compelling alternative narrative of slavery organized around the experiences of women. Despite these impressive innovations, *Kindred* was initially overlooked by critics—unlike Toni Morrison's *Beloved*—which uses similar strategies and was showered with praise as soon as it appeared. Nor was Butler's novel a bestseller—in very stark contrast to the instant popularity of *Roots* in 1976.

Alex Haley's *Roots*

Alex Haley's epic narrative *Roots* concerns the capture of a youth named Kunta Kinte from the Mandinka village of Juffure in 1787 and his subsequent enslavement in America. The text details the travails and triumphs of Kunta and his descendants (including his daughter, Kizzy, and his grandson, Chicken George) over two centuries. The phenomenal popular success of *Roots*—in book and TV form—significantly altered the common perception of slavery and slaves in America.[2] As Leslie Fiedler says, "with *Roots*, a Black American succeeded for the first time in modifying the mythology of Black-White relations *for the majority audience*" (71). The sheer popular appeal of Haley's text is not its only notable characteristic. *Roots* engages in a promising and intriguing dialogue with Elkins's conception of slavery and slave psychologies. Unfortunately, however, Haley's exploration and critique of the historian's ideas is ultimately plagued by inconsistency, a lack of development, and a disappointing retreat from its own best insights. The potentially revolutionary depictions of slavery and slave subjectivities in *Roots* are finally compromised by the text's reliance upon traditional literary conventions and generic structures.

There has been considerable critical disagreement about the relationship between *Roots* and Elkins's ideas about slavery and slave identities. Leslie Fishbein claims that Haley's book "effectively debunks many of the stereotypes of slave life" propounded by the historian. In contrast to Elkins's claim that the rigors of slavery and dependence upon the white master class reduced African American slaves to the level of "Sambo," Fishbein praises *Roots* for showing that "slaves had a remarkable ability to avoid this role, that the institution of slavery was neither coherent enough nor oppressive enough to coerce predominantly Sambolike behavior. Kunta Kinte never becomes servile despite repeated punishments" (287).

A number of black critics, however, complain that Haley's work actually replicates rather than challenges many of Elkins's assertions. In May 1977, *The Black Scholar* published a symposium addressing the television adaptation of *Roots*. While four of the five writers involved critique the TV series for diluting, distorting, or deviating from Haley's book, Robert Chrisman's article questions the overall narrative trajectory of *Roots*, something that is common to both book and TV adaptation. Chrisman acknowledges the power of the early sections of *Roots*, with their vivid portrait of "the despicable slave trade and the subsequent brutalization of black people," but he is concerned that the central message of the story as a whole is "'survival by any means necessary.' In the case of Kunta Kinte and his descendants, this meant submission to floggings, rape, murder, the destruction of the family, and the brutality of forced labor. A mood of resignation to any kind of calamity pervades the *Roots* film. . . . Tomming is first presented as a tactic used by the slaves to assuage the guilt, fear, and suspicion of whites, but as *Roots* unfolds, it becomes the way of life for black peoples, their primary response to critical situations" (41). In other words, Chrisman argues that *Roots* actually shows that the physical and psychological rigors of slavery were ultimately quite successful in brutalizing people and reducing them to docility—just as Elkins claims.

This is not the only such interpretation of Haley's text. Elkins, we should recall, acknowledges that it "was possible for significant numbers of slaves, in varying degrees, to escape the full impact of the system and its coercions upon personality," but he emphasizes that such individuals were conspicuously exceptional (*Slavery* 137, 139). Harold Courlander's reading of *Roots* interprets Kunta Kinte as just such an anomaly. Courlander argues that "Kunta becomes and remains the undiluted Mandinka warrior, in contrast to his more typical shipboard companions and the docile fellow slaves on the plantation. . . . Haley's basic theme is that despite the pressures of two New World cultures—the white master society and the black slave society—Kunta forever remains an unreconstructed African" ("Kunta" 298, 299). In Courlander's reading, Kunta is an exceptional figure who rejects the Samboism of his fellows and is "contemptuous of those slaves who had adapted and found their own ways of surviving. . . . While there are black individuals whom Kunta learns to respect and even love, as a group the black community remains beyond his acceptance" ("Kunta" 300).[3] Haley's use of the traditional figure of the exceptional slave in *Roots* thus seems to confirm rather than question Elkins's view of slave personality. Indeed, in Courlander's formulation, Kunta even sounds uncomfortably similar to Styron's Nat Turner—who can love individuals, such as Willis and Hark, but is largely contemptuous of "my black shit-eating people" (27).

Some scholars, then, see *Roots* as a comprehensive refutation of the Elkins thesis, and others as a mere confirmation of it. In fact, Haley's book is ultimately both and neither. In its early chapters, *Roots* stages a promising, judicious, and sophisticated exploration of Elkins's ideas. The narrative vividly dramatizes Elkins's vision of slavery only to complicate the historian's claims about the institution's effects upon human identity. It achieves this through the evolving perspective of the increasingly acculturated Kunta Kinte. At the book's midpoint, however, *Roots*'s portrayal of the nature of slavery fundamentally changes, causing its critical dialogue with Elkins to founder.

Haley's text initially presents slavery precisely as Elkins imagines it—as a black equivalent of the Holocaust and an insidious system of control. It also shows, however, the ways in which individuals caught inside this system might resist descending into passive docility. The form of slavery that Kunta initially encounters in *Roots* is every bit as devastating as Elkins claims it was in reality. The historian asserts that—like the inmates of the Nazi death camps—"every African who became a slave underwent an experience whose crude psychic impact must have been staggering" (*Slavery* 87–88, 98). *Roots* vividly dramatizes the series of traumatic shocks that make up the process of enslavement: capture, transport, and introduction to the New World. The book's protracted and graphic depiction of the horrors of the Middle Passage has yet to be surpassed in fiction, and its presentation of a defamiliarized and alien America from Kunta's disoriented perspective is also extremely powerful.[4] *Roots* initially shows slavery to be entirely ruthless and the influence of the master class to be utterly pervasive. As a habitual runaway, Kunta faces frequent and harsh physical punishment, culminating in the casual amputation of his foot by slave-hunters. Throughout these grueling and dislocating experiences, however, Kunta refuses to accept his status as slave and resists the psychological pressures that slavery exerts upon him.

This alone is not sufficient refutation of Elkins's theories, however. While asserting the significance of the initial trauma of enslavement, Elkins is also careful to emphasize that "it is possible to overrate . . . this shock sequence in the effort to explain what followed," and that "it took something more than this to produce 'Sambo.'" After all, as Elkins acknowledges, those who were born into slavery in America did not experience the traumatic process of enslavement (*Slavery* 102). Elkins draws upon contemporary psychological theories in an effort to explain the development of the Sambo personality within slavery, specifically the importance of significant others to the development of identity and the ways in which social expectations determine individual roles and behavior (*Slavery* 119–21, 124–25).

Roots both dramatizes and refutes Elkins's view of slave personality by having Kunta initially see African American slaves in entirely Elkinsian terms: "It sickened him to think about how these black ones jumped about their work whenever they saw a toubob [white person], and how, if that toubob spoke a word to them, they rushed to do whatever he told them to. Kunta couldn't fathom what had happened to so destroy their minds that they acted like goats and monkeys. . . . Kunta vowed never to become *like* them" (186). Slavery is thus as alien to Kunta as it is to the twentieth-century reader of *Roots*. The great accomplishment of Haley's text is its construction of slavery from the perspective of an outsider whose attitude toward slave identities changes as he gradually becomes a slave himself. Kunta develops from being an alienated spectator—who is simply horrified by the brutality of slavery and the accommodation of its subjects to the institution—to an insider who learns how to survive the system and begins to appreciate the degree to which enslaved people maintain a measure of individuality and integrity despite all the compromises they must make to survive. In sum, *Roots* shows an exceptional slave becoming integrated into the slave community. Kunta's progress, we might say, mirrors the shift in historiography from Elkins's theories to the studies of the 1970s that focused upon the dynamism of slave communities and the agency of slaves as individuals.

Kunta gradually becomes aware that his fellow slaves are not the "goats and monkeys" he initially took them for. His friendship with the storytelling musician, Fiddler, and his marriage to the plantation cook, Bell, assimilate him into slave society. Kunta then becomes aware of acts of black resistance, conscious of a secret communications network within the slave community, and alert to evidence that slave rebellions are a clear and constant danger to the white master class. Finally, Fiddler explains to Kunta that the Sambo persona is a protective mask: "Reckon since you been born I been actin' like de no-good, lazy, shiftless, head-scratchin' nigger white folks says us is" (190–91, 246–47, 296–97, 217).

The development of Kunta's perception of the slave community and comprehension of slave psychologies is not an entirely smooth process, however. It sometimes seems that Kunta will never quite be able to stop believing that "any kind of respect or appreciation for themselves had been squeezed out of [the slaves] so thoroughly that they seemed to feel that their lives were as they should be" (212). While at one moment Kunta is quite aware of the existence of slave militancy, at another he seems to deny its frequency and significance: "There were a few young rebels among them but the vast majority of slaves were the kind that did exactly what was expected of them, usually without even having to be told. . . . Why, there were some right there on the plantation he was sure the massa could leave unguarded for a year and find them there—still working—when he returned. It wasn't because they were content; they complained constantly among themselves. But never did more than a handful so much as protest, let alone resist" (247–48). After an argument with Bell, Kunta finally gains a full understanding of his fellow slaves: "Though they never showed it except to those they loved, and sometimes not even then, he realized at last that they felt—and hated—no less than he the oppressiveness under which they all lived" (284). Kunta thus discovers that his attitude toward slavery is not exceptional after all. Kunta has gradually become like the other slaves and, in the process, has discovered that they are more like him than he initially acknowledged. Ostensibly obedient and content, Kunta and his fellow slaves are anything but Sambos on the inside. Haley's book thus acknowledges that the docile Sambo persona may have been widely visible on southern plantations, as Elkins suggests, but this does not mean that it was an accurate indication of slaves' identities. In *Roots*, Sambo is never more than a mask.

The implication of this narrative trajectory is that Elkins's conception of slave personality is superficial. Kunta, like the twentieth-century white historian, sees only Sambo—until he is sufficiently integrated into the black community to develop a deeper understanding of individual slaves. This is an extremely compelling complication of the Elkins thesis. Haley's text vividly shows the cultural and psychological pressures that forced slaves to conform to the demands of the system and to enact certain roles, but it also shows how slaves had identities and communities of their own—and significant others beyond their masters. The slaveholders of *Roots* have every reason to believe that their human property is loyal, docile, and content, but the slaves have unspoken depths that are unknown to all but their most intimate friends and family members.

There are, however, limits to Haley's dialogue with Elkins. Ultimately, *Roots* glosses over several crucial questions. For example, if Fiddler has been playing "de no-good, lazy, shiftless, head-scratchin' nigger" for decades, might not such long-term and constant role-playing have had a genuine effect upon his identity? If such an exceptionally militant individual as Kunta can be rendered at least superficially docile by the rigors of slavery, might it not be possible that the institution could have even more profound effects upon others? If Kunta's militancy can be pushed beneath a surface of apparent passivity in just a few years, what might have been the psychic impact of generations of slavery?

Roots evades rather than engages with such questions, and it does so by dramatically altering its portrayal of the institution of slavery. By the time the book reveals that Kunta (and, by extension, Elkins) was wrong to assume that slavery turned African Americans into Sambos, its portrait of the institution has softened considerably. For over a hundred pages the text focuses upon Kunta's bewildered view of the unrelenting oppression and random violence of slavery. The amputation of his foot, however, forces Kunta to begin the process of assimilation. At this point in the narrative, anonymous blacks and "toubob" become individualized. The cruel but nameless whites who have dominated Kunta's life since he arrived in America recede into the background and the slave community moves into the foreground.[5] Slave-traders and hunters are replaced by the kindly master, William Waller—who plays a small role in the story—while Bell and Fiddler become the book's significant secondary characters. The cruelty and violence of slavery all but evaporate after Kunta's wound liberates him from field work, and he becomes a gardener and then Waller's coachman. In these episodes, *Roots* is increasingly organized around Kunta's relatively harmonious domestic and community relationships. In just a few pages, then, the book takes the reader from Elkins's Holocaust and "perverted patriarchy" to a form of slavery that is not especially distinguishable from the benign institution of *Gone with the Wind* (Elkins, *Slavery* 104).

It is true that cruelty continues to occasionally explode into the narrative. After a lengthy interlude of relative peace, Waller's sale of Kunta's daughter, Kizzy, and her subsequent rape by her new master are shocking. But the book swiftly neutralizes such horror in its depiction of the life of Kizzy's son, the roguish Chicken George. As a child, George's antics and mimicry amuse the whites, while as a youth, his tomcatting around the local plantations becomes legendary. All the while, George enjoys the privileged occupation of trainer of his master's fighting roosters, making several thousand dollars in the process—all of which he squanders in his roistering (456–57). Haley, meanwhile, has squandered the power of Kunta Kinte's early experiences in slavery and Kizzy's suffering under an exploitative new master by increasingly depicting the institution in relatively mild terms. We should not be surprised, then, at Fishbein's description of the "surprisingly upbeat" tone and fundamental "optimism" of *Roots* (276, 278).

To some degree, *Roots* suffers from the same problems as the histories of slavery published in the 1970s that were designed to critique Elkins's ideas. In order to locate within slavery sufficient space for slave identities and communities to flourish, historians of the 1970s often tended to de-emphasize the brutality and oppression of slavery that previous historians had focused upon, and to assert its relative material comfort. These histories countered Elkins's idea that slavery was a "closed system" that had a drastic impact on slave subjectivities by arguing that slavery was not a "closed system" at all.

At one point in *Roll, Jordan, Roll,* for example, Eugene Genovese essentially recites the arguments of antebellum slaveholders when he emphasizes that enslaved Americans probably worked slightly shorter hours than their free white counterparts in northern factories—and enjoyed a comparable diet and, on average, superior medical care (60–62). John Blassingame, meanwhile, begins the second edition of *The Slave Community* with the story of George Bentley, a Tennessee slave who earned a salary of $700 as preacher in a white Baptist church (vii). Peter Kolchin has argued that some such histories come "dangerously close to replacing a mythical world in which the slaves were objects of total control with an equally mythical world in which slaves were hardly slaves at all" (148–49).

Kolchin overstates the argument as far as 1970s historiography is concerned, for several scholars, including Genovese, remained highly sensitive to the considerable influence of the slaveholder. Kolchin's statement, however, applies very well to the second half of *Roots.* After initially presenting slavery as sheer horror, the book abruptly abandons the idea that slavery could have brutalized its subjects by simplistically suggesting—a third of the way into the narrative—that the institution was not especially brutal after all, once one had adapted to it. In *Roots,* the actual process of enslavement and the slave trade are cruel and traumatic, but everyday plantation life for slaves tends to involve little physical coercion or psychological control. Consequently, it should come as no surprise to Kunta that his fellow slaves are not really Sambos—what, after all, might have made them so? Fishbein makes a similar point when she asks, "if slavery never robbed Kunta Kinte's heirs of their essential dignity, how oppressive could the 'peculiar institution' have been?" (282).

The inability of *Roots* to fulfill its promising exploration and critique of Elkins's ideas is largely a result of the literary genres Haley selected for his story. As Helen Taylor observes, one reason for "the extraordinary [popular] success of *Roots* lies in its affinity with other bestselling works set in the plantation South" (50). Haley's book has been called "a contemporary *Uncle Tom's Cabin*" and "the black *Gone with the Wind*" (quoted in Taylor 51). In other words, *Roots* exploits pre-existing, populist genres concerned with slavery; but this strategy also makes the book subject to the same literary conventions that govern such works. Taylor's incisive analysis of the way in which Haley's choice of genre becomes an ideological straitjacket is worth quoting at length:

Roots has been received as a response to and rejection of the plantation epic saga, but it has not supplanted it. It has adopted and
adapted the rules of the genre so that it may legitimately be read as
"a black *Gone with the Wind*": a family saga, a survival and success
epic, with a structure that begins in an Eden-like innocent, formal
and ordered society (Juffure—the equivalent of the plantation novel's
"glorious days before the War"); proceeds to the Paradise Lost of the
Middle Passage and enslavement (for which read the Civil War and
loss of the plantation); followed by gradual restitution of black pride,
self-worth, economic and social order (read Redemption of white supremacy). Working within the terms of the master narrative, Haley
does not seem to have escaped its structure, parameters and thus ideological power. (51–52)

In short, *Roots* does not appropriate traditional white literary conventions and styles of representing slavery—they appropriate it. The plantation
epic is not the only genre that Haley's book resembles, as its original subti-
tle, "The Saga of an American Family," clearly indicates. In this respect, *Roots*
is as much in the tradition of *East of Eden* (1952), *The Godfather* (1969), and
James A. Michener's *Centennial* (1974) as that of *Uncle Tom's Cabin, Black
Thunder, The Confessions of Nat Turner*, and *Flight to Canada*. As Fishbein
observes, Haley believed that "the universal appeal of *Roots* derived from the
average American's yearning for a sense of heritage" (280). David L. Wolper,
the producer of the TV adaptation, rejected the idea that "*Roots* is a black
drama for black people. . . . It's a drama *about* black people for everybody"
(quoted in Wolper and Troupe 172). James Monaco confirms this opinion:
"Black Americans are not alone in their search for ethnic roots, and it seems
likely that millions of white viewers were attracted [to *Roots*] as much by
the saga of immigration and assimilation as by the racial politics" (quoted
in Fishbein 280). Fishbein notes that: "The interest in genealogy [stimulated
by the TV adaptation] may well have eclipsed the concern with slavery for
many viewers. Significantly, when Haley himself appeared on *The Tonight
Show* following the broadcast of *Roots*, he did not want to discuss slavery
or its evils but instead appeared obsessed with genealogy and with the notion that blacks could be integrated into American society because they too
had families" (281). The attitude that Haley demonstrated on *The Tonight*

Show is indicative of the emphases of the second half of *Roots*. When Kunta marries Bell, the narrative shifts its focus from slavery to the family. Indeed, slavery increasingly becomes a mere backdrop for the saga of Kunta and his descendants, not the central topic of the book. One might say that, following the thirty-three chapters dedicated to Kunta's life in Juffure, chapters 34 to 67 of *Roots* comprise a powerful (if incomplete) novel about slavery, while chapters 68 to 120 constitute a rather formulaic family saga, albeit one that is interesting and unusual for being about an African American family.

This is not the only way in which working within established generic boundaries and conventions limits Haley's exploration of slavery. Like *Gone with the Wind* before it, *Roots* focuses predominantly on the privileged class of slaves. Kunta is a gardener and then coachman, Bell a cook, Chicken George a rooster trainer, and George's son, Tom, a blacksmith. As David Gerber notes, "theirs is not the life of the masses of slaves, men and women, who worked from sunrise to sunset with the lucrative staple crops which were slavery's reason for being" (92). While the field hand class is not as invisible in *Roots* as in *Gone with the Wind*, both novels focus upon the lives of the slave elite and thus are not obliged to address many of the harsher experiences of slavery.

Another limitation of Haley's book is its almost exclusively masculine emphasis. Many of the twentieth-century white novelists who wrote about slavery before the 1980s were women (Mary Johnston, Mitchell, Gaither, Willa Cather), while most African American fiction about the institution in these years—with the exception of *Jubilee*—was the work of males (Charles Chesnutt, Arna Bontemps, Harold Courlander). *Roots* is no more immune from a discourse of masculinism than Bontemps's *Black Thunder* or the Ten Black Writers' responses to Styron's *The Confessions of Nat Turner*. Gerber rightly complains about "Haley's unsatisfactory development of too many of his female characters. . . . Haley's women are mere foils for the demonstration of the strength, wisdom, and self-control of his men" (94). As Merrill Maguire Skaggs puts it, "Haley leaves out half the horror and grief and agony which are part of this American story—the female part" (50). She goes on: "In his stirring family history, Haley first excludes losers from the story and then equates winning with maleness. He further defines maleness in terms of the most traditional and familiarly macho American sexual stereotypes. His males control themselves, their families, and, sooner or later, their enemies. . . . To construct this new, revisionist version of black history, however, Haley must downplay the losers of his story—who are often the women. So the focus shifts away from raped and degraded Kizzy almost as soon as Chicken George is born to replace her" (50). This is a persuasive critique. After dominating four hundred pages of the narrative, Kunta Kinte abruptly disappears to be replaced by Kizzy, who becomes the book's central figure—for the mere twenty-six pages it takes for her to be raped by her new master, give birth, and have her son grow up to become the novel's next protagonist.[6]

Haley's portrayal of slavery is, in short, somewhat compromised by the structures, the populist features, and the traditional emphases of the genres in which he chose to write. Neither, for all its power and popularity, does *Roots* fulfill its initially promising dialogue with Elkins's theories about slavery and slave personality. It is seriously hindered by its inconsistent and increasingly cursory portrayal of slavery, the generic trajectories and conventions of the plantation epic and family saga, its overemphasis of male protagonists, and its consequent diminishment of women.

Ishmael Reed's *Flight to Canada*

Published the same year as *Roots*, Ishmael Reed's *Flight to Canada* concerns the escape of black poet Raven Quickskill from the Camelot plantation owned by Arthur Swille. While Quickskill heads to Ontario with a pretentious Native American socialite named Princess Quaw Quaw, significant events unfold at Camelot. Swille entertains such luminaries as Abraham Lincoln and Queen Victoria, aided by his obsequious and apparently loyal manservant, Uncle Robin. Meanwhile, Mammy Barracuda, Swille's slave lover, forces Swille's sickly wife to abandon her feminist inclinations and assume the airs and duties of plantation mistress. Swille is eventually killed, apparently in "Fall of the House of Usher"-fashion by his deceased sister, although one suspects the real killers to be his slaves.[7] Uncle Robin, furthermore, has altered Swille's will and so inherits Camelot. As even this brief summary should suggest, *Flight to Canada* utterly reinvents the novel of slavery by eschewing the traditional generic conventions to which *Roots* so rigidly adheres. Reed's novel offers instead a playful metafictional fantasia, in which the antebellum era is anachronistically constructed in terms of the present. Thus Quickskill considers escaping from bondage by Greyhound bus and jet plane, and he watches the assassination of Lincoln live on TV.

While *Flight to Canada*'s inventive postmodern approach succeeds in transcending the clichés of slavery fiction, it does not provide a way of engaging directly with contemporary historiographical debates about slavery. Indeed, several critical analyses suggest that *Flight to Canada* is best interpreted as a meditation on race relations in the present via the literary works of the past. While Reed's novel explicitly signifies upon nineteenth-century texts, such as the fugitive slave narratives (specifically those of Frederick Douglass and William Wells Brown), *Uncle Tom's Cabin*, and the fiction of Edgar Allan Poe, the book's central concern seems to be black culture and resistance in the late twentieth century. As Matthew R. Davis puts it, *Flight to Canada* "serves the dual purpose of revising historical knowledge while simultaneously critiquing contemporary society" (746). This is a common critical approach to the novel. Norman Harris interprets Reed's characters as analogues of black neoconservatives and Black Nationalists in the present day (116–21). Rushdy similarly sees the novel as a "critique of Black Power," which asserts that revolutionary violence is "meaningless without a supplementary strategy for controlling the shifting of economies" (*Neo-slave* 115). Finally, in a 1971 interview, Reed himself stated that he was "getting more and more interested in slavery as a metaphor for how blacks are treated in this civilization. . . . The Irving Howe crowd and the liberals in New York are the abolitionists" (quoted in Beck 134).

At the very least, Reed is more concerned in this novel to wage, as he says, "artistic guerilla warfare against the Historical Establishment" than to participate in measured debate with it. To Reed, Elkins is merely guilty of portraying slaves as "fawning, cringing, and shuffling darkies" (quoted in Rushdy, *Neo-slave* 110, 102). *Flight to Canada* asserts instead that, behind a mask of loyal docility, slaves were very much dedicated to resistance and freedom—but the novel does so more as an exploration of the literary stereotype of "Uncle Tom" than as a sustained historical argument against Elkins's Sambo thesis.

When Swille asks what Robin knows of Canada, the slave replies, "I do admit I have heard about the place from time to time, Mr. Swille, but I loves it here so much that . . . I would never think of leaving here. These rolling hills. Mammy singing spirituals in the morning before them good old biscuits" (19). Robin even claims that it is an "honor to serve such a mellifluous, stunning and elegant man" as Swille. Such eloquence reverses the traditional literary stereotype of unsophisticated slave dialect, and also hints that there is more to this particular servant than meets the eye. The slaveholder fails to pick up on such suggestions, however, choosing to believe that Robin is "a simple creature" who lacks the "thought powers" for deviousness (20, 34). Robin even expounds upon the joys of slavery to Abraham Lincoln (although he noticeably lapses back into the slave vernacular when addressing the Great Emancipator): "Good something to eat when you wonts it. Color TV. Milk pail fulla toddy. Some whiskey and a little nookie from time to time. We gets whipped with a velvet whip, and there's free dental care and always a fiddler case your feet gets restless" (37). The narrative eventually reveals, however, that the supposedly subservient Robin has been slowly poisoning his master all along, and has even altered Swille's will so as to inherit the plantation. In the book's final paragraph, Robin reflects upon his status as a supposed "Uncle Tom": "*Yeah, they get down on me an Tom. But who's the fool? Nat Turner or us? Nat said he was going to do this. Was going to do that. Said he had a mission. . . . Now Nat's dead and gone for these many years and here I am master of a dead man's house. Which one is the fool?*" (178).

The purpose of the novel, in other words, is to interrogate black cultural stereotypes. It is not concerned with Nat Turner as a historical figure but as a literary symbol. *Flight to Canada* dismantles discourses about and representations of slavery rather than making historiographical arguments about the probable reality of slavery and slave identities. The book's characterization of Robin is not a specific refutation of Elkins's thesis, and would not be a very substantial or compelling one if it were. Slaves, after all, could not inherit plantations, and, as Aptheker's *American Negro Slave Revolts* repeatedly demonstrates, where there was ever any suspicion of the murder of whites, slaves were usually arrested and often executed.

Reed's novel, in fact, boldly eschews traditional depictions of both the cruelty and the pervasive influence of the master in slavery. In this playful metafiction, no slave character ever seems to be in any real peril. The only physical abuse that occurs within slavery in the novel is directed, ironically, at white women. Arthur Swille whips Queen Victoria for refusing him a barony and Mammy Barracuda verbally and physically assaults Mistress Swille. This is a liberating reversal of conventions, but is also potentially problematic. While transcending the clichés of slavery fiction, *Flight to Canada* necessarily glosses over the very real physical suffering that bondage often involved. Furthermore, the book's emphasis on the abuse of white women—along with its patronizing attitude toward the socially ambitious Quaw Quaw—is evidence of a rather masculinist perspective in the text, if not outright misogyny, as one critic suggests (Marcus 129).

Flight to Canada, then, is an explicitly postmodern fiction, one that, unlike *Roots*, shuns traditional conventions for representing slavery, such as the emotional appeals that have been the hallmark of classic slavery literature since *Uncle Tom's Cabin* and the fugitive slave narratives. Reed questions our expectations of and reliance upon such conventions and demands new ways of imagining slavery that are not predetermined by existing representations. Some readers, however, have found Reed's satire to be a little lacking. Greil Marcus observes that when Raven "finally makes it to Canada, Reed surrenders the tale to an actual quote from a man who ferried escaped slaves from Buffalo to Ontario. His description of what he saw when his passengers reached the other side is so shattering—'They seemed to be transformed; a new light shone in their eyes, their tongues were loosed, they laughed and cried, prayed and sang praises, fell upon the ground and kissed it, hugged and kissed each other, crying Bless de Lord! Oh! I'se free before I die!'—that it lifts a reader right out of the novel, almost trivializing Raven's story, capsizing it" (128). Marcus does not mention that the novel's use of this passage is entirely ironic. Only a few pages later, Raven discovers that Canada is not the utopia of which he dreamed. "Man," one of his fugitive friends tells him, "they got a group up here called the Western Guard, make the Klan look like statesmen" (160). Nonetheless, Marcus has a point. The moving testaments of escaped slaves contain a powerful emotional core that is necessarily absent from the determinedly anti-realistic *Flight to Canada*.

Flight to Canada exposes the discursive stereotypes and clichés of cultural representations of slavery. Such an emphasis, however, precludes the novel from engaging in direct and productive dialogue with the discipline of history. As Matthew Davis observes, *Flight to Canada*, in true postmodern fashion, envisions slavery as "an entirely textualized discursive field" (746). Postmodern fiction's emphasis on history as a series of discourses and representations enables it to unmask and denaturalize the processes by which such discourses are made. Hortense Spillers discusses *Flight to Canada*'s engagement with a "slavery" that is "*primarily* discursive, as we search vainly for a point of absolute and indisputable origin, for a moment of plenitude that would restore us to the real, rich 'thing' itself before discourse touched it" (29). But *Flight to Canada's* emphasis on discourses and documents rather than historical reality means that it is neither concerned with nor equipped to engage with historiography's rather more prosaic debates about what the past actually may have been like. Despite postmodern and poststructuralist theory, the discipline of history inevitably remains concerned with the reality of the past as well as the ways in which it has been constructed in discourse. Reed's novel hilariously dissects *Uncle Tom's Cabin* and brilliantly reveals the ideologies, limitations, and suppressed content of existing discourses about slavery, but it does not contribute to debates about what slavery and slave identities might have been like in the 1850s. In short, *Flight to Canada* shares little in common with any previous fiction about American slavery.

Reed's novel speaks eloquently to black writers about the imperative to write about slavery, and it suggests innovative ways in which they might do so. Janet Kemper Beck asserts that, with *Flight to Canada*, Reed "has reclaimed the slave narrative tradition for the African American writer," while Marcus describes the novel as "Reed's bid to take back the story of Uncle Tom from Harriet Beecher Stowe—probably because Reed thinks it too valuable to leave to a white writer" (Beck 132; Marcus 128). *Flight to Canada* encourages black artists to counter such cultural appropriations as *Uncle Tom's Cabin* and *The Confessions of Nat Turner* by reclaiming and reinventing slavery literature. Precisely because of its original formal techniques and rejection of traditional representations of slavery, however, Reed's novel does not engage directly with fundamental ongoing questions about the institution and its subjects, and this satirically playful book is simply not interested in questions about the often-horrific realities of slavery. Thus *Flight to Canada* embodies the ultimate limits as well as the significant potentialities of postmodern historical metafiction.

Octavia E. Butler's *Kindred*

In her analysis of *Flight to Canada*, Spillers articulates a desire to "eat the cake *and* have it. I *want* a *discursive* 'slavery.' . . . At the same time, I suspect that I occasionally resent the spread-eagle tyranny of discursivity across the terrain of what we used to call, with impunity, 'experience'" (33). Octavia Butler's *Kindred* is a perfect literary example of having one's discursive historical cake while simultaneously biting deep into the real thing. *Kindred* emphasizes slavery both as field of representation and brutal actuality. Like *Flight to Canada*, this novel self-consciously signifies upon existing literary discourses about slavery—from the fugitive slave narratives to *Roots*. Simultaneously, however, *Kindred* engages in carefully researched and constructive dialogue with contemporary historiographical debates about the reality of slavery, and it stages a careful and consistent exploration and critique of Elkins's theories. Since 1979, many novels have followed the template established by *Kindred* and have modulated between formal experimentation and traditional realism in order to question previous discourses about slavery while also creating a realistic and feasible alternative to them.

Dana Franklin, the heroine of *Kindred,* is a contemporary African American woman who is mysteriously and unwittingly drawn back in time from 1976 to an antebellum Maryland plantation whenever her white slaveholder ancestor, Rufus Weylin, is in peril. Once stranded in the past, Dana is catapulted back into the present only at moments of extreme danger to her life. In this curious manner, Dana travels to and from the Weylin plantation at several points between 1811 and 1831—on one occasion accompanied by her white husband, Kevin—and she saves Rufus's life when he is both a child and an adult. As a grown man, Rufus sexually exploits a slave named Alice, a situation in which Dana is helplessly complicit because she knows that she is a descendant of the two, and thus would risk her own existence were she to intervene. Alice is driven to despair by Rufus's coercions and finally hangs herself. Rufus then turns his attentions to Dana, who stabs the slaveholder when he tries to rape her, bringing about her sudden and permanent return to the twentieth century.

Butler's novel can be read in relation to a diverse variety of texts about slavery.[8] One viable approach is to interpret *Kindred* as a critical rewriting of *The Confessions of Nat Turner* from the perspective of a contemporary black woman. Both, after all, are first-person narratives that explore the psychological traumas of enslaved people who ultimately rebel violently against their oppressors. The protagonists of both works are influenced by white significant others: Nat's psychology is largely attributed by Styron to his relationship with his paternalist master, Samuel Turner, and to his sexual fixation upon Margaret Whitehead. Dana is similarly affected by Rufus and by a rather more functional sexual relationship with a white person, her husband, Kevin. Both Nat and Dana rebel against slavery in ways that are detrimental for other black people. Dana's stabbing of Rufus leads to the burning of the Weylin plantation and the selling of its slaves, while the lawyer, Gray, observes in *The Confessions of Nat Turner* that Nat's rebellion led only to the slaughter of families, vicious reprisals against innocent blacks, and a tightening of slave laws (112–13). Just as Styron's novel ends with Nat's spiritual reconciliation with God and Margaret, so does *Kindred* end with Dana's reunion with her husband in the present. While Styron makes the risky imaginative leap of assuming the voice of a nineteenth-century African American, Butler is pointedly prepared only to speak for a contemporary black woman like herself.

For the purposes of my analysis, however, *Kindred's* most illuminating parallels are with *Roots* and Elkins's *Slavery*. Even the stark, one-word title of Butler's fiction clearly echoes that of Haley's novel. As their titles suggest, both *Kindred* and *Roots* are concerned with ancestry and genealogy, but while Haley seeks to recover and idealize his African heritage in his text, Butler's novel draws attention to the other significant forefathers of many contemporary African Americans—white slaveholders. Both novels depict slavery over a span of time: Haley's by providing an epic narrative covering several generations and Butler's by having its protagonist visit the Weylin plantation at different points in its history. *Kindred* and *Roots* both exploit the familiar literary figure of the exceptional slave, but in unusual and opposing ways. Haley's Kunta feels alienated among the acculturated African Americans he encounters because he has been brought to the United States directly from Gambia and still retains his Mandinka identity. He represents, in other words, a figure from the ancestral past of African American culture. Dana, on the other hand, is exceptional in the slave community of the Weylin plantation, not because she hails figuratively from the past, but because she comes literally from the future—although, unlike Kunta, Dana is eventually able to return home. Both protagonists are also concerned to ensure the continuance of their bloodlines. Kunta is determined to have offspring to carry on his name, while Dana must ensure that Rufus and Alice couple in order to guarantee her own birth. Just as Kunta loses his foot, thus ending his attempts at resistance and flight, so, at the very end of *Kindred*, does Dana lose her left arm when she returns to the present for the final time.

Kindred not only echoes Haley's book but also engages in critical dialogue with it. Butler's novel exposes the unresolved tensions between *Roots* and Elkins's ideas, critiques and offers an alternative to Haley's masculinist construction of slavery, and contrasts the traditional realism of *Roots*—its use of the conventions of the plantation genre and family saga—with an innovative fictional approach that provides new ways of representing slavery.

Kindred both explores and critiques Elkins's theories about slavery and slave identities, and completes *Roots*'s promising but unfulfilled interrogation of Elkins's ideas. Perhaps the most famous assertion in Elkins's book is that the "only mass experience that Western people have had within recorded history comparable in any way with Negro slavery was undergone in the nether world of Nazism. The concentration camp was not only a perverted slave system; it was also [like slavery] . . . a perverted patriarchy" (*Slavery* 104). Butler's novel explicitly incorporates Elkins's vision of slavery as Holocaust. Upon one of her first returns from the antebellum South to 1976, Dana feverishly reads "books about slavery, fiction and nonfiction," in preparation for the possibility that she will be drawn back into the slave past again (116). She finds herself, however, unexpectedly caught up in a book about World War II and the Holocaust: "Stories of beatings, starvation, filth, disease, torture, every possible degradation. As though the Germans had been trying to do in only a few years what the Americans had worked at for nearly two hundred. . . . Like the Nazis, ante bellum whites had known quite a bit about torture" (117). Elkins's argument is that slavery, like the concentration camps, demonstrates that "infantile personality features could be induced in a relatively short time among large numbers of adult human beings" (88). As Elkins summarizes the process, "Several million people were detached with a peculiar effectiveness from a great variety of cultural backgrounds in Africa. . . . It was achieved partly by the shock experience inherent in the very mode of procurement but more specifically by the type of authority-system to which they were introduced and to which they had to adjust for physical and psychic survival" (*Slavery* 88). The trajectory of Butler's novel mirrors this process—as do the early sections of *Roots*—but *Kindred* ups the ante further. Butler's fiction does more than demonstrate how enslaved Africans and African Americans in the past could be reduced to passivity by the pervasive control mechanisms of slavery: *Kindred* vividly shows how a sophisticated and independent twentieth-century woman with a confident knowledge of American history could become enslaved both physically and psychologically. As Dana muses at one point, "I tried to get away from my thoughts, but they still came. *See how easily slaves are made?* they said" (177).

When Dana travels in time, she undergoes a trauma similar to that of Kunta Kinte, one that severs her from the only reality she has ever known. Robert Crossley even likens Dana's time traveling to the Middle Passage, suggesting that in "her experience of being kidnapped in time and space, Dana recapitulates the dreadful, disorienting, involuntary voyage of her ancestors" (xi). Elkins, however, attributes much of slavery's influence on personality not to the "shock sequence" of enslavement, but to the everyday workings of a system "in which all lines of authority descended from the master and in which alternative social bases that might have supported alternative standards were systematically suppressed," and in which the available social roles for slaves were extremely limited in number and rigorously defined (102, 128). Butler's fiction follows Dana's adaptation to these limited roles and her increasing acceptance of the pervasive influence of the slaveholder. During her third visit back in time to the Weylin plantation, Dana spies on white and black children playing together and is deeply shocked when she realizes they are re-enacting a slave auction. Dana's white husband, Kevin—who travels back into the past with her on this occasion—disputes the importance of this game, telling her that the children "are just imitating what they've seen adults doing. . . . Dana, you're reading too much into a kids' game." Dana, on the other hand, understands the social and psychological conditioning that such games achieve. "I never realized how easily people could be trained to accept slavery," she broods (99, 100, 101).

At this point in the narrative, however, Dana does not fully understand that nineteenth-century African Americans are not the only ones to be conditioned in this way. Even as she speaks, Dana too is unwittingly and unconsciously beginning to conform to the system. In order to survive antebellum Maryland, Dana adapts to the role of a hard-working domestic slave: "I cleaned and plucked a chicken, prepared vegetables, kneaded bread dough," she reports. Dana defends her capitulation to the role of slave by arguing that it is worth "putting up with small humiliations now so that I can survive later." She even becomes appreciative of her relative comfort as a slave on the Weylin plantation, observing, "I'm not being treated any worse than any other house servant . . . and I'm doing better than the field hands" (81, 83).

Dana consciously performs this slave role for her own safety and security: "I played the slave, minded my manners probably more than I had to because I wasn't sure what I could get away with" (91). Butler powerfully explores the possibility that *Roots* evades—that roles and behaviors adapted for survival may ultimately infiltrate and dominate the individual. Dana is disturbed when she suddenly comprehends the degree to which she and Kevin (who is masquerading as Dana's master) have been accepted into the Weylin household—and the degree to which they in turn have accepted their places in it. "How easily we seemed to acclimatize," Dana muses. "Not that I wanted us to have trouble, but it seemed as though we should have had a harder time adjusting to this particular segment of history—adjusting to our places in the household of a slaveholder." Increasingly, during those brief intervals in which she returns to the present, Dana finds the America of 1976 alien and unreal. "I felt as though I were losing my place here in my own time. Rufus's time was a sharper, stronger reality." Indeed, on her fourth journey back in time to the Weylin plantation, Dana is "startled to catch myself wearily saying, 'Home at last'" (97, 191, 127).

The narrative emphasizes the degree to which Dana has adapted to slavery by pairing her with other slave characters. Dana teaches Alice to peel potatoes just as the slave cook, Sarah, earlier taught Dana the same task. The reader understands that in this scene Dana has taken Sarah's place, which is to say that she has become a slave. A few pages later, Dana yells at some slave boys to stop fighting, only to have them respond that she sounds "just like Sarah," a characterization Dana desperately rejects even as the reader again understands the implication (155, 159). While Dana at this moment possesses a superficial resemblance to Sarah, her true double in the novel is, as Sandra Govan argues, Alice (93). The two characters are virtual mirror images of each other, identical yet opposite. Dana does not realize that she has become a slave, while Alice loses her memory and forgets that she is enslaved after a traumatic mauling by dogs. When Alice ultimately rediscovers the truth of her own situation, she cries, "But I'm supposed to be free. I was free. Born free"—an ironic echo of a statement that Dana made to Alice's mother on her second journey into the past: "But I'm free, born free, intending to stay free" (156, 157, 38).

Alice, however, ultimately proves more militant and more resistant to slavery than Dana. It is the uneducated nineteenth-century woman who points out that the sophisticated twentieth-century woman has become fully acculturated to slavery. After a draining morning of field work, imposed upon her as punishment for a transgression, Dana clings desperately to her position as Margaret Weylin's maid, whatever compromises are required. Alice, however, is chagrined at Dana's obsequiousness. "You run around fetching and carrying for that woman like you love her. And half a day in the fields was all it took. . . . The way you always suckin' up to that woman is enough to make anybody sick." Dana's close relationship with Rufus is an even greater source of tension between the two women. Because Dana knows that the child of Rufus and Alice will be her grandmother, she can offer little comfort when Alice asks what she should do about Rufus's increasingly aggressive sexual overtures. Dana's failure to help finally causes Alice to angrily explode, "That's what you for—to help white folks keep niggers down. . . . They be calling you mammy in a few years. You be running the whole house when the old man dies." Later, Alice tells Dana that she is planning to flee the plantation because "I got to go before I turn into what you are." Dana, in Alice's view, has completely capitulated to the slaveholders. The independent woman from the enlightened future has become an obedient mammy. Alice's impassioned criticisms make Dana realize that she no longer controls the roles that she plays. "Was I getting so used to being submissive?" she muses, "When had I stopped acting? Why had I stopped?" (220, 167, 235, 221). After but a few months under slavery, Dana has learned to tolerate her enslavement and accept her slave status.

It is not merely the roles that Dana is obliged to play that seduce her into slavery. *Kindred* vividly dramatizes the psychological influence of the patriarchal slaveholder in similar terms to Elkins. While Kevin is able to accompany Dana on one of her journeys into the past, her real significant male other in the novel is Rufus Weylin, the young slaveholder. It is, after all, for Rufus's very welfare that Dana is repeatedly plucked from the present into the past, and she saves his life on five occasions. Why Dana is inexplicably transported to the past whenever Rufus is in danger remains a complete enigma, but because he becomes her protector in the past and the potential key to her return to the present, Dana adopts the role of loyal and affectionate slave to please him. As she explains to Kevin during one of her first visits into the past, "I'll have a better chance of surviving if I . . . work on the insurance we talked about. Rufus. He'll probably be old enough to have some authority when I come again. Old enough to help me. I want him to have as many good memories of me as I can give him now." Because he is a child and she is an adult when they first meet, Dana's relationship toward Rufus is initially maternal in nature. The adult Rufus, however, comes to dominate her life. Dana even takes to referring to the antebellum past specifically as "Rufus's time." Despite his cruel and oppressive behavior, Dana cannot help but care for Rufus. She diligently and lovingly tends to him whenever he is hurt or sick, and, even as Rufus attempts to rape her, is tempted to submit, realizing "how easy it would be for me to continue to be still and forgive him even this. . . . But it would be hard to raise the knife, drive it into the flesh I had saved so many times" (82–83, 191, 259–60).

Butler's narrative is thus a chilling exploration of how an exceptionally strong and knowledgeable individual can be reduced, both physically and psychologically, to the status of a slave. In this respect, *Kindred* is very much a dramatization of Elkins's ideas about the psychological effects of slavery. As Dana's eventual act of resistance reveals, however, the novel rejects Elkins's ultimate conclusion that the end result of this process was to render those who were enslaved to the level of Sambo, characterized by "infantile silliness" and a "childlike attachment" to the master. (*Slavery* 82). Slavery has a profound effect upon Dana, but it does not make her into a dependent child. In order to survive, Dana—like the other Weylin slaves—makes many compromises and largely accommodates herself to what the system and her master demand. But she will not completely surrender herself, no matter what the cost. She tells Kevin that Rufus "has to leave me enough control of my own life to make living look better to me than killing and dying" (246). Rufus finally steps over that line, pushing Dana past the limits of her ability to compromise for the sake of survival, and she kills him.

Dana, of course, is quite unlike the other enslaved characters in the book, precisely because, in an unusual modification of the figure of the exceptional slave, she hails from the twentieth century. Dana's exceptionalism, however, raises questions that Haley largely avoids in *Roots*: if slavery could seriously affect such uncommon individuals as Dana and Kunta, how might it impact the average person? If Dana and Kunta can be forced to accommodate psychologically to slavery in a short span of time, what might the effects of the institution have been over generations? *Kindred* provides more compelling answers to such questions than *Roots*. It achieves this partly by maintaining a more consistent portrayal of the nature of slavery than Haley's book presents. Butler's characters always struggle against an Elkinsian institution rather than the initially brutal but subsequently moderate form of slavery depicted in *Roots*. More importantly, *Kindred* constructs its argument by undermining the apparent exceptionalism of its protagonist. In one interview, Butler explained that she got the idea for her novel when "the Black Power Movement was really underway . . . and I heard some remarks from a young man who was the same age I was but who had apparently never made the connection with what his parents did to keep him alive. He was still blaming them for their humility and their acceptance of disgusting behavior on the part of employers and other people. . . . That was actually the germ of the idea for *Kindred* . . . I wanted to take a character . . . back in time to some of the things that our ancestors had to go through, and see if that character survived so very well with the knowledge of the present in her head" (quoted in Rowell 151). Butler's thesis in *Kindred* is that, for all her knowledge of the past, Dana is less equipped to resist the rigors of slavery than her ancestors. She is anything but superior to them in her ability to survive. She knows that her "ancestors had to put up with more than I ever could" (51). Hailing from the relative luxury of the late twentieth century, Dana believes that she lacks the hardiness and reserves of endurance necessary for life as a slave. Unlike Kunta, Dana does not view her fellow slaves contemptuously; instead, she makes greater compromises to adapt to slavery than any of them.

Luke, the slave driver, is singularly unimpressed by Dana's twentieth-century ideas about emancipation and her high-handedness, muttering, "Like we so dumb we need some stranger to make us think about freedom." Luke counsels a surreptitious defiance to slavery: "'Don't argue with white folks,' he had said. 'Don't tell them "no." Don't let them see you mad. Just say "yes, sir." Then go 'head and do what you want to do.'" In other words, Luke plays Sambo for whites and expresses his own character covertly. Sarah, the Weylin cook, is similarly unimpressed by the white master class. She dismisses Margaret Weylin, the plantation mistress, as a "bitch," and, assuming that Kevin is Dana's master, advises the latter to "try to get him to free you now while you still young and pretty enough for him to listen." Sarah, furthermore, runs the entire household in the absence of the mistress and she "managed the house as efficiently as Margaret had, but without much of the tension and strife Margaret generated." The other slave characters are also highly capable individuals and resistant to the institution that oppresses them. Even Nigel, Luke's studious son, quietly fantasizes about escaping to the North. Meanwhile, Isaac, Alice's husband, beats Rufus to a bloody pulp when the white man first tries to rape the slave's partner (74, 96, 72, 96, 144, 151, 117–19). Unlike Kunta Kinte, Dana discovers a slave community that is not less but more militant than she is.

Kindred, however, does not exaggerate or romanticize slaves' resistance to the system that oppressed them. The novel argues that a slave's rebellious streak would have been fragile, hard-won, and under constant assault. Even such limited resistance as Luke shows is ruthlessly punished. As Rufus explains it, Luke "would just go ahead and do what he wanted to no matter what Daddy said. . . . Daddy said it would be better to sell Luke than to whip him until he ran away." Neither does Butler's novel deny that slaves could be reduced to childlike docility. Alice suffers a debilitating psychological trauma as the result of a ruthless mauling by dogs. Dana tells us that "Alice was a very young child again, incontinent, barely aware of us unless we hurt or fed her. . . . She called me Mama for a while" (138, 153). The novel emphasizes, however, that Alice's infantalization is a temporary response to a specific and extreme trauma, not a permanent condition. *Kindred* thus rejects the idea that the everyday operations of slavery, whatever their long-term impact on the human psyche, could reduce an individual to a literal Sambo.

Butler's fiction presents a clear and carefully developed argument about slavery. It assents to Elkins's theories about the nature and the processes of the institution, and acknowledges that slavery did have a profound psychological impact upon its subjects. Butler, however, differs from Elkins on the extent of slavery's ultimate effects. Dana may accommodate to slavery, she may accept the roles that it imposes on her, and she may become dangerously dependent upon Rufus, but neither she nor any of the other slave characters ever come close to becoming Sambo figures. There are significant and painful limitations on individual character within slavery, but none of Butler's characters are "docile but irresponsible, loyal but lazy, humble but chronically given to lying and stealing . . . full of infantile silliness" (Elkins, *Slavery* 82). Butler, in short, carefully distinguishes between Elkins's theories about slavery—which she finds persuasive and which she dramatizes compellingly—and his ideas about slave psychologies, which she modifies and complicates in the pages of *Kindred*. The narrative denies the simple correspondence that Elkins asserts between a Holocaust-like slavery and the Sambo personality described by southern slaveholders. In *Kindred*, the pervasive effects of slavery may lead to psychological accommodation, but not to "childlike conformity" (Elkins, *Slavery* 128).

Butler thus disagrees as much with several of the slave community historians of the 1970s as she does with Elkins. Both black and white historians in the 1970s risked understating the harshness of slavery and tended to emphasize its relative material comfort in order to argue that the institution provided space for an active slave community to flourish—which is ultimately what *Roots* does as well. Robert Crossley locates *Kindred* in the tradition of the 1970s histories of the slave community when he suggests that the enslaved African Americans on the Weylin plantation "constitute a rich human society. . . . Although the black community is persistently fractured by the sudden removal of its members . . . that community always patches itself back together, drawing from its common suffering and common anger a common strength" (xviii–xix). Certainly, Butler's novel presents a slave community of sorts, but, contrary to the arguments of many 1970s historians, this community is severely limited, continually struggling to assert itself against the control of an institution that is potentially as omnipresent as Elkins suggests. Crossley somewhat overstates the vitality of the slave community in *Kindred*, for the narrative refuses to make bold claims about its autonomy or the agency of its members.

There are glimpses of community in the novel, such as at the corn shucking party. Dana tells us that "People working near me around the small mountain of corn laughed at my blisters and told me I was being initiated. A jug went around and I tasted it, choked, and drew more laughter. Surprisingly companionable laughter." Equally, when Liza, a slave who hates Dana, betrays her escape attempt, Dana's friends retaliate by giving Liza a beating (229, 178). There are diverse personalities among the slaves of the Weylin plantation. There is much loyalty and companionship, but also some enmity and hostility.

Ultimately, however, the slave community still remains relatively marginal in the novel. Butler's text uses Dana's exceptional status and relative separation from the slave community to deemphasize its importance. Furthermore, *Kindred* shows that what an individual might have to do in order to survive the system of slavery frequently works against the solidarity of the slave community. Some slaves resent the power of Sarah, the cook, who, in return, considers them "[l]azy niggers." When Dana asks her why slaves should bother working hard, Sarah responds, "It'll get them the cowhide if they don't. . . . I ain't goin' to take the blame for what they don't do" (144). Furthermore, Dana's individual liberation from slavery is extremely destructive to the slave community. After her final return to the present, historical research reveals to Dana that the Weylin plantation burned down the night she killed Rufus. In the aftermath, many of the Weylin slaves were abruptly sold—while some are simply unaccounted for (262–63). Dana may have achieved freedom, but at great cost to her fellow slaves.

Butler's novel acknowledges the potential of the slave community, but is pessimistic about its agency and autonomy in practice. Nobody could reasonably claim that *Kindred* replaces "a mythical world in which the slaves were objects of total control with an equally mythical world in which slaves were hardly slaves at all" (Kolchin 148–49). The book complicates the idea implicit in some 1970s historiography and in the later parts of *Roots* that, in order to critique Elkins's claims about slave psychology, it is necessary to suggest that the institution of slavery was not as insidiously affecting as he suggests. In *Kindred*, Kevin argues that slavery is less appalling than he imagined it might be, but Dana sees that the institution is both brutal and brutalizing. Kevin observes that "this place isn't what I would have imagined. No overseer. No more work than the people can manage."

Dana cuts in, saying, "no decent housing. . . . Dirt floors to sleep on, food so inadequate they'd all be sick if they didn't keep gardens in what's supposed to be their leisure time and steal from the cookhouse. . . . And no rights and the possibility of being mistreated or sold away from their families for any reason—or no reason. Kevin, you don't have to beat people to treat them brutally" (100).

In short, the narrative argues that Elkins could be largely correct about the operations of slavery as an institution and about its pervasive psychological power, but that he is in error about its ultimate effects upon slave character. This is Butler's great contribution to the cultural dialogue about the nature of slavery and slave personality. Her novel acknowledges the existence of the slave community, but is reluctant to advance great claims for it, and it dissents from the implication that the existence of an active community necessarily means that slavery was not a Holocaust. By depicting both the debilitating effects of slavery *and* a potentially vital slave community, *Kindred* vividly dramatizes the dialogue between Elkins and succeeding historians in the 1970s, and demonstrates that their arguments are not necessarily as diametrically opposed as some commentators have assumed.

The work of historiography to which *Kindred* is most closely aligned is Eugene Genovese's *Roll, Jordan, Roll* (1974). While Genovese explores the achievements of the slave community like other historians of his era, he is careful not to overexaggerate its autonomy or agency. Like Butler, Genovese also draws upon and revises Elkins's ideas in order to stage an innovative analysis of the ways in which American slaves negotiated between the accommodation necessary to survival and resistance against dehumanization. Just as *Kindred* emphasizes Rufus's influence upon Dana, so does *Roll, Jordan, Roll* address the importance of the slaveholder as *paterfamilias*—the patriarch or significant other in Elkins's terminology (Genovese, *Roll* 483; Elkins, *Slavery* 104, 122, 132). Slaveholders, according to Genovese, developed a paternalist doctrine of reciprocal duties according to which they were obliged to care responsibly for those upon whose involuntary labor they depended. In return for their paternal generosity, masters expected their slaves to be loyal and grateful for the kind treatment they received. Enslaved Americans, however, subtly reinterpreted this doctrine: "To the idea of reciprocal duties they added their own doctrine of reciprocal rights. . . . From their point of view, the genuine acts of kindness and material support . . . were in fact their due." Genovese concludes that the "slaves' acceptance of paternalism, therefore, signaled acceptance of an imposed white domination within which they drew their own lines, asserted rights, and preserved their self-respect" (*Roll* 91, 146, 147). The problem, Genovese believes, is that while slaves were thus able to build "an Afro-American community life in the interstices of the system. . . . their very strategy for survival enmeshed them in a web of paternalistic relationships which sustained the slaveholders' regime. . . . The slaves' success in forging a world of their own within a wider world shaped primarily by their oppressors sapped their will to revolt" (*Roll* 594). While Genovese rejects the Sambo stereotype and the parallels between slavery and the Holocaust advanced by Elkins, he is clearly building upon his predecessor's ideas. Genovese modifies Elkins's "perverted patriarchy" into a milder doctrine of paternalism. Where Elkins describes slaves as being merely subject to patriarchy, Genovese shows how slaves actively responded to paternalist doctrine in order to secure benefits for themselves. Yet Genovese also emphasizes the extent to which slaves psychologically accommodated to the system, and, elsewhere, he has acknowledged that the "enduring strength of Elkins' case . . . lies in its delineation of the demonic logic of slavery" ("Meditation" 214). *Roll, Jordan, Roll*, is, in short, less in opposition to Elkins's *Slavery* than it is in dialogue with it—as is Butler's novel.

Kindred thus stages a more fully developed engagement with, and modification of, Elkins's ideas than previous slavery fiction. Butler's novel, furthermore, also responds to Haley's and Reed's emphases on male experiences in slavery and their marginalization of women. *Kindred*, in fact, was the first significant novel published by a black woman in the twentieth century that is entirely concerned with slavery.[9] Butler uses *Kindred* to expose and to challenge the masculinism of modern black discourses about slavery, as epitomized by the works of such male predecessors as Arna Bontemps, the Ten Black Writers who responded to *The Confessions of Nat Turner*, Ishmael Reed, and Alex Haley.

Kindred demonstrates that specifically masculine stereotypes have proven insufficient as ways of conceptualizing slave subjectivities or for providing viable models of resistance to slavery. Butler's novel rejects the notion that slaves were *either* militant rebels, like Nat Turner, Kunta Kinte, Stowe's George Harris, Frances Gaither's Scofield, and Bontemps's Gabriel, on one hand, *or* docile accommodationists like Uncle Tom, Sambo, Bontemps's Ben Woolfolk, and, arguably, Chicken George, on the other. Butler challenges the practicality of either approach. After all, while servile submission achieves nothing, rebels like Turner, Scofield, and Gabriel all end up dead—and Kunta's potentially suicidal resistance is ended by the amputation of his foot. Butler has revealed that "I began with a man as main character [in *Kindred*], but I couldn't go on using [him] . . . because I couldn't realistically keep him alive. So many things that he did would have been likely to get him killed. He wouldn't even have time to learn the rules . . . of submission . . . before he was killed for not knowing them. . . . The female main character, who might be equally dangerous, would not be perceived so. She might be beaten, she might be abused, but she probably wouldn't be killed" (quoted in Rowell 51). Butler's novel rejects the cliché of the doomed militant for a figure who endures and who usually resists within the system rather than fighting suicidally against it—and it specifically identifies this figure as a woman. Butler, as I noted earlier, claims that the novel's genesis was her response to a male Black Power activist's condemnation of previous black generations for their humility. The author found such condemnation inadequate, given her own growing appreciation for the compromises that her mother was prepared to make which "kept me fed, and . . . kept a roof over my head." "I started to pay attention," Butler says, "to what my mother and even more my grandmother and my poor great-grandmother . . . went through" (quoted in Rowell 51).

In *Kindred*, the male characters are relatively minor and do not endure. The stubborn Luke and the brave Isaac alike are sold. Sarah and Alice, however, are at the forefront of the novel. Sarah is a survivor. She has had all but one of her children sold away from her, but she continues to run the household and, more significantly, constantly suggests ways in which Dana can resist within the system. Butler's novel, however, also refuses to idealize the stoic endurance and quiet resistance of African American women in slavery. Alice survives a traumatic mauling, rape, and seeing her husband mutilated and sold away from her. She maintains a resistant attitude toward slavery in the face of all her suffering, but she finally can tolerate no more when she is led to believe that Rufus has sold her children. In despair, Alice hangs herself. *Kindred* thus rejects the "survival by any means necessary" view of slavery for which Chrisman criticizes *Roots* (41). Neither does Butler give her characters any easy solutions, in contrast to Reed in *Flight to Canada*. Poisoning Weylin and altering his will are simply not options. Dana escapes finally, but at a severe cost. Butler's text emphasizes the importance of pragmatic everyday resistance over both servile accommodation and the grand militant gestures of previous slave heroes. *Kindred* is not concerned with the Kunta Kintes or the Chicken Georges of the world, but aims, instead, to restore the abused and marginalized figure of Kizzy to centrality in the discourse of slavery.

The other great achievement of Butler's novel is its reinvention of formal strategies for representing slavery in fiction. While Haley tends to obscure or gloss over the ambivalent and problematic generic status of *Roots*, caught, as it is, between novel and nonfiction, *Kindred* deliberately draws attention to its own fictionality by meshing the apparently contradictory genres of science fiction (which is usually concerned with a speculative future) and the historical novel (which traditionally explores the documented reality of the past).[10] *Kindred*, furthermore, transcends the conventional realism and tired family saga/plantation genre clichés of *Roots*, as well as the playful metafictional cleverness of more experimental works like *Flight to Canada*. Christine Levecq notes that "*Kindred*, unlike previous, more traditional historical novels of slavery . . . clearly flaunts its experimentation with genres" and "questions all forms of historical knowledge, by demonstrating the inescapable shaping or silencing of the past by perception, ideology, and language" ("Power" 542, 527–28). At the same time, Levecq notes, the novel's postmodern skepticism and intertextual signifying do not "stand in the way of a very realistic account of life under slavery. . . . In spite of the repeated emphasis on history's textuality, it is precisely the confrontation with reality that constitutes the main appeal of the novel. Notwithstanding its fantastic premise, *Kindred* has a realistic, even documentary streak. . . . The novel also depicts Dana's encounter with slavery with a poignancy and a physical immediacy that enhance its realistic effect" ("Power" 528, 529, 530). Levecq's insight into the novel's generic character is crucial, although she does not locate Butler's achievement specifically within the history of the slavery novel. *Kindred*, we might say, builds upon the strengths of both *Flight to Canada* and *Roots* while evading their limitations. In the process, it created new possibilities for the American novel of slavery.

Toni Morrison's *Beloved*

While few scholars or writers seemed to pay much attention to *Kindred* when it first appeared, the majority of slavery novels published since 1980 use strategies and conventions similar to those of Butler's work. Like *Kindred*, much recent slavery fiction relies upon intertextual signification and other self-conscious techniques that emphasize slavery as a discursive field, while simultaneously providing believable portrayals of slavery, realistic characters about whom the reader is able to care, and an informed engagement with debates about the historical reality of slavery. Much of this literature, furthermore, has been written by women, who continue to challenge the previously marginal status of black females in fiction about slavery.[11] The most renowned such work, of course, is Toni Morrison's *Beloved.*

Morrison's novel modifies the techniques of *Kindred*. Where Dana literally travels in time back to slavery, Morrison's protagonist, Sethe, remembers the horrors of slavery from the vantage point of 1873. While Butler defamiliarizes slavery by merging science fiction with the historical novel, Morrison draws upon the tradition of the ghost story in order to construct slavery in a new and striking way. Like *Kindred*, *Beloved* contains fantastic elements, but the reader also believes in and cares about the novel's characters and their experiences. *Beloved* responds to other texts, both historical and literary, such as the fugitive slave narratives and the historical source material for the novel, the story of Margaret Garner.[12] *Beloved* approaches history both as discursive field and horrifying reality. When Rafael Perez-Torres argues that *Beloved* and similar novels "diverge from classically postmodern texts . . . in their relation to socio-cultural realities," he is identifying the very innovation that *Kindred* first brought to fictional representations of American slavery (92).

Morrison's novel also engages with the theories of Elkins in a very similar way to *Kindred*. Rather than dismissing the historian's ideas as merely racist, like some black writers and critics, Morrison flirts with the horrific possibility that slavery might indeed have had a profound effect upon human identity. Morrison also fully accepts Elkins's comparison of American slavery to the Nazi Holocaust. At the time of *Beloved*'s publication, Morrison observed that "[i]f Hitler had won the war and established his thousand-year Reich . . . the first 200 years of that Reich would have been exactly what that period [slavery] was in this country for Black people" (quoted in Washington 235). Indeed, some critics of the novel were displeased with the parallels Morrison implied between the Nazi death camps and slavery in her book's dedication to "sixty million and more."[13]

Beloved also depicts the traumatic shocks of slavery very vividly. Just as *Kindred* emphasizes the psychic disorientation of its heroine's physical return to the era of slavery, so does Morrison's text seek to create a similar experience for its readers. Morrison's own description of her book's abrupt opening paragraphs declares that the "reader is snatched, yanked, thrown into an environment completely foreign. . . . Snatched just as the slaves were from one place to another . . . without preparation and without defense" ("Unspeakable" 228).

While emphasizing the sheer horror of slavery, *Beloved* also acknowledges that there were milder forms of the institution. However, where *Roots* abruptly shifts from a brutal slavery to a relatively benign one, Morrison's fiction shows that wildly different forms of slavery could result simply from different masters. Life at the Sweet Home plantation in Kentucky is at least endurable for Sethe and her family and friends under the stewardship of the benevolently paternalist Garner. When he dies, however, slavery becomes a vicious nightmare under the auspices of the new master of Sweet Home: Garner's brother, the sadistic Schoolteacher. Morrison's novel, however, astutely identifies the gravest psychological effects of slavery with the kindly paternalist rather than with the brutal sadist. Schoolteacher's cruelty simply drives the Sweet Home slaves to attempt flight. The generosity of Garner, on the other hand, has a significant impact upon their identities. Paul D recalls that he and his brothers were "encouraged to correct Garner, even defy him. To invent ways of doing things; to see what was needed and attack it without permission. To buy a mother, choose a horse or a wife, handle guns, even learn reading. . . . [T]hey were believed and trusted, but most of all they were listened to" (147). But Paul D simultaneously realizes that Garner, for all the freedom he gave his slaves, had made them psychologically dependent upon his paternal generosity: "[T]hey were only Sweet Home men at Sweet Home. One step off that ground and they were trespassers among the human race. Watchdogs without teeth; steer bulls without horns; gelded workhorses. . . . Garner called and announced them men— but only on Sweet Home, and by his leave. Was he naming what he saw or creating what he did not? . . . Oh, he [Paul D] did manly things, but was that Garner's gift or his own will?" (147–48, 260). By having Paul D recognize Garner as the significant other upon whom his manhood and identity depended, Morrison's novel does nothing less than boldly dramatize the Elkins thesis.

However, *Beloved*, like *Kindred*, also complicates Elkins's ideas about slavery. For all the horrors of slavery under Schoolteacher and for all the psychological dependence fostered by Garner, Morrison's fiction asserts that slaves were not helpless Sambos but were able to assert their individuality and forge communities to some degree, however limited. Furthermore, the narrative vividly dramatizes how black cultures and communities might flourish outside of slavery—in contrast to some commentators who misread Elkins as claiming that the psychological chains of slavery continued to impede African Americans after emancipation. When Sethe becomes a virtual prisoner of Beloved in 1873, it is the black community that steps in, providing food and, ultimately, exorcizing the ghost of her daughter.

Indeed, one might even say that the character Beloved, the spirit of Sethe's murdered baby, represents the ghost of slavery itself—as Elkins conceives it. After all, Beloved enslaves Sethe and makes her dependent, childlike, and docile: "At first they played together. . . . Sometimes coming upon them making men and women cookies or tacking scraps of cloth on Baby Suggs' old quilt, it was difficult for Denver to tell who was who. . . . her mother sat around like a rag doll (282, 283, 286). Morrison's novel exorcises this ghost and complicates Elkins's simplistic thesis.

In short, the conception and presentation of slavery in *Beloved* shares a great deal in common with that in *Kindred*. Morrison sees slavery as comparable to the Holocaust, and she dramatizes the debilitating psychological effects of slavery, but she also provides an informed and persuasive alternative to the notion that slavery reduced enslaved African Americans to the level of Sambo. Like Butler's novel, Morrison's text depicts American slaves as struggling against an institution that sought to render them mere subjects. They may be profoundly affected by the power of slavery, but they are not dehumanized by it. *Beloved*, like *Kindred*, thus negotiates persuasively between the arguments of 1950s and 1970s historians.

Kindred never received the popular attention given *Roots*, nor the critical plaudits awarded *Beloved*. It is only since the early 1990s that scholars have begun to pay attention to the novel. Yet *Kindred* played a crucial and central role in the literature of slavery. Historians, until recently, have either tended to emphasize the vibrancy of the slave community at the cost of remembering the cruelty of slavery, or have focused so thoroughly upon the horrors of the institution that slaves themselves seem little more than passive victims. Butler's novel, in contrast, coherently argues that slavery could have been as appalling as its most impassioned critics suggest but that a functional if limited community might still have been able to assert itself. This insight has permeated novels about slavery ever since. Equally important has been Butler's act of restoring women to the center of narratives about slavery. Dismissing the centrality of both Sambo and Nat Turner, *Kindred* emphasizes instead those who sought a balance between individual integrity and the compromises necessary to survive. Such figures—usually female—have become an archetype of contemporary slavery fiction. Finally, Butler developed a way to mesh a sophisticated postmodern critique of historical discourses with a powerfully realistic depiction of the experience of slavery within the covers of a single book. In any reasonable canon of twentieth-century fiction about slavery, *Kindred* should be located at the very center.

4

Scarlett and Mammy Done Gone

COMPLICATIONS OF THE CONTEMPORARY NOVEL

OF SLAVERY, 1986–2003

Kindred's innovative strategies for representing American slavery in fiction swiftly became predominant. Virtually all novels concerned with the peculiar institution published since the 1970s combine conventional realism with postmodernist intertextuality, and thus engage with slavery both as contested historical reality and as a tradition of conflicting cultural representations. Such fiction demands careful and nuanced interpretation. The reader must be sensitive to the fundamental distinctions between a novel's arguments about the actualities of slavery and its responses to established textual conventions for representing slavery. In this chapter, I explore the complicated relationship between slavery as historiographical debate and slavery as a set of discursive conventions in two novels, Sherley Anne Williams's *Dessa Rose* (1986) and Valerie Martin's *Property* (2003).

There are good reasons for considering these two particular works of fiction together. The many critics who have discussed *Dessa Rose* tend to focus upon the manner in which the book's eponymous African American heroine evades both the literal and the linguistic chains of slavery: Dessa not only leads a rebellion and escapes to freedom, but she also tells her own story about life inside and outside the institution.[1] In terms of literary history, Williams's novel is also notable for its rehabilitation of a figure that had become even more marginal in slavery fiction than the female slave: the plantation mistress. *Property* goes a step further in this regard by having its entire narrative told from the perspective of Manon Gaudet, the wife of a

Louisiana slaveholder—a point of view previously unexplored in the modern novel of American slavery.[2]

Property is additionally significant for being the first novel of substance about slavery by a white writer published in more than thirty years. *The Confessions of Nat Turner*—or, more specifically, the critical reaction to it—essentially shut down all opportunities for a fruitful discourse between black and white writers of slavery fiction. African American critics, exemplified by the Ten Black Writers, were justified, of course, in condemning William Styron's unqualified acceptance of the questionable conclusions of Stanley Elkins in his fictionalization of the Turner insurrection. However, the virulence of some of the attacks on *The Confessions of Nat Turner* apparently discouraged white novelists from engaging with the subject of slavery at all for three decades.[3] In some respects, this was an advantageous, even necessary, development. Slavery fiction of the first half of the century had been dominated by white writers (with *Black Thunder* and *The Foxes of Harrow* being rare exceptions to the rule). With white novelists reluctant to address the subject after the Styron debacle, African American writers made the best of the opportunity of a now-open field, and constructed a powerful literature and discourse of their own about slavery. Beginning with Margaret Walker's *Jubilee* in 1966, the final third of the twentieth century saw a resurgence in black fiction about slavery that has produced some of the most powerful books in contemporary American literature, including *Kindred, Beloved,* and, most recently, *The Known World.*

After more than twenty-five years of such achievements by African American authors, however, the omission of white novelists from the cultural conversation about slavery in the United States has become a limitation. Notably, both *Dessa Rose* and *Property* are fundamentally concerned with the notion of constructive interracial debate about slavery. In the absence of a dialogue about slavery between white and black novelists in the late twentieth century, *Dessa Rose* imaginatively projects just such an interracial dialogue into the antebellum era, by creating a dynamic fictional relationship between a plantation mistress and a female slave. *Property,* meanwhile—as the work of a white novelist—initiates a new interracial conversation between black and white writers on the subject of slavery for the twenty-first century.

Property and *Dessa Rose* also appear to be instances of the hybrid form of slavery fiction exemplified by *Kindred*. Both seem to combine the conventions of realism with explicit intertextuality, and to engage with slavery as both discursive tradition and historical reality. *Dessa Rose*, for example, directly responds to works of history, such as Herbert Aptheker's *American Negro Slave Revolts*, as well as works of fiction, specifically *The Confessions of Nat Turner*. *Property* implicitly interrogates the depiction of interracial friendships between women in previous American fiction, such as *Dessa Rose* itself and Kate Chopin's *The Awakening* (1899) while simultaneously advancing an informed counter-revisionist historical argument in line with the thesis of Elizabeth Fox-Genovese's *Within the Plantation Household: Black and White Women of the Old South* (1988).

In both *Dessa Rose* and *Property*, furthermore, there is a significant tension between the treatment of slavery as a discursive tradition and as grim reality. For all its apparent historical and psychological realism, *Dessa Rose* is, finally, not a book that makes a consistent argument about the actuality of slavery. Indeed, in Williams's novel, the emphasis upon the potential for interracial relationships—both in the antebellum South and in contemporary American culture—leads it to abandon historical feasibility altogether as the narrative progresses. While the novel's opening section provides an informed and convincing re-creation of the conditions of slavery, the purpose of *Dessa Rose* is ultimately closer to that of *Flight to Canada* than that of *Kindred*. While much more formally realistic than Reed's text, the primary concern of *Dessa Rose* is to respond to and react against the ways in which slavery has been represented in discourse, not to make an argument about what the institution may have been like in reality.

Property is almost the reverse of *Dessa Rose* in this respect. In formal terms, it appears to be a traditionally realistic historical novel, seemingly lacking the postmodern discursive knowingness and self-consciousness that we find in the pages of *Kindred* and its ilk. Yet *Property* is also best illuminated in terms of its intertextual relationships with such works of imaginative literature as *The Awakening* and *Dessa Rose*. It does not, however, signify upon these texts in order to make an argument about how slavery has been constructed in discourse. The book's central concern is the reality of the past, and *Property*'s differences with other fictional works about slavery are directed toward a counter-revisionist historical analysis of the nature of relationships between black and white women on antebellum American plantations. The irony is that this informed counter-revisionism pulls the book's narrative toward a series of extremely traditional literary stereotypes about the plantation mistress—even as the novel breathes new life into those stereotypes by telling its tale directly from the perspective of the slaveholding white woman.

The Plantation Mistress in American Fiction

Jubilee anticipated and *Kindred* spearheaded a new cultural discourse emphasizing the voices and experiences of African American women—which has subsequently involved such novels as *Beloved, Dessa Rose,* and *The Wind Done Gone,* as well as historical studies including Deborah Gray White's *Ar'n't I a Woman?* (1985).[4] Similarly, historiography of the 1970s and 1980s—such as Anne Firor Scott's *The Southern Lady* (1970) and Catherine Clinton's *The Plantation Mistress* (1982)—focused new attention upon white women in the antebellum South. The culmination of such scholarship, Fox-Genovese's *Within the Plantation Household,* also provided a comprehensive analysis of relationships between black and white women during slavery. In fiction, however, the plantation mistress has remained what she has always been—a rather marginal figure. While the unmarried daughters of the plantation have been commonly prominent in slavery novels—from Nina Gordon in Harriet Beecher Stowe's *Dred* (1856) to Scarlett in *Gone with the Wind* and Fannie in *The Red Cock Crows*—the female authority on the plantation, when not altogether absent, has usually been relegated to the margins of fiction. Furthermore, on those occasions when slaveholding white women have played a prominent role in novels, they have frequently been reduced to one-dimensional stereotypes, usually portrayed either as selfless, dedicated, and sexless angels of the plantation, or as sadistic, selfish, and sexually repressed (or wildly jealous) hypochondriacs.

Uncle Tom's Cabin relegates its plantation mistresses to the periphery, while also exploiting both of these stereotypes. The noteworthy members of the planter class in Stowe's famous novel are the male patriarchs, from the sympathetic Augustine St. Clare to the evil Simon Legree. The most important and prominent white female in *Uncle Tom's Cabin* is St. Clare's young daughter, Eva—who, significantly, is doomed not to grow into slaveholding adulthood. Even St. Clare's northern relative, Ophelia, plays a larger role in the narrative than any plantation mistress. Those slaveholding women who do appear in Stowe's novel, furthermore, are simplistic archetypes.[5] Emily Shelby, the wife of the Kentucky master who sells Tom at the beginning of the novel, is an avatar of nineteenth-century American womanhood—the four cardinal virtues of which, in Barbara Welter's famous formulation, were "piety, purity, submissiveness and domesticity" (151). Stowe's Mrs. Shelby is "a woman of high class, both intellectually and morally. To that natural magnanimity and generosity of mind . . . she added high moral and religious sensibility and principle. . . . Her husband . . . reverenced and respected the consistency of hers, and stood, perhaps, a little in awe of her opinion. Certain it was that he gave her unlimited scope in all her benevolent efforts for the comfort, instruction, and improvement of her servants" (52–53). Emily's attitude toward her slaves is one of maternal duty. She claims that, "as a Christian woman . . . I have cared for them, instructed them, watched over them, and know all their little cares and joys" (83). When she challenges her husband's intentions to sell Tom, she may not seem especially submissive, but it is her piety, purity, and dedication to domestic order that cause her to challenge his authority and actions. Furthermore, her dissent manifests itself very modestly: she pleads rather than quarrels with her husband (81–86).

While Stowe's abolitionist novel makes use of the stereotype of the slaveholding woman as maternal angel, this archetype also enjoyed a long life in the pages of pro-slavery fiction. Minrose Gwin observes that Stowe's depiction of plantation mistresses is virtually identical to that in one of the first and most popular southern pro-slavery responses to *Uncle Tom's Cabin*, Mary Eastman's *Aunt Phillis's Cabin* (1852) (20–21). This particular stereotype of the plantation mistress culminated, of course, in the character of Ellen O'Hara in *Gone with the Wind*. Scarlett regards her mother "as something holy and apart from all the rest of humankind. When Scarlett was a child, she had confused her mother with the Virgin Mary, and now that she was older she saw no reason for changing her opinion" (60). Ellen runs the plantation at Tara with rigorous efficiency and unfailing serenity. She keeps accounts and supervises overseers, while also finding time to philanthropically devote her energies to caring for sick slaves and the poor whites of the neighborhood. Scarlett, of course, is utterly unable to live up to such a role model.

The other traditional archetype of the plantation mistress is the very opposite of Emily Shelby and Ellen O'Hara. Nineteenth-century antislavery literature often used this counter-type to assert the corrupting influence of slavery upon the white master class. When, in *Uncle Tom's Cabin*, the Shelbys reluctantly sell Tom to the St. Clare plantation in New Orleans, the text provides a portrait of the plantation mistress as selfish, lazy, hysterically hypochondriac, and heartlessly racist in the form of Marie St. Clare. Marie sorely lacks all those qualities of the nineteenth-century ideal of American motherhood—self-sacrificing dedication and a healthy moral influence upon her family, black *and* white. She is instead a "faded, sickly woman, whose time was divided among a variety of fanciful diseases, and who considered herself, in every sense, the most ill-used and suffering person in existence." Applauding Emily Shelby's housekeeping, Stowe notes that, in stark contrast, Marie is "[i]ndolent and childish, unsystematic and improvident." Marie's lack of affection for her daughter, Eva, is matched only by her callous exploitation of slaves: she separates Mammy from her husband and children so as to be able to constantly enjoy the services of the former, and, indeed, she obliges Mammy to attend her hourly throughout the night. Marie remains, however, utterly oblivious to the devotion of her slaves and the burdens and sacrifices that she imposes upon them. She claims that African American slaves are "the plague of my life. . . . a provoking, stupid, careless, unreasonable, childish, ungrateful set of wretches" and members of a "degraded race." Once her liberal husband dies, Marie wastes no time in sending her servants out to a "whipping-establishment" for punishment. Although her late husband had promised Uncle Tom his freedom, Marie refuses to release him (243, 309, 261, 260, 267, 268, 459, 464).

Such a stereotype of the white slaveholding woman was common in nonfiction of the antebellum era as well as in novels. In Frederick Douglass's narrative, Sophia Auld, who never owned a slave before she became Douglass's mistress, is initially presented as the very epitome of true womanhood. Sophia even begins to teach Douglass to read, until her husband bans the lessons. Unfortunately, slavery "proved as injurious to her as it did to me. When I went there, she was a pious, warm, and tender-hearted woman. There was no sorrow or suffering for which she had not a tear. She had bread for the hungry, clothes for the naked, and comfort for every mourner that came within her reach. Slavery soon proved its ability to divest her of these heavenly qualities. Under its influence, the tender heart became stone and the lamblike disposition gave way to one of tiger-like fierceness"

(31). The corrupting influence of slavery thus causes a pious and industrious equivalent of Emily Shelby to degenerate into another Marie St. Clare.

We meet another such slaveholding woman in the pages of Harriet Jacobs's autobiographical *Incidents in the Life of a Slave Girl*. Harriet's mistress, Mrs. Flint, is a relatively peripheral figure in the narrative, but instantly recognizable as a type. Mrs. Flint resembles Stowe's Marie in that she is "totally deficient in energy. She had not strength to superintend her household affairs; but her nerves were so strong, that she could sit in her easy chair and see a woman whipped, till the blood trickled from every stroke of the lash." Mrs. Flint even spits in cooking pots "to prevent the cook and her children from eking out their meagre fare with the remains of the gravy and other scrapings." What Jacobs adds to the stereotype is the jealous rage of a woman whose husband is sexually abusing his slaves. Mrs. Flint, however, does not blame her husband for his infidelity and rapacity but projects her anger instead upon the unfortunate slave woman. Mrs. Flint, Jacobs reports, "pitied herself as a martyr; but she was incapable of feeling for the condition of shame and misery in which her unfortunate, helpless slave was placed.... I was an object of her jealousy, and consequently of her hatred" (9, 10, 33, 34).

As works of nonfiction, the narratives of former slaves suggest that all too many Marie St. Clares existed in fact, although, of course, the explicit anti-slavery purpose and rhetoric of such works had little use for any more complex characterization of the slaveholding woman. In both fiction and nonfiction of the nineteenth century, polemicism was largely responsible for reducing the plantation mistress to a simplistic stereotype.

The plantation mistress fared little better in twentieth-century fiction. Not a single white female member of the planter class appears, for example, in Bontemps's *Black Thunder*, while the ailing Lillian Garner has a negligible role in *Beloved*. Even in fiction by southern white women, the plantation mistress often has been a marginal figure. The emphasis in both *Gone with the Wind* and *The Red Cock Crows* is not on the plantation mistresses, but upon their daughters. The same is true of *The Confessions of Nat Turner*, in which Nat becomes sexually fixated upon the young Emmeline Turner and Margaret Whitehead, whose mothers barely appear in the narrative.

Furthermore, while fiction since *Gone with the Wind* has largely rejected the celebratory stereotype of the plantation angel—which has no relevant ideological function in the modern era—it has still tended to thoroughly depend upon the old, negative stereotype of the white slaveholding woman as selfish, cruel, hypochondriacal, and sexually repressed (or, alternatively, sexually disturbed). The title character of Willa Cather's *Sapphira and the Slave Girl* (1940) is an invalid who becomes erroneously convinced that her husband is having an affair with a young slave named Nancy. She responds by inviting her nephew to the farm in the hope that he will rape the girl. Salina Dutton, the plantation mistress in the first half of *Jubilee*, cruelly abuses Vyry, as a way of taking revenge for her husband's sexual relationships with slaves. Salina is also coldly asexual. She tells her husband that "sex, to her mind, was only a necessary evil for the sake of procreation. When she had presented him with a son and a daughter, she further informed him that her duty as a wife had ended" (10). In the opening pages of Ernest J. Gaines's *The Autobiography of Miss Jane Pittman* (1971), the eponymous narrator reports that the master, rather than punishing Jane himself for a perceived infraction, "gived my mistress the whip and told her to teach me a lesson." This is not, however, sufficient to assuage the mistress's rage. "Take her to the swamps," she tells her husband, "and kill her" (9). Even Octavia Butler's portrayal of Margaret Weylin in *Kindred* is reminiscent of the Marie St. Clare/Mrs. Flint stereotype. Margaret is a high-strung woman, who, Dana observes, is "priming herself for a nervous breakdown." Margaret brutalizes the children that her husband has fathered with slaves, callously sells other slaves simply in order to buy new crockery, and angrily throws scalding coffee over Dana. Eventually, she becomes a reclusive laudanum addict (83, 85, 95, 81, 218).

One of the few characters in fiction to have evaded these rules of representation is Flo Hatfield, in Charles Johnson's *Oxherding Tale* (1983). Hatfield, the female matriarch of the Leviathan plantation, is an insatiable nymphomaniac who ravishes her male slaves. This is hardly, however, a sophisticated reimagining of the female slaveholder, but merely a simplistic reversal of the traditional stereotype of the sexually repressed mistress. Even as late as the 1980s, therefore, one could search American fiction in vain for a complex depiction of a white slaveowning woman.

Sherley Anne Williams's *Dessa Rose*

Since African American women were rarely central to twentieth-century U.S. fiction about slavery until the 1960s, and since white slaveholding women were marginalized and stereotyped in novels until even later, there has obviously been little scope for significant interracial relationships in literature between women of the antebellum South. *Dessa Rose* has been justly celebrated, therefore, for its innovative portrayal of black and white women during slavery. Not only does the novel transcend conventional stereotypes for representing both enslaved African American women and white slaveowning females, but its depiction of a rich and rewarding relationship between an escaped slave and a plantation mistress is also essentially unprecedented.

Dessa Rose is divided into three parts. In the first section, the racist author Adam Nehemiah—who is planning to write a study of slave insurrections—interrogates the pregnant Dessa, a slave woman who was captured after leading a rebellion. In the second part of the narrative, Dessa escapes from enslavement, gives birth, and seeks shelter at Sutton's Glen, a plantation owned by Rufel (or Ruth Elizabeth), whose debt-ridden gambler husband has deserted her. Rufel even acquiesces to the presence of an entire band of fugitive slaves at Sutton's Glen in return for their working her land. One of these former slaves, Nathan, eventually begins a love affair with Rufel. In the third section of the novel, Nathan persuades Rufel to join the fugitives in an elaborate scam in which the plantation mistress repeatedly "sells" the "slaves," who promptly escape to be sold again and again until a fortune has been amassed, and the fugitives can flee forever into a life of freedom in the West. Dessa and Rufel become increasingly close during this caper, and when the tenacious Nehemiah eventually catches up with Dessa, Rufel helps her to evade him again.

The narrative consistently rejects simplistic and traditional archetypes, and, in Rufel, presents the most complex and interesting plantation mistress to have appeared in American fiction. Rufel initially harbors runaway slaves largely because of her financial needs, and her racial attitudes are, at first, far from enlightened. She addresses black characters as "wench," "darky," or "nigger," even when she knows their names (145, 142, 99). She tends to conceive of African Americans in the most crudely stereotypical terms; even the house servant with whom she shares close personal contact Rufel associates "with the stock cuts used to illustrate newspaper advertisements of slave sales and runaways: pants rolled up to the knees, bareheaded, a bundle attached to a stick slung over one shoulder, the round white eyes in the inky face giving a slightly comic air to the whole" (140). Rufel refuses to believe stories of slaveholder brutality, and assumes that Dessa is responsible for her own plight, even speculating that Dessa "was making up to the master; that's why the mistress was so cruel" (136). Rufel, however, undergoes considerable development in the course of the narrative, unlike the static stereotypes who preceded her in slavery fiction.

Through Dessa and Nathan, Rufel slowly learns to overcome the racist orthodoxies of her culture. In her conversations with Nathan, Rufel finally comes "to know something of the people who lived in her Quarters" (147). In addition, when Rufel speaks of her beloved and recently deceased "Mammy," a delirious Dessa mistakenly thinks that the white woman is referring to her own mother and argues with Rufel about Mammy. Although this is a case of mistaken identity, Dessa's blunt words cause Rufel to realize that her own "Mammy" was more than just a devoted servant. Rufel now comprehends that her nurse possessed a name beyond the maternal title that denoted her role, and she wonders if this individual might have had children that were sold away from her (128). In short, Rufel moves beyond seeing "Mammy" only as a servant and begins to appreciate that she was a human being named Dorcas.

Dessa's attitude toward the privileged white woman also evolves. Initially hostile and defensive, Dessa eventually helps Rufel fight off a would-be rapist, and she begins to soften toward the mistress of Sutton's Glen, realizing that Rufel "was subject to the same ravishment as me." Their friendship finally blossoms, with Dessa telling the reader, "I wanted to hug Ruth. I didn't hold nothing against her, not 'mistress,' not Nathan, not skin." While the two eventually go their separate ways, Dessa recalls, "I have met some good white men. . . . But none the equal of Ruth" (201, 232–33, 236).

Much existing scholarship on *Dessa Rose* traces and celebrates Rufel's gradual racial enlightenment and the trajectory of her relationship with Dessa in considerable detail. A few critics, however, have acknowledged that the novel's portrayal of nineteenth-century women uniting across racial barriers may be somewhat romantic and unrealistic. Ann Trapasso describes the latter part of the novel, in which Rufel, Dessa, and the other fugitives embark upon their campaign to con purchasers of slaves out of their money, as "fantastic," and she observes that the novel "increasingly resembles an adventure story" (222, 227). Elizabeth Meese makes an implicitly disparaging value judgment about the novel when she declares that it is "a romance of race, a u-topic fiction of hope and a 'happy ending'" (quoted in Rushdy, Neo-slave 149). Finally, Donna Haisty Winchell quotes one reviewer's complaints that Dessa Rose is characterized by "wishful thinking" and that it "finally shirks history in favor of romance." Winchell is troubled by this harsh evaluation, but struggles to answer it. "Is the novel overly romanticized?" she asks. "Probably, but at least in Williams's case, readers are left wishing that it could have happened that way rather than, with Styron's Nat Turner, hoping that it didn't" (736–37). Winchell's apologetic conclusion is, however, an entirely insufficient defense of the novel's more problematic elements. It is hard to take seriously the suggestion that we should just accept the novel's apparent idealism and lack of historical veracity purely because it tells us what we want to hear: that black and white women in the antebellum South could develop significant friendships despite slavery, and that they could even resist patriarchal power together.

More considered defenses of the romantic and utopian elements of Dessa Rose identify the existence of certain limitations in the relationship between Rufel and Dessa. Ashraf Rushdy argues against the simplistic "happy ending" reading of Dessa Rose. He points out that when, in the final section of the novel, Dessa is arrested and threatened with a body search, she is quick to remind Rufel that it is she—the black woman—who has possession of the money belt containing the wealth they have amassed. Rushdy opines that Dessa simply cannot trust Rufel "to act on entirely disinterested motives. . . . Whatever basis there is for the friendship between Rufel and Dessa—and it is a friendship more in remembrance than in the experience— it is important to note that Dessa cannot completely trust Rufel without referring to Rufel's own material interests" (Neo-slave 149). Nancy Porter likewise points out that, while "black and white people in Dessa Rose confront and transcend racial and class perceptions to become real to one another, the ending of the novel is not utopian. Ruth does not join the new order of free blacks in the west where some 'good white men' are invited to eat at Dessa's table" (264).

The critical debate, in short, centers upon the historical feasibility of Dessa's and Rufel's friendship. Is this, scholars ask, an impossibly utopian relationship, or is it sufficiently limited to remain believable? The terms of this debate, however, rest upon the largely unexamined assumption that

Dessa Rose must (or should) be aiming for historical verisimilitude, and that any nonrealistic elements in the novel are thus potentially problematic. The challenge for critics is to find a way to account for and explain the romanticized elements of Williams's tale that does not simply argue for or against the book's historical veracity, or that does not merely accept the book's content as appealing, if unrealistic, wish-fulfillment.

Such an interpretation should begin with careful consideration of the manner in which the novel adapts and alters its source material. In her "Author's Note" at the beginning of the book, Williams reveals that "*Dessa Rose* is based on two historical incidents. A pregnant black woman helped to lead an uprising on a coffle . . . in 1829 in Kentucky. . . . In North Carolina in 1830, a white woman living on an isolated farm was reported to have given sanctuary to runaway slaves. I read the first incident in Angela Davis' seminal essay, 'Reflections on the Black Woman's Role in the Community of Slaves.' . . . In tracking Davis to her source in Herbert Aptheker's *American Negro Slave Revolts* . . . I discovered the second incident. How sad, I thought then, that these two women never met" (5). This passage clearly indicates that Williams is rather less focused upon contemporary historiographical debates than novelists like Butler, Morrison, and even Styron. She significantly identifies not a modern study as her ultimate historical source, but Aptheker's text, which, for all its undeniable importance and influence, was more than forty years old by the time *Dessa Rose* appeared, and the conclusions of which had been thoroughly challenged by contemporary historians.[6] It is significant, furthermore, that the two women Aptheker describes not only failed to meet in actuality, but that there is also no historical data to suggest that two women even vaguely like them ever met under any such circumstances. Aptheker argues that there is much evidence of interracial alliances against slavery along class lines, but he offers no instance of such a coalition based upon gender solidarity. As Williams suggests, her fiction is an imaginative attempt to compensate for the fact that, historically, such women as she describes did not meet or create partnerships.

In addition, Mary Kemp Davis, one of the few scholars to have addressed the relationship between *Dessa Rose* and its documentary sources, notes that Aptheker's story about the escape from a slave coffle that inspired the character of Dessa actually involved *two* African American women: one who rebelled and one who helped raise the alarm to ensure the capture of the rebellious fugitive and her accomplices (Davis, "Everybody" 546; Aptheker, *American* 287). Davis draws no conclusions from this discrepancy between the historical source material and the content of *Dessa Rose*, but it is striking that the novel erases a figure that would have significantly complicated its portrayal of slave women as militantly resistant to slavery. This suggests that *Dessa Rose*'s purpose is more ideological than strictly historical in nature.

Furthermore, Aptheker's account of the white woman who gave sanctuary to runaway slaves differs in significant ways from *Dessa Rose*'s adaptation of it. According to the historian, a band of fugitive slaves planned a general uprising in North Carolina, but whites captured one of their number and forced him to reveal that arms were stored at a nearby place that, according to a letter to the governor, was "in possession of a white woman living in a very retired situation—also some meat, hid away & could not be accounted for—a child whom the party [of citizens] found a little way from the house, said that his mamy [*sic*] dressed victuals every day for 4 or 5 runaways, and shewed the spot . . . where the meat was then hid" (quoted in *American* 289). Aptheker reports that the local militia discovered and burned the fugitive slaves' encampment, and hunted down and killed the survivors (*American* 289–90). What became of the white woman who fed them and stored their arms is unrecorded. *Dessa Rose* presents a much more optimistic and empowering version of events in which the fugitive slaves and white female ally escape to permanent freedom instead of being ruthlessly eliminated. Furthermore, while Williams elects to imagine the anonymous white heroine of the historical record as a plantation mistress in *Dessa Rose*, there is no documentary evidence to suggest that she was actually anything of the kind in reality. In her summary of Aptheker's account, Williams describes an "isolated farm," whereas the historical report actually refers only to "a house." The white woman may have been a farmer or planter and might even have been a slaveholder. She could, however, just as easily have been a lower-class white woman who helped fugitive slaves because she felt a sense of class solidarity with them. This, however, is not a possibility toward which Williams's novel is drawn. *Dessa Rose* is more concerned with twentieth-century identity politics than nineteenth-century class politics.

Dessa Rose's portrayal of interracial female relationships in the antebellum South has been further complicated by recent historical studies about plantation mistresses and interracial female relations during slavery—most notably Fox-Genovese's *Within the Plantation Household*. If one accepts the conclusions of this counter-revisionist study, the relationship between Dessa and Rufel, whatever its ultimate limitations, would have been quite extraordinary had it occurred in reality. Fox-Genovese concludes that the "privileged roles and identities of slaveholding women depended upon the oppression of slave women." She argues that "Slaveholding women were elitist and racist. . . . From my reading of the diaries and private papers of the slaveholders, I have sadly concluded that the racism of the women was generally uglier and more meanly expressed than that of the men. . . . To view slaveholding women as the opponents of southern social relations is to extrapolate from their depictions of slavery as a personal burden to an assumed opposition to the social system as such" (35, 349, 338). Rushdy acknowledges the problem of the disparity between the portrayal of inter-racial relationships in *Dessa Rose* and historical evidence on the subject. In response to Fox-Genovese's claims, he asserts that the antebellum South "was, nonetheless, a world providing rare and fleeting instances of friend-ships between black and white women—friendships that might well have taken the metaphor of a communal, interracial 'family' as a serious tenet" (*Neo-slave* 148). This, however, is little more than optimistic speculation. Rushdy provides no historical evidence of even "rare and fleeting" friend-ships between white and black women during slavery.

Given the formidable barriers to the development of interracial friend-ships in the antebellum South, Williams's novel has, in fact, to contrive an entirely unorthodox set of circumstances to create an environment in which an intimate association between an aristocratic white woman and a fugitive female slave might flourish. The narrative erases the mistress-slave dynamic from the relationship between Dessa and Rufel. The latter does not own the former; she has simply given the fugitive slave shelter. The story also expels the plantation patriarch from the novel so that Rufel has space and freedom in which to develop intimacies with both Dessa and Nathan.

I do not deny the possibility that strong relationships might have devel-oped on rare occasions between black and white, and even between slave-holding and enslaved women in antebellum America. It is precisely such relationships that are most likely to have evaded documentary records be-cause they would necessarily have been private friendships. Neither am I suggesting, as several critics have implied, that *Dessa Rose* is necessarily flawed simply because it is organized around a historically unlikely situation and relationship. Many novels have pushed the limits of historical verisimilitude to far greater extremes than *Dessa Rose*. Williams's book does not, for example, distort history in the way that Styron's novel does, because Dessa and Rufel—unlike Nat Turner—are not actual historical figures.

My point is that a comparison of *Dessa Rose* to its documentary sources and to other historical evidence illuminates precisely what kind of novel it is. In formal terms, *Dessa Rose* is indeed seemingly reminiscent of *Kindred*, in that it is both intertextually postmodern and conventionally realistic. As several scholars have observed, for example, Williams's novel explicitly signifies upon *The Confessions of Nat Turner*. Rufel and Dessa are, however, also believable characters about whom the reader is invited to care. Given this formal blending of the realistic and the postmodern, it is not surprising that critics tend to read *Dessa Rose* as a novel that addresses history as both discursive field and material reality. By acknowledging that the novel's plot was inspired by historical events, Williams even seems to encourage such a reading. Scholars seem to assume, therefore, that the novel challenges existing discourses about slavery while also advancing a sustained and substantiated argument about what the past was really like. In fact, despite its formal hybridity, it is my contention that, in its depiction of the relationships between black and white women, *Dessa Rose* is essentially concerned with history primarily as discourse, not as actuality, and, in these terms, it is closer to Reed's *Flight to Canada* than to *Kindred* or *Beloved*.

Williams's "Author's Note" makes this quite clear. It states that *Dessa Rose* is a response to "a certain critically acclaimed novel . . . that travestied the as-told-to memoir of slave revolt leader Nat Turner" (5).[7] Indeed, the short story that Williams later expanded into *Dessa Rose* was even entitled "Meditations on History," a direct reference to Styron's own description of *The Confessions of Nat Turner* in *his* book's "Author's Note." *Dessa Rose* signifies upon Styron's fiction in a number of ways. For example, the racist white writer Nehemiah is clearly intended as a caricature of both Nat Turner's questioner, Thomas Gray, and Styron himself. In addition, Williams's book contains several intertextual jokes, such as the fact that Nehemiah refers to his projected magnum opus, *The Roots of Rebellion in the Slave Population and Some Means of Eradicating Them*, by the diminutive *Roots*. Williams also describes a slave named Thomas who betrayed a slave rebellion conspiracy, and she later notes that his master referred to him affectionately as "Uncle Tom"—this in a novel set mostly in 1847, five years before the appearance of Stowe's famous fiction (23, 32, 27).

Such openly parodic moments should alert the reader to the extent to which *Dessa Rose* is primarily concerned with the ways in which slavery has been represented in literature, not as it may have been in reality. The realistic dimensions of the novel, however—especially the first section's portrayal of Dessa's life as a slave—make it very easy to mistake the book for one that is as much concerned with the historical actuality of slavery as it is with the ways slavery has been portrayed in literary discourse.

In fact, the novel's first section—set on the Hughes Farm owned by Terrell Vaugham—does engage very successfully with specific questions about slavery raised by historians. *Dessa Rose*'s treatment of the relationship between house servants and field hands on the Hughes Farm is a good case in point. Nehemiah observes only separation between these two classes of slaves. He recalls Dessa saying that she "work[s] the field and neva goes round the House," implying a rigid division between laborers and servants. Nehemiah, however, also acknowledges to the reader that he is often so distracted when interrogating the captive Dessa that he forgets to record her statements and is obliged to reconstruct her answers in writing later. It is entirely possible, then, that Nehemiah has recreated Dessa's words in the light of his own assumptions about slave communities and subjectivities. He certainly remains quite unaware of close relationships that the novel reveals do exist between the two slave classes. One house servant, for example, smuggles "special fixings from the white folks' supper table" to the imprisoned Dessa. The narrative makes the connection between the two classes of slaves even clearer through the figure of Dessa's husband, Kaine, who, as gardener, occupies a liminal position between house servant and field hand. As Dessa describes Kaine, "He been round the House, most a House nigga hisself—though a House nigga never say a nigga what tend flowas any betta'n one what tend corn." Kaine himself is amused by the fact that even the white master class seems confused about his social status. The women of the house consider a full-time gardener necessary, while the master complains that he "*couldn't afford to have a nigga sitting around eating his head off while he waited for some flowers to grow.*" The mistress angrily responds that her husband "*don't know the difference between a gardener and a common field hand.*" Even Nehemiah is not so oblivious that he fails to understand that a figure like Kaine bridges the slave classes. The white historian concludes that "an argument ought to be made for a stricter separation between house servants and field hands" in his book (18, 54, 34, 40).

Dessa Rose's depiction of slave classes and the relationship between them is historically informed and illuminating. Revisionist historians have argued that the divisions between slave classes have been much overstated by earlier scholars, and that there was much greater intimacy between slaves of different social status and more fluidity between slave classes than has traditionally been suggested.[8] The white planter class, however, was concerned to assert rigid class distinctions between slaves as a way of discouraging solidarity among their bondspeople. Where unreconstructed white southerners— including Margaret Mitchell—continued in the twentieth century to deploy the idea that there was little contact between different classes of slaves to ideological advantage in their fiction, *Dessa Rose* persuasively asserts the existence within slavery of blurred class lines and strong relationships across them. The novel also vividly demonstrates how southern whites sought to erect rigid class barriers between slaves, both in practice and in discourse.

The historical analysis present in the first section of *Dessa Rose* is not, however, sustained throughout the novel. When Dessa escapes to Rufel and Sutton's Glen, she leaves behind not only slavery but historical probability as well—even as the narrative becomes less focused upon intertextual signification and increasingly realistic in the psychological development of its characters. If one mistakenly assumes that the book aims to provide a compelling and historically substantiated portrait of what women's interracial relationships within slavery could really have been like, then *Dessa Rose* does indeed seem to be a sentimental, idealistic, and utopian romance.

However, if we read *Dessa Rose* as a text that is ultimately concerned primarily with slavery as it has been represented in fiction, not as it may have been in reality, claims about the narrative's idealism and lack of historical feasibility seem misplaced. If we approach Williams's novel as one that is concerned with literary conventions for representing history more than it is with history itself, then it is simply not a problem that the relationship between Dessa and Rufel is a historically unlikely one. Like Ishmael Reed in *Flight to Canada*, Williams does not reconstruct the reality of the past, but deconstructs existing literary stereotypes about the past. Williams is not a writer like Nehemiah, who privately acknowledges that he is more a compiler and editor of existing ideas than a creator (25). Instead, she rejects and replaces existing archetypes. In place of the traditionally male slave rebel, Williams presents Dessa. Instead of the plantation mistress as either domestic angel or sexually repressed sadist, she creates the psychologically complex Rufel. The friendship between Dessa and Rufel, furthermore, transcends stereotypical relationships between female slaves and white women in American literature—whether the maternal attitude of an Emily Shelby or Ellen O'Hara toward dependent slaves, or the cruelty of a Marie St. Clare or Salina Dutton toward slave victims, or the unquestioning dedication of a Mammy toward her beloved Scarlett. Williams's novel, like Reed's, provides ways of thinking about slavery that are not determined by preexisting discourses, historical or literary.

In order to transcend such stereotypes and conventions, however, Williams, like Reed before her, ultimately sidesteps—rather than engages with—historiographical discourses. The circumstances and community at Sutton's Glen are as historically bizarre in their way as Uncle Robin's inheritance of Swille's estate in *Flight to Canada*. Reading *Dessa Rose* in relation to Fox-Genovese's study suggests that Williams has constructed an anomalous and historically unlikely situation in order to create a textual environment in which black and white women can find an opportunity to gradually develop a greater understanding of each other. In other words, *Dessa Rose* does not posit a productive relationship between black and white women within the conventional circumstances of American slavery. Instead, the book imagines a fantastic situation within slavery in which such a friendship could develop.

Dessa Rose also resembles *Flight to Canada* in prioritizing the relevance of its tale to the present over any question of historical veracity. Susan Goodman suggests that Williams's novel "especially appealed to reviewers" in the 1980s because the relationship between Dessa and Ruth promises "a new era of interracial sisterhood" (24). Angelyn Mitchell similarly observes that "Williams presents to her readers her feminist engagement with race, so that we can imaginatively consider what might have been in terms of interracial feminist coalitions during slavery as well as what should be in terms of interracial feminist coalitions now" (65). Jane Mathison-Fife, meanwhile, suggests that Williams "wants to offer a 'black' version of the story of slavery that will be more empowering to African American children than the traditional depiction of slavery in literature and history written by whites" (32). The novel, in other words, aims to be polemical and inspirational, not historical and factual. *Dessa Rose* is a historical novel, certainly, but it is not so much about the past as it is about the present; or, we might say, it is a romance about the past that is directed toward contemporary political realities. *Dessa Rose*, in short, constructs a friendship between a gradually enlightened white woman slaveholder and an escaped female slave in the past in order to explore the possibility of productive interracial relationships and alliances between women in the present day.

For all the parallels I have noted, however, *Dessa Rose* differs from *Flight to Canada* in one significant and ultimately problematic way. While, like Reed's novel, it approaches slavery as a discursive field and articulates an argument about race relations in the present, it does not take the form of a comical and overtly metafictional fantasia. While *Flight to Canada's* characters are largely caricatures and types, Dessa, Rufel, and Nathan are convincing three-dimensional human beings about whom the reader cares. While the playful, postmodern dimensions of *Flight to Canada* eschew the horrible realities of slavery, *Dessa Rose* graphically represents its cruelties. When Dessa is captured, whites punish her by locking her into a sweatbox. "I had cried a long time in that box, from pain, from grief, from filth," she recalls. "Laying up there in my own foulment made me know how low I was. And I cried. I was like an animal; whipped like one; in the dirt like one." Rufel is shocked when she spies the scars inflicted upon Dessa by whites. Rufel notices that Dessa's "loins looked like a mutilated cat face. Scar tissue plowed through her pubic region so no hair would ever grow there again. Rufel leaned weakly against the door, regretting what she had seen. The wench had a right to hide her scars, her pain, Rufel thought, almost in tears herself" (191, 154). The emotional impact that Greil Marcus finds lacking in *Flight to Canada* is a fundamental aspect of *Dessa Rose*. Where Reed's novel emphasizes parodic comedy over the brutality of slavery, Williams's work is an involving, powerful, and moving book.

The psychological realism and emotional impact of Williams's fiction is, however, problematic if it encourages readers to assume that the portrayal of the past in *Dessa Rose* is thus historically credible. Goodman argues that it is a "sentimental book" precisely because, she claims, it "prompted readers to suppose that relationships such as Dessa and Ruth's most likely did exist in the antebellum South" (26). The danger, in other words, is that although *Dessa Rose* is centrally concerned with history as discourse rather than reality, its compelling realism may divert readers from understanding it as such. As I have noted, even astute literary critics have become mired in questions about the novel's historical veracity.

The novel risks confusing readers in this way because of a disjunction between its formal style and its approach to history. Paradoxically, *Dessa Rose* is at its most historically feasible and persuasive in its early scenes, when it is also most self-consciously explicit about its status as revisionist fiction. However, as the novel becomes increasingly realistic in stylistic and psychological terms and less oriented toward interextual parody, it also moves away from historical verisimilitude and a concern with the reality of the past and engages instead in the project of revising literary and textual representations of slavery.

The first section of *Dessa Rose*, set on the Hughes Farm, signals the book's emphasis upon slavery as discourse through its use of Nehemiah, an unreliable white historian, as viewpoint character and through parodic allusions to other fiction about slavery, such as *The Confessions of Nat Turner*, *Roots*, and *Uncle Tom's Cabin*. Simultaneously, however, this section's informed, realistic, and substantiated portrayal of the slave community also seems to promise a consistent engagement with slavery as historical reality throughout the text. The second section of the novel, set at Sutton's Glen—with its close psychological portrait of Rufel and the tensions she experiences with Dessa—is the most realistic part of *Dessa Rose* in formal terms. It is this portion of the narrative, however, that involves the various historically anomalous contrivances that create an unrealistic environment in which Dessa and Rufel can gradually come to understand each other.

Only in the third and final section is the novel's treatment of history really in synch with its formal style. At this point, the style of the book moves away somewhat from the intense psychological realism of the second section and revels with joyous self-consciousness in the "fantastic" genre of the romantic, comic, and suspenseful "adventure story," to use Trapasso's terms (222, 227). It is at this point as well that the novel rejects the tragic inevitability of many historical studies about slavery. *Dessa Rose* bypasses the brutal logic of Elkins's American Holocaust and rejects the bleak fate of the historical model for Dessa, who, as Williams acknowledges in her

Author's Note, was captured and hanged. Instead, the novel ends with the triumphant freedom of its fugitives from slavery. This conclusion also transcends the conventions of many existing twentieth-century fictional depictions of slavery. *Dessa Rose* will not accept that slave resistance must end in death, unlike those novels about black rebellion that attempt to hew closer to the historical record, such as *Black Thunder* and *The Confessions of Nat Turner*. Neither will it accept the notion that African American freedom depended upon legal abolition, as in *Jubilee* and *The Autobiography of Miss Jane Pittman*—books in which the narratives must follow their heroines into the era of Reconstruction in order to see them liberated from slavery. Even Dana, in *Kindred*, can escape slavery only by returning to the twentieth century. *Dessa Rose*, in contrast, boldly asserts the possibility of permanent and empowering self-liberation in the antebellum era.

Like *Flight to Canada*, then, Williams's novel very effectively explores new ways of thinking about slavery and race by radically revising and recreating conventions for representing slavery and race. Unlike Reed's novel, though, *Dessa Rose* also provides a frequently realistic and emotionally involving reading experience. Ironically, this very quality risks deflecting readers from an appreciation of the book's primary purpose. If we try to read *Dessa Rose* as a recreation of the realities of slavery—and often the novel itself seems to encourage us to do so—we are apt to miss the point.

Superficially, *Dessa Rose* may resemble *Kindred* and *Beloved*, but it is fundamentally different from either of them, and thus must be read in a different manner. While *Kindred* and *Beloved* involve fantastic elements, such as time travel and ghosts, they engage directly and compellingly with contemporary historiographical debates and theories about slavery. On the other hand, while *Dessa Rose* becomes increasingly naturalistic in formal terms, it presents extraordinary circumstances that were most likely unknown in nineteenth-century America and for which historians have found no evidence. Butler and Morrison place extraordinary figures—a time-traveling woman and a ghost—into the ordinary circumstances of slavery, while Williams places her psychologically realistic characters into an extraordinary context within slavery.

Dessa Rose thus reveals the complexities and the tensions involved in mediating between traditional and postmodern approaches to historical fiction—between addressing history as reality and as discourse. For all our knowledge of postmodernism, most readers remain inclined to assume that the subject of historical fiction is history itself, not the textualization of history. Despite our contemporary appreciation of the fact that we have access to the past only through constructed narratives, it is hard to put aside our expectation that a historical novel should portray the past in ways that we consider to be believable and accurate. *Flight to Canada*'s blatantly surreal mixing of the past and present serves to thoroughly disrupt such expectations. If it is a less emotionally involving novel than *Dessa Rose*, it nonetheless sufficiently distances its readers from questions of historical truth so that we are directed to focus upon issues of historical representation in literature and culture. Conversely, *Kindred* and *Beloved*, for all their postmodern characteristics, do not need to disrupt our assumptions about historical fiction in such a manner because they are primarily concerned with the nature of slavery in reality rather than in discourse. Their metafictional techniques are largely directed toward arguments about the historical conditions of slavery—most obviously in terms of their debates with Stanley Elkins. It does not matter that we become absorbed in the realism of these novels' characters and situations—despite their fantastic elements—because the ultimate subject of both books is the reality of slavery. *Dessa Rose*, in comparison, is a problematic text. It signals that its central concern is with the discourse, not the reality, of slavery in a variety of ways, but its postmodern and parodic elements are not sufficiently disruptive to neutralize our habitual inclination to assume that the primary subject of historical fiction is the reality of the past. Indeed, in its compelling opening portrait of the slave community on the Hughes Farm, *Dessa Rose* even encourages our tendency to expect historical fiction to recreate the past accurately and persuasively. Thus diverted from the novel's central purpose, we are apt to descend into largely irrelevant questions about the historical feasibility of interracial relationships between antebellum women, rather than attending to *Dessa Rose*'s polemical interrogation of traditional conventions for representing slavery or the empowering nature of the alternatives that it provides.

Valerie Martin's *Property*

Property's portrayal of interracial female relationships in slavery illustrates very different tensions inherent in the contemporary historical novel's treatment of the past than those exemplified in *Dessa Rose*. *Property*'s narrator is Manon Gaudet, the mistress of a Louisiana plantation in the 1820s, who harbors a deep bitterness toward her husband for fathering a child with a house slave named Sarah. During a slave uprising, rebels kill Mr. Gaudet and Sarah escapes. Although she achieves as a widow the independence she has always desired, Manon obsessively fixates upon the fugitive Sarah and goes to considerable lengths to recapture her. *Property* thus addresses relationships between black and white women within slavery in much bleaker terms than does *Dessa Rose*. As Martin observes in an interview, "I think the current vogue of circumscribing the past within the context of our enlightened sensibilities (such as they are) is largely a result of contempt for readers, who are perceived as too weak-minded to face the fact that . . . our forebears were not us in the making, but rather stubborn supporters of the status quo" ("Orange"). Martin's opinion, in other words, is that historical fiction should ultimately be about the reality of the past, not about contemporary identity politics, nor about history as primarily a discursive field. While Martin does not name any of the novels that she identifies with the "current vogue" about which she is so dismissive, *Dessa Rose* clearly represents precisely that kind of fiction.

Indeed, *Property* is best illuminated by being read as an intertextual commentary on the portrayal of interracial female relations in previous American fiction. While Martin has not acknowledged that this is the case, it seems quite evident that consideration of two particular novels are crucial to interpreting the meanings of *Property*. Martin's novel boldly emphasizes its treatment of race relations among southern women, an issue that is merely implicit or even repressed in one classic nineteenth-century American text, *The Awakening*. Simultaneously, *Property* can be read as a critical reaction to the idealism of the depiction of friendship between a white slaveholding woman and a black female slave in a twentieth-century novel of slavery, *Dessa Rose*.

What is important, however, is that *Property*'s strategy of intertextual signification is anything but overt. The novel, for example, contains no sly, parodic jokes comparable to *Dessa Rose*'s satirical allusions to *The Confessions of Nat Turner*, *Roots*, and *Uncle Tom's Cabin*. Instead, *Property* presents itself as an entirely conventional realistic novel without any explicitly self-conscious or metafictional dimension. Nonetheless, the novel's meanings are largely illuminated by focusing upon its intertextual dialogues with *The Awakening* and *Dessa Rose,* however veiled, implicit, and unacknowledged these dialogues remain in the narrative. In the book's acknowledgments, Martin lists a variety of historical sources that informed her writing of the novel (including the ubiquitous Aptheker), but does not mention the two novels to which, I argue, *Property* should be read in relation.

In short, *Property* seems to be a work of fiction that is concerned to conceal its postmodernist, intertextual tendencies and which avoids disrupting the realism or credibility of its tale, or emphasizing its own textual nature. In this it differs not only from the manifest metafictionality of *Dessa Rose* and, especially, *Flight to Canada,* but also from the combination of postmodern textual self-consciousness and straightforward realism that characterizes novels like *Kindred* and *Beloved. Property,* in other words, seeks to distinguish itself formally as well as ideologically from other contemporary fiction about slavery, which its author criticizes for "circumscribing the past within the context of our enlightened sensibilities" ("Orange"). If such novels are often characterized by textual self-consciousness, *Property* differentiates itself by obscuring its own use of that same strategy.

Martin's open acknowledgment of her historical sources—in contrast to her text's entirely implicit treatment of its literary predecessors—signals *Property's* primary purpose as a historical novel. The book's latent allusions to other works of fiction are not directed toward an analysis of traditional literary conventions for representing slavery but toward building a persuasive and informed argument about the historical conditions of the institution. *Property's* portrayal of Manon Gaudet's relation to Sarah advances a parallel argument to that which Fox-Genovese makes so compellingly in *Within the Plantation Household*: "The hard truth is that slave and slaveholding women occupied antagonistic positions.... [Slaveholding] women lived—and knew they lived—as privileged members of a ruling class.... Overwhelmingly, they supported slavery and its constraints as the necessary price for their own privileged position.... [They] accepted and supported the social system that endowed them with power and privilege over black women" (98, 145, 243). Initially in Martin's novel, Manon tentatively identifies with Sarah as a fellow victim of white patriarchy, but her ultimate loyalties lie with the ruling race and gender. Within existing social structures, Manon enjoys considerable privileges and powers, and thus she finally chooses to identify with patriarchy for all that it grants her. She joins the ranks of the oppressors rather than align herself with the oppressed, for she refuses to consider herself the equal or ally of an enslaved black woman.

While Martin cites no fewer than nine historical studies in her acknowledgments (as well as several primary sources, including fugitive slave narratives and plantation journals), *Property*, as I have suggested, largely advances its argument about the past by signifying upon other fiction about slavery and white southern women. *The Awakening* may seem a curious choice of literary allusion, given that Kate Chopin's famous novel is a late-nineteenth-century fiction about the postbellum South, but recent critics have focused much attention upon the repressed or implied racial component of *The Awakening*. *Property* unearths the racial subtext of Chopin's novel by telling a parallel story set in the same southern location a few decades earlier than *The Awakening*. Martin's fiction encourages the reader to consider what kind of person Chopin's famous proto-feminist heroine, Edna Pontellier, might have been had she been born a generation or two earlier—as a slaveholder.

While *Property* is not explicit about its intertextual strategies, its relationship to *The Awakening* is nonetheless palpably apparent. Carol Shields, in one of the first reviews of Martin's novel, observes that Manon "is as complex and disaffected as Edna Pontellier in Kate Chopin's *The Awakening*" (quoted on book jacket of *Property*). It is more than just that the books' two protagonists are similarly disillusioned with their lot in life—the parallels between the two novels are, in fact, numerous and significant. The opening scene of *Property* even obliquely evokes the beginning of *The Awakening*. Chopin's narrative commences with Léonce Pontellier watching from a distance as his wife approaches from the beach. She and her companion then relate what he considers "utter nonsense; some adventure out there in the water" (45). *Property* reverses the roles and begins with its female protagonist watching her husband through a spyglass as he indulges in his own "adventure out there in the water," playing a sadistic sexual game upon his male slaves in the river.

Property and *The Awakening* are both set in Louisiana, but at opposite ends of the nineteenth century, and both concern white aristocratic women chafing against the restrictions of patriarchy.[9] The female protagonists of both novels are accused of failing to fulfill their roles as wives and mothers. Edna is categorically "not a mother-woman," and her husband is irritated by what he considers her neglect of her children. Edna concedes that by "all the codes which I am acquainted with, I am a devilishly wicked specimen of the sex," even as she rejects the values that inform her culture's condemnation of her (51, 48, 50, 138). Manon, meanwhile, is appalled to receive "another lecture on my failings as a wife," and is even less a "mother-woman" than Edna, for she fails to conceive a child and eventually refuses to sleep with her husband altogether (69). Both women seek rooms of their own. Manon is relieved when her mother dies and she inherits her "little house" in New Orleans, while Edna moves into her small "pigeon house" in the same city (Martin 93; Chopin 151). The husbands of both women respond to their wives' "unbalanced" behavior by consulting doctors (Chopin 117–19; Martin 56–57). Meanwhile, the brief flirtation that Manon enjoys with the hedonistic Joel Borden is reminiscent of Edna's fling with the playboy Alcée Arobin.

In *Property*, furthermore, Martin inverts the motif of awakening that recurs throughout Chopin's text. There are several literal awakenings in Chopin's novel that represent Edna's gradual dawning of consciousness, such as when she wakes after an afternoon nap at Madame Antoine's, refreshed, hungry, and ready to face a new world. "How many years have I slept?" she asks. "The whole island seems changed. A new race of beings must have sprung up" (85). Michele Birnbaum observes that Edna is also repeatedly overcome by drowsiness in *The Awakening*, and that "her feminine liberation is narcoleptic, a movement in and out of consciousness" (301). Manon, in contrast, is an insomniac who experiences little drowsiness, few satisfied awakenings, and develops no sense of feminine liberation in *Property*. Indeed, Manon needs to take a tincture in order to sleep at all. Furthermore, she is constantly startled into wakefulness in the middle of the night, once to find the mill on fire, and once to emerge from a nightmare only to discover Sarah staring fixedly at her. "I thought, She has been watching me like that this entire night" (31, 39, 71, 44–45, 14).

This moment at which Manon becomes conscious of Sarah's surreptitious surveillance is highly relevant to *Property's* invocations of *The Awakening*. Although Chopin's novel is most commonly discussed as a proto-feminist text, several critics in the last decade have explored its repressed racial dimensions. Rebecca Aanerud notes that, "while Edna's position in the gender hierarchy is constraining, this constraint is offset by her position in the race and class hierarchies. Her abundant leisure time is made possible by women of color" (42). Barbara Ewell similarly observes that the "labor and presence of black people are systematically assumed in the novel. Edna's spiritual journey is directly supported by nameless black servants who care for her children and cook her meals and drive her carriages while she tries to figure out how to be a lady and still have a self" (34). Elizabeth Ammons likewise argues that Edna's freedom "comes at the expense of women of other races and a lower class, whose namelessness, facelessness, and voicelessness record a much more profound oppression in *The Awakening* than does the surface story of Edna Pontellier" (75). Finally, Joyce Dyer suggests that there is "evidence on nearly every page that *The Awakening* is a silent meditation on the dangerous subject of race.... [T]here is an enormous black presence, often menacing, and sometimes capable of sabotaging not only the white characters in Chopin's novel, but also the very text itself" (140). For Dyer, the black servant characters in the novel "are not always what they seem to be.... They are discontent, detached from their roles and the world they have been forced to occupy—and we sense their potential for explosiveness" (143).[10]

Martin brings all these issues fully to the surface by setting her revision of *The Awakening* in the era of slavery. Sarah, in *Property*, is as silent as the servants in Chopin's novel, but hers is a more central and explicit racial presence. Manon, while eventually discounting Sarah's humanity, obsesses about her on almost every page of the narrative. The novel thus constantly encourages the reader to imagine, as Manon apparently cannot, what the silent, stony-faced Sarah is thinking and feeling as the narrative unfolds. Sarah's silence in *Property* is quite deafening.

Just as the independence for which Edna strives in postbellum Louisiana involves being waited upon by servants, so does the independence that Manon achieves in New Orleans in 1828 necessarily involve the service of slaves. Unable to break out of the patriarchal chains that bind her, Chopin's Edna commits suicide. *Property*, however, provides Manon with everything that might have saved Edna: an absence of children, financial independence, widowhood, and a disfigurement received during the slave rebellion that discourages men from pursuing her. Despite all this, however, Manon still has no more sense of freedom than Edna. Even in her independence, Manon begins to feel "as if an iron collar, such as I have seen used to discipline field women, were fastened about my skull" (182). The entrapped Edna, meanwhile, reflects that marriage and motherhood entail "the soul's slavery" (175). For all their disillusion with the status quo, then, both characters remain psychologically enslaved, despite their very different material circumstances, because neither has been able to develop her personal complaints into a coherent rejection of the system of patriarchy that holds her in bondage. For all the power that men have over them, as upper-class women administered by a retinue of servants, Manon and Edna benefit too much from patriarchy to wish to challenge it.

For much of *Property*, Manon blames her misery upon her husband, whom she sees as an exceptional hypocrite and failure. Toward the end of the narrative, however, she discovers that Joel Borden, a glamorous local planter to whom she is attracted, is as guilty as her husband of sexually exploiting women of color. Furthermore, although Manon is initially excited to discover the journal of the long-dead father whom she has always idealized, his cold, compassionless memoirs drive her to disillusion. It is at this point that she imagines the ghost of her husband "leaning over me, turning the screw of the hot iron collar tighter and tighter until my skull must crack from the pressure." Manon's sense of male hypocrisy remains, however, at the level of bewildering psychological pain, not insight. She is outraged by the "lie at the center of everything," but, as far as she is concerned, this "great lie" is simply the failure of individual men to live up to the values and rhetoric of patriarchy, not the system itself. Rather than seeking to liberate herself from patriarchy, Manon chooses to perpetuate it, claiming for herself the patriarchal authority to which she was once subject. Hence she is determined to recapture her escaped maid, even refusing a monetary offer from one of the fugitive's allies that is "twice what Sarah was worth" (183, 179, 169). Manon sees herself as a victim of patriarchy, but she is really an instrument and beneficiary of it. Thus she must continue to oppress Sarah as her husband did before her.

Property explicitly argues what *The Awakening* represses: that to equate the situation of people in slavery with that of women under patriarchy is a false analogy. While the titular heroine of *Dessa Rose* discovers that black and white women are "subject to the same ravishment," Martin's fiction asserts that this is about all they have in common—and that white women can oppress and, as we shall see, ravish too (Williams 201). Karen Sanchez-Eppler critiques the way that many nineteenth-century feminist works compare the situation of women to that of slaves. By using the slave to represent the oppression of white women, she argues, the antebellum feminist "asserts her right to speak and act, thus differentiating herself from her brethren in bonds. The bound and silent figure of the slave metaphorically represents the woman's oppression and so grants the white woman access to political discourse denied the slave" (quoted in Birnbaum 304). Applying this insight to Edna's claim about the "soul's slavery" in marriage and motherhood in *The Awakening*, Birnbaum asserts that by "initiating her escape from gender convention through the rhetoric of racial oppression, Edna reinforces rather than razes class and race differences" (304). When Edna and Manon compare themselves to slaves, they are doing little more than repeating the questionable complaint of the lazy, selfish, and callously exploitative Marie St. Clare in *Uncle Tom's Cabin*, who suggests that "it's we mistresses that are the slaves" (260).

While *Property* thus vividly excavates the suppressed racial subtext of *The Awakening*, it completely reverses the narrative structure, perspective, and trajectory of *Dessa Rose*, as well as the psychological development of its white female protagonist. Martin's novel is almost a negative photo-image of Williams's text. Although both *Dessa Rose* and *Property* portray relationships between white and black women during slavery, and while both are concerned with slave rebellions, *Dessa Rose* never takes the reader directly into the mind of the plantation mistress. The third section and epilogue of Williams's novel are narrated from Dessa's standpoint, and the first section consists largely of Nehemiah's journal entries. Rufel is certainly the viewpoint character for much of the book's second section, but Williams never narrates directly from her perspective. Conversely, in *Property*, the equivalents of Nehemiah and Dessa—Manon's husband and Sarah—are rendered marginal while Manon's voice dominates the story. *Property* thus reverses the emphases of *Dessa Rose*, just as Williams's novel itself reverses existing literary stereotypes.

Property also depicts a very different process of character development for its plantation mistress. Rufel initially accepts the racial orthodoxies of her culture, then learns to see beyond them and to appreciate the humanity of people of color as *Dessa Rose* progresses. In contrast, Manon, at the outset of *Property*, is a fairly sympathetic character who shows signs of sloughing off southern ideology. Her later involvement with slave rebels and a female slave runaway, however, do not contribute to her enlightenment, but cause her to cement her relationship with the white patriarchal status quo.

At the very beginning of *Property*, Manon seems to reject her husband's assumption that black people "are brutes and have not the power of reason." She also has a close relationship with her cook, Delphine, talking to her frankly and openly. Entering the kitchen, Manon observes that "It's hell in here," and asks Delphine, "How can you stand it?" Despite the heat, however, Manon says that she feels more at ease in the kitchen "than in my own room. Delphine is the only person in this house I trust at all." Later, during the slave insurrection, Manon seems concerned for Delphine, hoping she is "safe in the kitchen" (4, 40, 107).

While Manon is close to Delphine, Mr. Gaudet suspects his wife of actively conspiring with Sarah, the maid he is exploiting sexually. In one scene, Gaudet's "good humor evaporated. He looked from Sarah to me and back again. 'All you women do is talk,' he said" (15). This is reminiscent of Nehemiah's declaration at the end of *Dessa Rose*, "You-all in this together . . . womanhood" (232). Manon, in fact, seems to desire the very alliance with Sarah that her husband fears and which Rufel and Dessa develop in Williams's novel. Manon sees herself as a victim, a sister-sufferer to Sarah. She considers every day under her husband's authority to be a humiliation and she longs for his financial failure and even his death. She understands, furthermore, that Sarah hates Gaudet "as much as I do." When there are no servants present, Gaudet demands that his wife serve him as if she, too, were a slave. Manon responds to such treatment by staring at her husband "for a few moments blankly without comment, as if he was speaking a foreign language. This unnerves him. It's a trick I learned from Sarah" (17, 54, 38, 8).

Ostensibly, then, Manon seems to have at least as much potential as Rufel to develop a meaningful relationship with a woman of color. Furthermore, Manon frequently attempts to engage Sarah in candid conversation, but these attempts are largely met with stony silence from the slave. Manon is frustrated and perturbed that Sarah appears to hate her mistress as much as she does her master. "She wishes us both dead," Manon concludes mournfully. Events prove Manon correct on this score. During the slave rebellion, Sarah betrays both Gaudets to the rebels while taking the opportunity to escape herself. Manon is quite bewildered by this behavior: "My husband is dead, I thought. Why would she run now, when she was safe from him? It didn't make sense" (63, 127).

In fact, Sarah's flight makes perfect sense, for the slave understands something about her mistress that Manon does not know about herself: that the white woman is as much a part of the power structure of slavery as her husband. Manon is maddened by the lies and hypocrisies that underlie patriarchal power, but she fails to comprehend that she is part of this system and depends upon the privileges it bestows—that she, too, is an oppressor (63, 179–80). Early in the novel, Manon fantasizes about what she would do were her husband to die. Her first step, she decides, would be to sell all the slaves and erase her husband's debts—and she is even astute enough to imagine that Sarah probably knows she would do this (16). Despite such knowledge, however, Manon is still unable to understand Sarah's refusal to confide in her:

> Eventually I grew bored and tried talking to her, a largely hopeless enterprise. "You went down to tend Leo?" I said.
> "I did," she replied.
> "Is he bad?"
> "He'll live."
> "Who did the whipping?"
> "I don' know."
> So much for conversation. (7)

As this exchange demonstrates, the plantation mistress's efforts to engage the slave in dialogue are always made from an explicit position of authority. In this scene, Manon is clearly not concerned for Leo's welfare; she is merely curious. To her, a harsh physical punishment inflicted upon a slave is merely an occasion for conversation. Manon is not seeking to exchange confidences with a confederate; she really requires a loyal servant, a frank but subservient informant, and an audience for her discontent. She is not, however, prepared to give anything in return. Sarah's silence is an understandable survival tactic. She knows that Manon has no real human concern for her and cannot be trusted as an ally. Manon presumably likes Delphine so much because the cook responds so agreeably to her orders (40–41).

While Manon relies upon the care of black women, her true allegiances lie with the white patriarchal power structure. After being injured in the slave rebellion, Manon depends upon the nursing skills of Delphine and

Rose, but she is apparently most relieved when an ineffectual posse of planters turns up. "Blessed Providence," she thinks excitedly, "There are still white men alive." Furthermore, after Sarah has escaped, Manon can conceive of her only in terms of property, as the patriarchal slavocracy encourages her to do: "I don't think of her as having run away . . . I think of her as having been stolen." The final words of the novel confirm Manon's absolute commitment to conventional southern hierarchies. After she has been recaptured and restored to her duties as maid, Sarah describes being served coffee by Quakers in the North. Manon imagines an abolitionist couple attending to Sarah in such a manner and reflects, "It struck me as perfectly ridiculous. What on earth did they think they were doing?" (122, 171, 193).

Ultimately, then, Manon does not reject patriarchal power, but craves a share of it herself. Widowhood provides Manon with privileges normally only accorded males, such as the right to own property. This is not, however, sufficient for Manon, and she is especially annoyed that Sarah, by disguising herself as a white man during her escape attempt, has experienced a freedom that a white woman can never know (189). In one scene, Manon even exploits Sarah in precisely the same way as her husband has:

> The drop of milk still clung to the dark flesh of her nipple. . . . I dropped to my knees on the carpet before her. . . . I leaned forward until my mouth was close to her breast, then put out my tongue to capture the drop. . . . I guided the nipple to my lips and sucked gently. . . . This is what he does, I thought. . . . How wonderful I felt, how entirely free. . . . I opened my eyes and looked at Sarah's profile. She had lifted her chin as far away from me as she could, her mouth was set in a thin, hard line, and her eyes were focused intently on the arm of the settee. She's afraid to look at me, I thought. And she's right to be. If she looked at me, I would slap her. (76–77)

Oppressing another woman, then, makes Manon feel "wonderful" and "entirely free." What is especially striking about this scene is that we now see from the oppressor's point of view what we saw from the perspective of the oppressed in another novel. In *Beloved*, no act of brutality in slavery outrages Sethe more than the occasion when Schoolteacher's sadistic nephews "took my milk. . . . Held me down and took it" (19). This act is a double violation: it is a form of rape that also defiles a woman's maternal role. It is, in other words, an instance of misogynistic violence that simultaneously projects both white southern stereotypes of enslaved women upon an individual—the sexually available Jezebel and the nursing Mammy.[11] This act thus embodies both the literal and figurative exploitation and cruelty of slavery, especially in relation to women, like no other—and it is this very violation that Manon perpetrates against Sarah. This scene in *Property* contrasts sharply with Rufel's suckling Dessa's baby in *Dessa Rose* (88, 101–2, 117). Williams's novel subverts racial conventions and taboos by having the white woman serve as "Mammy" to a black baby, thus paving the way for Rufel to overcome other southern racial orthodoxies. In *Property*, on the other hand, Manon imposes the "Mammy" role upon Sarah in what is also an act of sexual violation, demonstrating that Manon is no different from her patriarchal husband in her attitudes and her behavior toward female slaves. In this scene, Manon clearly desires to understand not the position of an enslaved black woman, but that of the patriarchal husband she and Sarah always despised. In abusing Sarah, Manon assumes the power of the dead patriarch.

Edna's relations with her servants in *The Awakening* do not remotely resemble Manon's oppression of her slaves in *Property*, but Martin's novel nonetheless illuminates the ways in which Chopin's novel reveals the limits of nineteenth-century feminism. *The Awakening* may powerfully portray the frustrations of wealthy white women in a rigidly patriarchal society, but it cannot imagine a substantial relationship between its female protagonist and any woman of color. Ammons may be correct that, "as Edna awakens, black characters change from nameless parts of the scenery to individuals with names and voices" (310). It is even true that Edna erases the boundaries between herself and her servants to some degree. The day that Edna moves into the pigeon house, Alcée Arobin finds her "with rolled sleeves, working in company with the house-maid" (140). Despite such behavior, however, Edna simply does not develop a relationship with a black woman that is at all equal or even vaguely comparable to the friendship that develops between Dessa and Rufel in Williams's novel. Edna's exchanges with her servant, Celestine, more resemble the relationship between Manon and the loyal cook, Delphine, in *Property*. Celestine hardly appears in *The Awakening* directly, and whenever she is mentioned it is in relation to her duties: "Old Celestine, who works occasionally for me, says she will come stay with me and do my work. . . . Arobin had sent [the flowers], and had had Celestine distribute them during Edna's absence. . . . She hurried away to tell Celestine to set an extra place. She even sent her off in search of some added delicacy" (134, 149, 157). Edna paradoxically desires to assert her independence as a woman while still seeking to retain all the privileges accorded to white women by patriarchy. As Ewell points out, "Even her most dramatic attempt to move out of the social place assigned to her . . . results in an ironic reaffirmation of the larger systems that define female status. The pigeon house is, after all, purchased with Edna's father's money and staffed by a black servant" (35).

Just as *The Awakening* ultimately demonstrates the lack of potential for genuine relationships between black and white women in the South after slavery, so does *Property* make a specific argument about the nature of such relationships during slavery. Where *Dessa Rose* largely transcends historicity in its construction of the friendship between Rufel and Dessa, Martin's novel depicts the interactions between slaveholding and enslaved women in the antebellum South in ways that accord with contemporary historical studies such as Fox-Genovese's: as a relationship between oppressor and oppressed. *Property* provides a chilling and compelling case for this thesis.

For all the complexity of the characterization of Manon, however, *Property*'s counter-revisionist historical interpretation ironically rests upon a recycling of the traditional stereotype of the plantation mistress as a cruel, cold, and sexually disturbed individual. On one hand, then, Martin's novel constructs a sophisticated argument informed by current historical scholarship about the limited potential for friendships between black and white women during slavery, and it implicitly critiques fiction that seeks to transcend such historical realities. On the other hand, *Property*'s depiction of Manon is also curiously reminiscent of such dated and simplistic literary predecessors as Marie St. Clare and Salina Dutton. The achievement of *Property* is that it redeems this familiar stereotype from one-dimensional villainy, providing a startling portrait of the psychology and the motivation of such a figure. Yet one must also question the extent to which *Property*'s historical counter-revisionism encourages it to simply recite existing literary archetypes. Even if Fox-Genovese is correct that plantation mistresses were often even uglier in their racism than their husbands, does it necessarily follow that they were also as sadistic and sexually repressed as they have been consistently represented in modern American fiction—*Dessa Rose*'s Rufel aside—from Sapphira Colbert to Manon Gaudet?

* * *

For all their similarities of subject matter, *Dessa Rose* and *Property* are very different works of fiction. Williams's novel powerfully dismantles existing cultural and literary stereotypes about women during slavery in order to advocate the necessity of interracial female friendships and alliances in the present; it also quickly abandons its brief engagement with historical evidence and contemporary debates about the nature of slavery. For all its parodic intertextual allusions, however, *Dessa Rose*'s emphasis upon slavery as a tradition of discursive conventions is problematized by its compelling psychological realism. The novel's metafictional elements do not sufficiently disrupt the credibility of the narrative. *Dessa Rose* involves rather than distances the reader, and thus risks being read as a feasible fictionalization of the past rather than a commentary on the cultural archetypes of slavery and their relevance to interracial feminist politics in the present.

Property, meanwhile, presents itself as a thoroughly researched and realistic fiction about slavery. While the novel seems to directly allude to both *The Awakening* and *Dessa Rose*, Martin's text does not flaunt its metafictionality or its dialogues with other works of fiction. If *Property* engages with slavery as a discursive field, it does so implicitly, perhaps covertly—so concerned is the novel not to distract the reader from its historiographical argument about the nature of the relationships between black and white women in the antebellum South. *Property* challenges *Dessa Rose*'s apparent suggestion that friendships between black and white women could and perhaps did occur in slavery, and it alludes to *The Awakening* in order to validate its argument that aristocratic white women of the nineteenth century were not inclined to develop friendships or alliances with women of color—even after slavery. While Williams's text engages in historiography only in the rather outdated and problematic form of Aptheker's *American Negro Slave Revolts*, Martin's book references a number of contemporary historical texts in addition to Aptheker—all of which its author cites as a demonstration of the historical veracity of her story. While *Property* avoids overt literary self-consciousness, however, it cannot evade the influence of literary traditions. In the process of making its historical argument, Martin's novel resurrects the very fictional stereotypes that *Dessa Rose* transcends. *Property* essentially takes us into the mind of a Marie St. Clare or Mrs. Flint. Manon may be more three-dimensional and more intriguing than such simplistically sketched predecessors, but she possesses identical qualities of character. While *Dessa Rose* complicates and contests stereotypical representations of slavery, *Property* simply portrays them in more sophisticated terms.

If the cultural discourse about slavery in the late 1960s was characterized by the hostile stand-off between Styron and his critics, then in the first decade of the twenty-first century that discourse is exemplified by *Property*'s constructive engagement with *Dessa Rose*. One hopes that this will just be the beginning of a long and productive conversation between black and white writers and between novelists and historians on the subject of American slavery. The dialogue between *Dessa Rose* and *Property*, however, is a curious and unexpected one. The African American writer asserts the white slaveholding woman's potential for racial enlightenment, whereas the white writer accuses the plantation mistress of being a racist oppressor incapable of human feeling toward a woman of color. This debate, furthermore, has clearly moved on from the struggles of the late 1960s over the ways that a white novelist represented the famous leader of a historical slave rebellion. Black and white writers today are not primarily arguing about what slavery may have been like in reality. Instead, *Dessa Rose* and *Property* advocate opposing forms of historical fiction—one that addresses history as reality and one that addresses history as discourse. This debate, however, is complicated and confused because Williams's novel is psychologically credible and—at least initially—is also concerned with the realities of slavery, while Martin's text represses its treatment of slavery as a tradition of literary discourses.

In some ways, this debate is quite moot. *Kindred* and *Beloved* vividly demonstrate that fiction can address historiographical questions about the nature of slavery while also signifying upon conventions for representing slavery in literature. Neither Butler's nor Morrison's novel confuses the reader by entirely suppressing its treatment of slavery as a discursive field, nor by insufficiently differentiating between its treatment of slavery as historical reality and as a tradition of cultural representations. In blunt terms, *Dessa Rose* is an extraordinary yet inspiring story about black and white women during slavery, while *Property* is a more historically credible but rather depressing narrative about them. Neither text offers the multiple and complex options that *Kindred* and *Beloved* present. Morrison's and Butler's novels are both fantastic *and* historically credible, traumatic *and* hopeful.

5

Mapping the Unrepresentable

SLAVERY FICTION IN THE NEW MILLENNIUM

In his famously dismissive comments about the historical novel, Henry James observed that the genre is "condemned . . . to a fatal *cheapness* for the simple reason that the difficulty of the job is inordinate" (quoted in Horne 360). James's own experience with the genre was indeed troublesome. Despite his avowed misgivings about the form, he began a work of historical fiction entitled *The Sense of the Past* when he was at his peak in 1900, swiftly abandoned it, then resumed it as a distraction from global war in 1914, only for it to remain unfinished at the time of his death in 1916. Confounded by the problem of plausibly recreating the mindset of a distant and psychologically alien era, James took the unorthodox step of making his one historical novel a tale about an American essayist in the present who, whenever he crosses the threshold of a particular London house, returns to the nineteenth century and encounters his British ancestors. Realizing that one cannot unproblematically recreate the past and that history is only accessible through a contemporary perspective, the master of sophisticated realism was driven to make his single foray into historical fiction a fantastic tale of time travel, thus thoroughly disrupting the traditions of the very genre he was exploring. While the novel itself was never completed, its narrative almost immediately became the basis of a popular play and, later, film entitled *Berkeley Square*.

The parallels between *The Sense of the Past* and *Kindred* are substantial. Both texts are concerned with the limitations of conventional mimetic representations of history and both use extraordinary time travel plots in order to engage with the past in an unconventional yet ultimately credible manner that transcends orthodox ways of representing and thus thinking about history. Just as *The Sense of the Past* was an unfinished failure that found instant popular acclaim when adapted into drama, so was *Kindred* initially largely neglected, then increasingly feted by scholars, and now, in this study, identified as a significant turning point in late twentieth-century American fiction about slavery. Butler's text asserts the need for novels not only to engage with existing discourses (both fictional and historical) about slavery, but also to transcend these discourses and to present slavery in new and unfamiliar ways that are not subject to the formal and thematic concerns of previous texts.

Before the 1980s, American novels about slavery largely worked within the plantation or family melodrama forms epitomized in the twentieth century by *Gone with the Wind*. Even though many novelists responded to this genre and Mitchell's work critically, they nonetheless tended to rely upon many of its conventions and archetypes. *The Red Cock Crows* creates a romantic Tara-esque ambience only to disrupt the placid complacency of a supposedly benign system of slavery with an armed insurrection and white vigilante violence. Even black-authored novels focusing upon the African American experience in slavery hew closely to the path set by Mitchell's fiction. As an historical epic set in the Civil War and Reconstruction but concerning the black Vyry instead of the white Scarlett, *Jubilee* upturns the conventions of *Gone with the Wind* without fundamentally eschewing them. *Roots* is a very similar case, with one critic even naming it "the black *Gone with the Wind*" (quoted in Taylor 51). From this perspective, *The Wind Done Gone* is merely a late entry in a very long tradition.[1]

Gone with the Wind's influence on subsequent slavery fiction raises the vexed question of where intertextual dialogue ends and dependency begins. While the aforementioned novels work, to some degree, as analytical interrogations and subversive reworkings of Mitchell's book, it is nonetheless apparent that they all operate within a twentieth-century tradition in which *Gone with the Wind* is regarded as the undisputed Ur-text. Mitchell's novel is easily parodied, but it is hard to evade. *Gone with the Wind* has influenced the form, the conventions, the archetypes, and the themes of many subsequent fictional portrayals of slavery. The very terminology "black *Gone with the Wind*" suggests the ways in which the continual evocations of Mitchell's novel, however critical in nature, may serve to perpetuate rather than dismantle its cultural power.

It is not surprising that scholars are uneasy with *Gone with the Wind*'s pervasive influence and have sought to establish a specifically African American antecedent for the contemporary novel of slavery. Recent critical studies have thus been inclined to characterize recent black-authored slavery novels as "neoslave narratives" (Bell 289; Rushdy, *Neo-slave* 3). While it is certainly true that the antebellum fugitive slave narratives have become one of several crucial sources for African American fiction about slavery over the last forty years, "neoslave narrative" is a fundamentally problematic label.

Bernard Bell coined the term to refer to "residually oral, modern narratives of escape from bondage to freedom" (289). Even this fairly general definition, however, does not apply especially well to particular novels about slavery. Bell calls *Jubilee* the "first major neoslave narrative," and while Walker's tale certainly emphasizes aspects of black folk culture, it is not particularly "oral" in formal terms, and it certainly does not possess the first-person perspective that defined the fugitive slave narrative. Neither does Walker's protagonist, Vyry, *escape* from slavery precisely. She achieves freedom as a result of the Union victory in the Civil War, and the last third of the text concerns Vyry's experiences during Reconstruction, thus departing significantly from the fugitive slave narrative, which is essentially concerned with the antebellum era. Similarly, Bontemps's *Black Thunder* has multiple viewpoint characters, an omniscient narrator, and a story that concerns doomed collective resistance against slavery rather than successful escape from it. Yet Bell still claims it as a "skillful adaptation of the conventions of the [slave narrative] tradition" (289, 103).

If we accept Ashraf Rushdy's seemingly more specific definition of "Neoslave narratives" as novels that "assume the form, adopt the conventions, and take on the first-person voice" of their nineteenth-century antecedents, very few texts meet the criteria (Rushdy, *Neo-slave* 3).[2] Rushdy's emphasis upon the centrality of the first-person voice instantly discounts *Black Thunder* and *Jubilee* as neoslave narratives—but it also technically excludes two of the four novels he addresses in his own study of the neoslave narrative genre. While all the texts he analyzes certainly respond to the fugitive slave narrative tradition in one way or another, *Flight to Canada* is told in the omniscient third-person (aside from its brief opening and closing monologues), and only the final section of *Dessa Rose* is narrated from its heroine's point of view. Both novels are as much concerned with white-authored portrayals of slavery—*Uncle Tom's Cabin* and *The Confessions of Nat Turner*, respectively—as they are with the fugitive slave narrative. If one defines the slave narrative in yet more precise terms as a first-person account of an individual's experiences in slavery and ultimate escape from the institution, then—of more than a dozen African American novels about slavery published since the mid-sixties—only Charles Johnson's *Oxherding Tale* really fits the bill.[3]

The overemphasis upon the questionable generic category of "neoslave narrative" in recent critical studies simply reveals a desire on the part of scholars to construct a coherent black literary tradition concerned with slavery that stands in stark opposition to a white canon of works on the subject. There is no denying that many contemporary black authors have found in the fugitive slave narrative a usable African American literary heritage. It is clearly the case that numerous works—including *Jubilee*, *Flight to Canada*, *Kindred*, and *Dessa Rose*—actively respond to that tradition. The suggestion, however, that recent black-authored novels about slavery are formal and thematic twentieth-century equivalents or direct descendants of the fugitive slave narrative is a rather dubious one. After all, the neoslave narrative is a novelistic genre, while its predecessor was autobiographical anti-slavery polemic. The fugitive slave narrative is, in fact, just one of multiple textual sources for slavery fiction today, not its ultimate template. When scholars assert a fundamental kinship between the fugitive slave narrative and recent works of slavery fiction, all they really seem to be suggesting is that both are black-authored and are primarily concerned with the African American experience in slavery. Black-authored fiction, however, cannot avoid alluding to such works as *Uncle Tom's Cabin* and *Gone with the Wind* or engaging with the ideas of white historians, including Elkins and Aptheker. Lest black texts seem overly dependent upon white discourses, critics quite understandably have tried to identify a specifically black literary progenitor for contemporary slavery fiction—however erroneously.

The long shadow cast by such works as *Gone with the Wind* and the critical enthusiasm for the notion of the neoslave narrative are indicative of an anxiety of influence that permeates the writing and reception of slavery fiction. African American writers may wish to avoid producing mere revisions of *Gone with the Wind*, but the concept of the neoslave narrative simply replaces a white literary ancestor with a black one. It does not suggest ways in which novelists today might move beyond previous discursive conventions for representing slavery. Literary influence is not only an issue for African American writers either. *The Confessions of Nat Turner* is problematic, for example, largely because it rehashes the conventions and ideologies of the fugitive slave narrative without sufficient sensitivity to that genre's original context, purpose, and audience.[4] Innovative for its use of the plantation mistress's perspective, *Property* ultimately seems entirely predictable because its protagonist so thoroughly resembles the archetype of the cruel and repressed female slaveholder with whom readers have long been familiar.

It is not merely concern about the ideologies of antecedents that makes it imperative for authors of new slavery fiction to distinguish their works from prior literary discourses about the institution. The continual use of standard, long-established strategies for representing slavery in literature risks making the institution seem commonplace and overly familiar, thus diminishing its impact. While comparisons of American slavery with the Nazi Holocaust are potentially problematic, the peculiar institution does resemble the Final Solution insomuch as it is "a scandal for rational representation" and "an event which tests our traditional conceptual and representational categories, an 'event at the limits'" (Kellner 399; Friedlander 389).[5] Existing textual conventions may simply be ill-equipped to express exploitation on such a huge scale and the inconceivable horrors it involved in any meaningful way. Half a century after the American Civil War, and a couple of decades before the beginnings of the Holocaust, Victor Shklovsky, the Russian formalist, argued that "as perception becomes habitual, it becomes automatic. . . . Habitualization devours works, clothes, furniture, one's wife, and the fear of war" (19, 20). Consequently, Shklovsky asserts, "the technique of art is to make objects 'unfamiliar,' to make forms difficult," to use an unorthodox approach to make things seem new and startling (20). In historical novels that rely upon traditional forms and familiar archetypes, habitualization is at risk of devouring slavery, rendering it conventional and our responses to it automatic. Postmodern fiction, meanwhile, uses intertextual critique to disrupt and defamiliarize existing means for representing slavery, but it often does not construct the reality of slavery itself in strikingly unusual or newly vivid ways.

Any novelist inclined to tackle the subject of slavery thus faces a substantial series of challenges. How does a novel address prior literary portrayals of slavery without also becoming subject to their tacit rules of representation? How can a novel respond to discursive traditions for representing slavery without reducing a complex reality to a familiar and banal series of literary conventions? How is one to engage in critical dialogue with an existing text about slavery—such as Mitchell's novel—without further confirming its inescapable immortality? How is a work of fiction to participate in existing scholarly debates about slavery and critically examine conventional literary modes for representing the institution without merely reproducing or else simplistically reversing previous discourses? How can a work of fiction engage in dialogue with other texts while also asserting its own innovative historical and literary vision?

Kindred is a landmark text precisely because it wrestles with and provides compelling answers to such questions. It demonstrates precisely how a novel might engage with historical sources and literary traditions while also representing slavery in a powerful and innovative new way. Butler's novel may signify upon works including the fugitive slave narratives and *Roots*, but it also radically defamiliarizes slavery through its unorthodox use of science fiction—the apparent antithesis of the historical novel genre—and the narrative perspective of a twentieth-century woman.

The plot of *Kindred* sounds more than faintly absurd when baldly summarized. Dana is miraculously and mysteriously transported from 1976 to antebellum Maryland to save her slaveholder-ancestor from peril, and she is catapulted back into the present with equally ludicrous convenience whenever her own life is in danger. No rational explanation is ever offered for these incredible occurrences. *Kindred* thus thoroughly disrupts conventional ways of depicting slavery. Yet the novel, while conscious of its blatant unfeasibility, also takes its fantastic premises entirely seriously and frequently asserts its own ultra-realism. As she watches patrollers beat a slave during her second journey into the past, Dana muses: "I had seen people beaten on television and in the movies. I had seen the too-red blood substitute streaked across their backs and heard their well-rehearsed screams. But I hadn't lain nearby and smelled their sweat or heard them pleading and praying, shamed before their families and themselves" (36). In *Kindred*'s rhetoric, a graphically violent and pictorially mimetic portrayal of slavery on TV is utterly unreal, characterized, for all the accuracy of its appearance and de-tails, by false notes—by "too-red blood" and "well-rehearsed screams." These customary ways of representing slavery generate only automatic responses. *Kindred*'s extraordinary plot, in contrast, constantly draws attention to the book's artificiality, provoking readers from the complacency of mechanical reactions. For all the implausibility of her circumstances, however, Butler's text also suggests that Dana's modern perspective of the slave past is strik-ingly authentic in comparison to other representations—"a sharper, stron-ger reality," as she says (191).

Kindred's portrayal of slavery is thus radically unusual, consciously arti-ficial, and yet strangely believable. It makes the peculiar institution a more vivid and horrifying actuality by rendering it less textually conventional. The book's startlingly original manner of portraying slavery allows it to engage with historiographical debates about slavery (such as the Elkins thesis) and conventional literary tropes for representing slavery (including the arche-type of the exceptional slave) without becoming subject to such discourses. *Kindred* does not recycle or simply invert existing textual conventions for representing slavery; it fundamentally reimagines the institution.

In sum, the problem for the novelist is to engage with slavery's historical actuality and its discursive traditions without becoming dependent upon conventional literary formulas for representing the institution and its sub-jects. The slavery novel is at its most illuminating when it transcends tradi-tional forms of expression, rules of representation, and pre-existing genre conventions. *The Confessions of Nat Turner* is a limited text not so much because Styron's Nat is a racist stereotype but because he is a bland cliché—yet another tragically doomed black male rebel in the tradition of Stowe's Dred, Bontemps's Gabriel, and Gaither's Scofield. Beginning in the 1960s, however, some novels—even if they may in other ways be subject to literary conventions for representing slavery—questioned this tired formula and provided intriguing alternatives. For all their traditional realism, *Jubilee* and *The Autobiography of Miss Jane Pittman* organize their narratives around the experiences of resilient black women protagonists both during and after slavery, instead of focusing upon militant but fated male revolutionaries. *The African* and *Roots*, meanwhile, make their black masculine rebels into enduring survivors. These texts emphasize that African Americans had op-tions beyond passive acceptance or futile violent resistance, and these imaginative alternatives to customary formulas encourage readers to think about slavery itself in new ways.[6]

Again, I should emphasize that such approaches are far from exclusive to the age of postmodernism or the post-1960s renaissance of African American fiction about slavery. Shklovsky, after all, first theorized defamiliarization in 1917 and located the technique in nineteenth-century Russian literature. Postmodernism's skepticism of grand universal metanarratives and African American resistance to white discourses have certainly encouraged writers of fiction to transcend common literary conventions and to blur generic boundaries. However, Harriet Beecher Stowe used a similar technique in *Uncle Tom's Cabin*, albeit rather less self-consciously than her twentieth-century successors. After several hundred pages of sentimental realism, the narrative's sudden shift to the gothic mode upon Tom's arrival at the Legree plantation denaturalizes the novel's presentation of slavery. This shift in literary style—from a sort of *Wide, Wide World* of slavery to an institution straight out of Edgar Allan Poe—prepares the reader for the appearance of a more brutal and lethal kind of servitude than the narrative has yet shown. Equally, one of the reasons why *Gone with the Wind* was so popular in its day and remains so enduring is that Scarlett O'Hara is anything but a formula figure. By the 1930s, the virtuous daughter of the plantation was a hoary cliché of plantation fiction—one that even *The Red Cock Crows* simplistically replicates. The willful, capricious, manipulative, self-deluding, and sexually liberated Scarlett, however, was and is a revelation. Much of *Gone with the Wind*'s complexity—and, for all its populism and repugnant white supremacism, it is a richly complicated text—derives from its heroine's moral ambiguity.

While such complexity is not new, *Kindred* nonetheless altered the fictional discourse about slavery in a number of ways. First, it encouraged an engagement with history both as discursive tradition and past reality in subsequent fiction. Second, novels about the institution that have appeared since Butler's text have frequently used the strategy of defamiliarization and have increasingly signified upon literary texts beyond the usual suspects of the fugitive slave narratives and *Gone with the Wind* (*The Wind Done Gone* being an anachronistic exception). *Beloved* is the most obvious example: another novel in which slavery paradoxically becomes more realistic through more fantastic treatment—in this case, through its use of the genre of ghost story. Like *Kindred*, Morrison's novel does not simply parody and critique existing formal conventions for representing slavery; it additionally provides original and arresting strategies for making slavery vividly real through unfamiliarity.

Other texts have followed in *Kindred's* and *Beloved's* footsteps. J. California Cooper's *Family* (1991) defamiliarizes its portrayal of the institution by making its narrator a dead slave. Clora, like Morrison's Sethe, tries to kill her children to save them from the horrors of slavery, but—unlike *Beloved's* protagonist—succeeds only in poisoning herself. She relates the stories of herself and her descendants as an omnipresent spirit. The modern female protagonist of Phyllis Alesia Perry's *Stigmata* (1998), meanwhile, is possessed by the ghosts of her slave ancestors, thus wrenching slavery vividly into the present in a narrative that is at once strikingly inventive and curiously reminiscent of Morrison's tale of haunting and Butler's time travel fable. One spirit that does not haunt any of these novels, however, is the ghost of *Gone with the Wind*.

Edward P. Jones's *The Known World*

In twenty-first-century slavery fiction, one particular novel already stands out for its confident negotiation between unique innovation and comprehensive engagement with existing discourses. This book confidently resists the influence of *Gone with the Wind*, and, although black-authored, cannot be contained by even the broadest definition of the term "neoslave narrative." The recipient of the 2004 Pulitzer Prize for Fiction, Edward P. Jones's *The Known World* participates in historiographical debates and addresses traditional literary constructions for representing slavery, yet it also portrays the institution in provocatively unfamiliar ways. It is skeptical about history as a discipline, and constantly highlights the artifice and limitations of historical studies. Simultaneously, however, the book draws upon the insights of contemporary historiography in its portrayal of slavery as a complex and multifaceted phenomenon rather than a coherent and monolithic institution. *The Known World* also responds actively to existing literary traditions for depicting slavery—particularly the archetypes used to portray nonslaveholding whites—but it thoroughly transcends conventional literary discourses about slavery through its radical defamiliarization of the institution, which is partly achieved through formal techniques, but also through the book's very subject matter: African American slaveholders. *The Known World* proceeds from the template established by *Kindred* and develops the possibilities of the contemporary novel of slavery still further.

It is not possible to provide a concise summary of Jones's vast, fragmented, and extremely populous novel set in fictitious Manchester County, Virginia. The central narrative strand, however, concerns the consequences of the death, in 1855, of a wealthy black slaveholder named Henry Townsend. As a youth, Henry chose his former white master, William Robbins, to be the central influence in his life, but his decision to become a slaveholder has brought him wealth at the cost of offending his free black parents, Augustus and Mildred. A significant secondary plot concerns John Skiffington, the pious local white sheriff, who considers slavery immoral but is obliged to accept a slave named Minerva as a wedding gift. Under pressure from Robbins and other local white planters, furthermore, Skiffington institutes slave patrols. After Henry Townsend's death, some of the patrollers destroy the proud Augustus's free papers and sell him into slavery, where he is killed. Meanwhile, Caldonia, Henry's widow, begins a sexual relationship with Moses, the Townsend driver. Moses comes to believe he will marry Caldonia and take his former master's place. To facilitate this plan, Moses encourages his wife and children to flee to the North, along with a supposedly insane slave named Alice. When Caldonia finally rejects Moses's overtures, he too becomes a fugitive, and finds shelter with Mildred Townsend. John Skiffington tracks Moses down, but there is a tense standoff when Mildred refuses to surrender him, and Skiffington accidentally shoots Mildred dead. In turn, Skiffington's deputy—hoping to seize the opportunity to plunder Mildred's rumored riches—kills the sheriff. The slave patrol cruelly hobbles the captured Moses, but his family and Alice successfully escape to Washington, D.C.

While *The Known World* provides a convincing and vivid portrait of American slavery, it is continually skeptical about the ability of human discourse to adequately represent the past, and the novel persistently emphasizes the limitations of the discipline of history. For example, the narrative satirically draws attention to the problematic nature of antebellum censuses—sources frequently utilized by contemporary historians.[7] The book claims that the state delegate who carried out the census of 1830 was

an unreliable alcoholic and that the 1840 census taker dramatically mis-
estimated the size of Manchester County because "he was unable to take
the measure of the land with the damn mountains in the way." Finally, the
narrative reports that the 1860 census taker utterly misreported the number
of slaves in Manchester County because he "argued with his wife the day
he sent his report to Washington D.C., and all his arithmetic was wrong
because he had failed to carry a one" (22, 23, 7). Censuses are not the only
historical documents about which Jones's text is skeptical. One white character owes a slave named Tom Anderson as payment to a neighbor, but
Anderson mysteriously vanishes in 1842. The neighbor, however, continues
to claim legal ownership of Tom, even enumerating him as an asset in an
1871 revision of his will—several years after the end of slavery. *The Known
World* constantly suggests that primary source documents are unreliable
and often provide no basis for accurate or meaningful historical narratives.
Jones's novel ultimately reveals that a 1912 fire destroyed the judicial records
of Manchester County, which are thus unavailable to historians (176). The
implication is that the notion of accurate history is a contradiction in terms.
Representations of slavery are always necessarily imaginative narratives, and,
the text implies, the creative omniscience of the novelist seems more compelling than the compromised empiricism of the historian.

The Known World features several fictitious historians of both the nineteenth and twentieth centuries. A Canadian named Anderson Frazier pub-
lishes a series of pamphlets in the 1880s entitled "Curiosities and Oddities
about Our Southern Neighbors," one of which concerns black slaveholders.
Frazier's interview with a black slaveholder and teacher named Fern Elston
highlights the limitations of his work, however, because Fern decides not to
be open with him and does not tell "*the truth as I know it in my heart*" about
slavery. We also encounter a historian named Roberta Murphy, author of
a 1979 study about Manchester County that seems to do little more than
obsessively rank the supposedly "momentous" events of the area from Skiffington's tenure as sheriff to the birth of five two-headed dancing chickens
in 1851 (106, 109, 43–44).

Historical studies are not the only form of discourse that the novel shows
to be inadequate to the task of representing the past accurately or mean-
ingfully. *The Known World* also dramatizes the inability of photography to
capture or explain the world. One character is enchanted by a photograph

of a New York family sitting on their porch, with a dog in the yard looking off to the right: "From the first second Calvin had seen the photograph he had been intrigued by what had caught the dog's attention and frozen him forever. He had a very tiny hope that when he got to New York he might be able to find the house and those people and that dog and learn what had transfixed him. There was a whole world off to the right that the photograph had not captured" (189). *The Known World* constantly explores that "world off to the right," the world beyond the immediate frame—which is to say, the world outside the temporal, geographical, and philosophical limits of its immediate subject: Manchester County in the last years of the antebellum era. The dramatic experiences of a few individuals in a single county in 1855 are both self-contained and inextricably connected to larger global and historical patterns. The novel contains multiple moments that place its local narrative in other contexts, including—to mention but a few of the book's myriad examples—the aforementioned studies by postbellum and twentieth-century historians, an immigrant smallpox carrier's family history in the Netherlands, an encounter with a harmoniously multiracial wagon train in Texas, and the future of two Townsend slaves as founders of a Richmond orphanage for whom a street is named in the twentieth century.

However, while the novel constantly emphasizes that human experience is too complex to be captured in language and while it insists that histories are undependable and limited forms of discourse, it also acknowledges that there is a significant and concrete reality toward which such texts gesture. *The Known World* accepts that history may only be available to us as unreliable narrative, but texts are finally the only kind of access we have to very real processes, events, and consequences. History, in other words, may well be bunk, but it is also vitally important. For all its skepticism about historical discourse, therefore, *The Known World* also engages very seriously with theories and debates in the discipline of history regarding American slavery. Even in this respect, however, Jones's novel is highly innovative. Contemporary slavery fiction—from *Jubilee* in 1966 to *Beloved* in 1987—has tended to engage with the Elkins thesis and with the counterarguments of 1970s historians concerned with the slave community, or, alternatively, has focused upon Aptheker's ideas about slave militancy. *The Known World*, in contrast, is the first major novel to address the body of post-1970s historiography that emphasizes the sheer diversity of American slavery.

The novel's fleeting allusions to the Elkins thesis are peripheral and play-fully satirical. Far from suggesting that a slaveholder's influence on a slave or a slave's identification with his master inevitably results in a passive Sambo figure, Jones's novel implies the very opposite. In selecting William Robbins as his significant other rather than his own father, Henry Townsend makes himself into an actively successful slaveholder, not a docile Sambo. In response to those who have extrapolated beyond the Elkins thesis to suggest that the effects of slavery have brought about the permanent retardation of the black race, *The Known World* emphasizes that there is nothing racially specific about Elkins's theories. The narrative describes a white woman named Elizabeth who lives in a remote part of Virginia and is imprisoned by her own slaves, who worked "her ragged with only a few hours rest each day.... When Elizabeth was finally rescued, she did not remember that she was supposed to be the owner and it was a long time before she could be taught that again" (11). Ironically, then, the only individual rendered passive and docile by the experience of slavery in Jones's novel is a white woman. It is as if the novel takes the inadequacy of Elkins's theories as a given, just as its portrayal of the slave community on the Townsend plantation seems to unquestioningly assume that active and functional (if often limited) African American societies and kinship networks existed in slavery.

With the Elkins thesis thoroughly refuted and the slave community studies of the 1970s now widely accepted, such ideas are much less important to *The Known World* than more recent theories about and approaches to slavery. While histories prior to the 1980s tended to make grand arguments about the fundamental natures of slavery and slaves, contemporary historiography asserts that the institution and its subjects were too complex and varied for any broad generalizations to be of particular value. Consequently, recent studies have focused upon specific aspects of slavery in particular times and places. A notable instance of such a work is Charles Joyner's *Down by the Riverside: A South Carolina Slave Community* (1985). Joyner complains that historians of American slavery have tended to "describe *the* slave community without having probed in depth any *particular* slave community" (xvi). *Down by the Riverside* is a corrective in which Joyner makes a comprehensive and detailed effort to recreate the everyday lives of the slaves of thirty-four plantations in the single parish of All Saints in South Carolina, primarily in the 1850s. While Joyner's study explores the applicability of larger theories about slavery—advanced by such scholars as Elkins and John Blassingame—to life in All Saints, it also frequently underlines the fact that this locality was anything but a typical slave parish, and that it would be inappropriate to generalize about slavery based upon this one community (or, correspondingly, to make inferences about any single slave community based upon any broad generalizations).

The Known World takes such notions yet further by emphasizing the very different forms that slavery takes in just one county over just a few decades. There is no monolithic slavery and no single slave community in Manchester, but instead multiple forms of slavery and diverse slave experiences, relations, and societies. Slave life on Robbins's plantation is clearly different from working under a black slaveholder like Henry, which in turn is distinct from being the single slave of a significantly less affluent master. The character of slavery in *The Known World* is extremely complex. It can be a horrifyingly cruel and oppressive system, as the brutal cropping of a fugitive's ear reminds us. But it can also be strangely benevolent and even kind. Barnum Kinsey is a lower-class white who works on the slave patrol and owns a single slave named Jeff. When Jeff falls sick, Barnum and his wife take loving care of him and entertain him by reading aloud from *Poor Richard's Almanac*. Frequently, the novel's characters are themselves confused by the multifaceted nature of slavery and its subjects. A white woman named Clara Martin derives evident sensual pleasure from having her devoted slave, Ralph, brush her hair. After emancipation, Clara's distraught tears cause Ralph to put aside his intentions to join relatives in Washington, D.C., so as to stay and keep his beloved mistress company until her death. For all the intimacy of this relationship, however, Clara actually spends most of her time with Ralph in mortal terror because she has heard tales about slave rebellions and a slave cook who put ground glass in her owner's food. Throughout twenty-one years of close habitation with Ralph, Clara cooks her own food "even though she knew no more about cooking than a bird sitting on a nest" and secures her door every night with nails (42, 151, 163, 164). To Clara, Ralph is a slave, a loyal friend, a loving family member, a life partner, and a potential murderer all at once.

In addition to emphasizing the sheer diversity of American slavery, *The Known World* explores one particular aspect of the institution that contemporary historiography has already highlighted. Among the many variations within slavery that historians have explored since the 1970s is the curious phenomenon of free African Americans who held human property. Michael P. Johnson and James L. Roark's *Black Masters* (1984) tells the story of William Ellison, a mulatto planter in antebellum South Carolina, while Larry Koger's *Black Slaveowners* (1985) focuses upon African American masters in that state.

Highly original as fiction, Jones's novel thus deals with issues that historiography thoroughly addressed twenty years earlier. Like *Black Masters*, *The Known World* explores race as an artificial cultural construct. As Johnson and Roark pithily put it, for a free black in antebellum America, "money sometimes whitened" (xii). They also note that William Ellison "confounds expectations we are tempted to project onto him from our own times. A brown-skinned man who would be called black today, Ellison did not consider himself a black man, but a man of color, a mulatto, a man neither black nor white, a brown man" (xi). The historians assert that the "first step toward understanding Ellison and his world requires abandoning the language of racial identification commonly used today. . . . To Ellison and his friends, a 'black' person had no white ancestors and was most likely a slave; a 'colored' person was the descendant of white and black ancestors and was more likely than a black person to be free" (xv).

The Known World similarly shows how the racial codes of antebellum slavery were at once rigidly fixed and legally codified, yet fluid and entirely arbitrary. Like Johnson and Roark, Jones uses the anomalous figure of the black slaveholder to dismantle such conventional binaries of slavery discourse as "black" and "white." Henry Townsend is richer than many whites in Manchester County, but is darker than his own slave, Moses. As far as his widow, Caldonia, is concerned, only free African Americans are "her people." Furthermore, after having sexual relations with Moses, Caldonia even wonders if she is guilty of "a kind of miscegenation." Meanwhile, Harvey Travis, one of the white patrollers, "wanted to make sure his own children were counted as white [in the 1840 census], though all the world knew his wife was a full-blooded Cherokee. Travis even called his children niggers." The census taker, however, thinks that Travis's children are "too dark for him and the federal government to consider as anything else but black. He told his government the children were slaves and he let it go at that, not saying anything about their white blood or their Indian blood." Locals claim that another lower-class patroller is saved "from bein a nigger only by the color of his skin." In this world, racial categories are not immutable biological facts but culturally constructed, contingent, and changeable labels. *The Known World* also emphasizes that, just as certain people of color could be slaveholders, so could some whites be slaves. In addition to the story of Elizabeth—the mistress enslaved psychologically and literally by her own human property—we learn of a white woman who puts her children on the market to finance a move to Paris and a Dutch immigrant who sells his wife into prostitution (5, 9, 291, 292, 22, 42, 56, 222).

The binary opposition between "black" and "white" is not the only one that the novel complicates. The tale of Elizabeth suggests that the distinction between "slave" and "free" is equally messy and often meaningless. To complicate matters further, the novel also blurs the boundaries between "slave" and "family member." Henry becomes free because Augustus purchases him from Robbins. Consequently, Henry is "listed forever in the records of Manchester as his father's property." Oden Peoples is a full-blooded Cherokee who has "four black slaves. One was his 'mother-in-law.' Another was his 'wife,' who was half Cherokee herself, and the other two were their children." A white couple in Philadelphia are imprisoned for "keeping two free black people as slaves" whom locals assumed were just "part of the family." When the anti-slavery Skiffingtons receive Minerva as a wedding present, they do "not feel like they owned her, not in the way whites and a few blacks owned slaves. Minerva was not free, but only in the way a child in a family is not free" (16, 155, 34, 43).

Despite this complex and multifaceted reality, however, the dominant white culture of the antebellum South sought to impose stark and simple racial codes upon the system of slavery. As Johnson and Roark put it, "Negroes were supposed to be slaves. Free people were supposed to be white" (xiii). The simplistic discourse of black/white and slave/free attempts to impose order upon a complicated and chaotic world. The very existence of a free black individual thoroughly disrupts this discourse. Consequently, Johnson and Roark note, "no free person of color could be confident of freedom in the antebellum South. Freedom marked a Negro as someone whites had to watch" (xv). Slaveholding for the free black protagonists of *The Known World* is essentially a way to codify and safeguard their freedom. It is an attempt to work within the binary oppositions that organize the South. To be a slaveholder is to be the opposite of a slave. If slaves are automatically black, then slaveholding makes one a little whiter, a little freer. *The Known World* notes that free blacks in the antebellum South "knew they were slaves with just another title," and Mildred observes that free papers "don't carry anough freedom," a claim confirmed by Augustus's fate. While the local patrollers intimidate and then enslave the legally free but nonslaveholding Augustus, they learn to leave slaveholding blacks alone after Fern Elston complains to prominent white landholders after the patrol has interrogated her. Fern acknowledges that slavery has forced her to choose a side, to align herself either with the ranks of the slaveholders or the slaves. Fern's conclusion is that she "would not fare very well as a dressmaker's apprentice.'Yessum' and 'Yessuh' do not come easily from my mouth. My hands, my body, they fear the dirt of the field" (252, 113, 131, 289). Jones's fiction is thus very much in accordance with Koger's argument that "free black masters embraced many of the attitudes of the white community even while they remained on the fringe of the [white] society" (3).

While frequently subverting and satirizing the limitations of the discipline of history, then, *The Known World* also acknowledges that we have no choice but to rely upon it to some degree. The book's treatment of literary conventions for representing slavery is very similar. It critically engages with traditional ways of portraying slavery while also thoroughly transcending previous dramatizations in its inventive and disorienting presentation of the institution.

Although Jones's novel is destined to be remembered for its portrayal of black slaveholders, it is also very concerned to interrogate the traditional rules for representing lower-class southern white males in fiction. Often, nonelite whites in the twentieth-century novel of slavery are brutish and usually anonymous foot soldiers of the system, such as the slave hunters who cut off Kunta Kinte's foot in *Roots*, the bigoted overseer of *Jubilee*, and the patrollers who assault Alice's mother in *Kindred*. Such portrayals are in stark contrast to Herbert Aptheker's claim that working-class whites often identified with African American slaves. *The Known World* refuses to portray its lower-class slave patrollers as a monolithic group of violent racists. While most of them are white, one is Cherokee. Some own at least one or two slaves, while some do not. Travis cruelly destroys Augustus's free papers and Oden casually crops ears and slices the tendons of fugitive slaves, but

Barnum Kinsey tries to save Augustus from being illegally sold and reports his abduction.

While slavery fiction and histories of the 1930s and 1940s addressed questions of class in the antebellum South, novels in the last few decades have tended to focus upon identity politics instead. Although it addresses issues of race, gender, and sexuality, *The Known World* reminds us that class was a fundamentally important factor in the social system of the antebellum South. After all, black slaveholders are not distinguished from their human property in racial terms but by the wealth necessary to purchase slaves. John Skiffington's position between the slaveholding aristocracy and the lower-class slave patrol is also revealing. If the Skiffingtons "stayed with a family of means similar to their own, the supper might include couples from the same class and perhaps one, but generally only one, from William Robbins's class. They also stayed with people in Robbins's sphere, but when they ate with them, Skiffington and [his wife] Winifred represented their class alone. As for the class that produced the patrollers, they were a hand-to-mouth people and invitations to anywhere were very rare" (147). Yet, for all the apparent social rigidity on display here, Skiffington's liminal position also reveals that class, like race, is a fluid category. Just as free blacks can become slaveholders, so is the social position of whites not fixed or stable. While Skiffington's social stock rises, his cousin, Counsel, descends from a complacent aristocrat to a hard-up sheriff's deputy.

Much of the novel's drama hinges around John Skiffington's precarious social position. The novel draws attention to the tragic absurdity of Skiffington's place in the class hierarchy, and the cultural pressures that cause him to act in ways that violate his moral principles. So, despite "vowing never to own a slave, Skiffington had no trouble doing his job to keep the institution of slavery going." He also desperately rationalizes his ownership of Minerva, after unexpectedly receiving her as a gift, arguing that the girl "might be better off with us than anywhere else" and choosing to see her not as a slave but as his "child" (43, 34). As sheriff and as the owner of a single slave, Skiffington enjoys relative social prestige, but this is entirely dependent upon the sponsorship of powerful elite whites. His privileged status can be stripped from him at any moment. What Skiffington never seems to understand is that he thus has something fundamental in common with the county's free blacks, whose social position is equally unstable, but because of race, not class.

While Skiffington is a sympathetic character, he, like the book's African American slaveholders, chooses the security of the slavocracy over his better instincts in order to protect his place in the social hierarchy. When order breaks down in Manchester County as fugitives flee the Townsend plantation, Skiffington's position as sheriff is on the line and his social status threatened. We then discover that even a pious and essentially good-hearted man might be capable of violent acts as an instrument of the law within the system of slavery. When he tracks down the fugitive Moses at Mildred's house, Skiffington—troubled by a painful toothache, and intimidated by the presence of his once-aristocratic cousin as his deputy—suddenly finds himself assuming the voice of the slavocracy, tentatively at first, but with increasing authority. He angrily tells Mildred, "I have not come all this way to be denied by a . . . by a nigger. . . . No nigger will stand between me and my duty." When he accidentally kills Mildred, his repressed racism floods out. "I asked nothing of that nigger, except what is proper and right," he says of the deceased Mildred, and tells Counsel to "bring that murderin nigger [Moses—who has not actually killed anyone] out here so we can take him to his owner, to his right and proper owner." Skiffington begins as a principled and humane striver and ends as an unwitting oppressor and tool of the system. In this respect, Skiffington is the white counterpart of Henry Townsend. Henry had once fantasized about being "a master different from any other, the kind of shepherd master God had intended . . . [providing] good food for his slaves, no whippings, short and happy days in the fields" (365, 366, 180). This is far from the ultimate reality for slaves on the Townsend plantation, however. Thus, planter, sheriff, and slave alike are trapped by the institution. Ultimately, then, Skiffington commits similar acts of violence against slaves as his literary predecessors, but he is a much more complex, sympathetic, and tragic figure than previous working-class white upholders of slavery in fiction.

While engaging with such archetypes of the slavery novel, however, *The Known World* is certainly not subject to the traditional rules for representing the institution. Indeed, the novel's portrayal of slavery is quite unique, and its narrative consistently defamiliarizes the institution. This is largely achieved through the book's subject matter. By dealing with black slaveholders, the novel instantly upends all of our most fundamental assumptions and prevents us from responding to the book's construction of slavery automatically. The representation of slavery in previous fiction has usually been predicated on the simple binary oppositions that Jones's novel dismantles. Traditionally, in literature, slaveholders are white and slaves are black. By subverting this custom, *The Known World* defamiliarizes slavery even more thoroughly than Butler's time-traveling protagonist or Morrison's ghost.

It is part of the project of this study, however, to emphasize that today's slavery fiction is never quite as unprecedentedly innovative as we are often tempted to assume. *The Known World* is, in fact, not the first novel to invert the racial hierarchies of slavery. As far back as 1924, Mary Johnston's *The Slave Ship* disrupted traditional expectations not by portraying black slaveholders, but by detailing the exploits of a white slave who becomes a slave-trader. Johnston's novel concerns David Scott, a Jacobite rebel shipped to Virginia for permanent indentured servitude alongside African American slaves, who escapes only to find himself aboard a slave ship. Wracked continually by guilt, Scott nonetheless spends ten years as a slaver, eventually becoming captain of the vessel, until, on landing in Virginia, he is recognized by his former master and returns to bondage almost gratefully. Johnston's novel provides a devastating portrait of slaveholder psychology and the way in which an owner of other humans rationalizes and justifies his power. Just like Jones's text, *The Slave Ship* depicts the temptations of slaveholding in a world in which one has to choose between joining the ranks of the oppressors or the oppressed—a view akin to that of Fern Elston in *The Known World*. The existence of Johnston's novel is yet one more reminder that inventive and unorthodox fiction about slavery is not simply a contemporary phenomenon, and that we need to rediscover and reexamine the forgotten literature of the past.

It is not only through its subject matter, however, that *The Known World* defamiliarizes slavery; its formal strategies are also crucial. In one of the first reviews of Jones's book, Jonathan Yardley describes it as "a Victorian novel transplanted to Ol' Dixie," complete with consciously anachronistic chapter subtitles that gesture obliquely toward the action to come, such as "A Mule Stands Up. Of Cadavers and Kisses and Keys. An American Poet Speaks of Poland and Mortality" (Yardley). *The Known World* is indeed a sort of *Middlemarch* of American slavery. This seems a fairly simple, if effective concept: the application of a nineteenth-century literary form (the large-scale British social novel) to a nineteenth-century subject (American slavery), but it is also a unique one—previous fiction about slavery usually having worked within the genre of historical melodrama or the American plantation romance, or, more recently, science fiction, ghost story, and post-modern fantasia. On one hand, this choice allows *The Known World* to pursue traditional social realism, but, on the other, the novel is also an ironic and parodic invocation of an earlier literary form.

Neither is the novel purely a faux-Victorian panorama. As Yardley also observes, there are "hints herein of Toni Morrison and Gabriel García Márquez, as Jones makes an occasional wry gesture toward the fantastic and moves smoothly back and forth in time" (Yardley). Episodes concerning two slave children who share identical dreams and another slave's encounter with a flying cabin during a thunderstorm are among those that disrupt the verisimilitude of the novel. Some reviewers were unimpressed by *The Known World*'s postmodernist or magical realist elements. Annoyed by the constant references beyond the story's immediate frame—such as the frequent mentions of later historians and the distant futures of the characters—Alan Cheuse complains that the "frequent insertion of the research materials into the story itself creates a persistently distracting temporal perspective. . . . Whether true or false, they distract a reader from the immediate narrative, breaking up the time frame and constantly reminding us that we are reading a reconstruction of a time and place. . . . Those interjected references to all the tomorrows that follow after the characters have long since passed away make for an annoying, sometimes even irritating narrative rhythm" ("When"). What Cheuse calls distraction and "irritating narrative rhythm," Shklovsky would call defamiliarization. The techniques Cheuse disparages are crucial to the novel's meanings. Jones's text creates a believable world that it also persistently disrupts in order to jolt the reader from automatic responses to a literary representation of slavery. *The Known World*'s commitment to traditional realism and its informed engagement with historiography is balanced by its skeptical attitude toward history as a discipline and its unsettling metafictional characteristics.

Nobody could mistake *The Known World* for a simplistic protest fiction that exists merely to critique the horrors of slavery. Jones's novel rebuffs any attempt to draw facile moral conclusions from the events it portrays. Its characters are complex, thoroughly evading any simplistic labels we might be inclined to impose upon them. *The Known World* refuses all generalizations about slavery and history. It also rejects easy binary oppositions, including the notion that radical countervisions of the institution challenge a hegemonic master narrative about it.

This becomes clear in the way in which the narrative contrasts two works of art: Skiffington's sixteenth-century woodcut map, "The Known World"—supposedly the first map to include the word *America*—and Alice's artistic renderings of Manchester County, which she displays in Washington, D.C., after her escape from slavery. North America, on Skiffington's map, "was smaller than it was in actuality, and where Florida should have been, there was nothing. South America seemed the right size, but it alone of the two continents was called 'America.' North America went nameless." When Caldonia's brother, Calvin, describes Alice's two works of art, he emphasizes their comprehensiveness and close correlation to reality. The first is a rendering of Manchester County, "*a map of life made with every kind of art man has ever thought to represent himself. Yes, clay. Yes, paint. Yes, cloth. There are no people on this 'map,' just all the houses and barns and roads and cemeteries and wells.*" The second work is a representation of the Townsend plantation, with "*nothing missing, not a cabin, not a barn, not a chicken, not a horse. Not a single person is missing.*" Calvin describes both of Alice's maps as showing "*what God sees when He looks down*" (174, 384, 385).

Some readers may well be tempted to interpret Alice's paintings of Manchester County as an authentic African American alternative to the dubious European metanarrative of Skiffington's "The Known World." Alice's artwork is authentic, unrefined folk art that possesses an omniscient and complete vision, whereas Skiffington's map is official, but inaccurate and outdated. Alice's paintings simply but imaginatively present the world without comment, whereas "The Known World" affixes artificial labels to a flawed but supposedly scientific rendition of it. Like many historical narratives, Skiffington's map presents itself as a factual representation, but is really an imaginative construction, a work of art. Just as some critics refer to a contemporary African American literature that challenges a traditionalist white historiography, so does Alice's creative, organic, and socially engaged black portrayal of reality seem truer and more meaningful than the grand, methodical, European depiction of "The Known World."

This study, however, is skeptical of readings organized around such simple oppositions. The contrasting canvasses that appear in *The Known World* constitute part of the novel's more complex negotiation with the discipline of history. While the superiority of Alice's paintings to Skiffington's map demonstrates the power of the literary imagination over the limitations of empirical discourse, these scenes also echo contemporary historiography's focus upon the specific and the local instead of the global and general. Alice's paintings are an artistic equivalent of a census in that they include all the houses of Manchester County and every person, cabin, and piece of livestock on the Townsend plantation. However, they are not statistical enumerations that are subject to massive human error, like the censuses of 1830, 1840, and 1860, but one individual's imaginative perception of a locality and its people. As we zoom in from the aerial view of Manchester County to that of the Townsend plantation specifically, we are able to see what is most important about the world, that which abstract studies effectively erase: the human figure. In Alice's art, each person's face is raised as though to look directly into the eyes of the viewer. Their simple humanity is unavoidable.

In this respect, Alice's art is akin to the project of contemporary historiography, in that it is focused upon the experiences of particular people in specific places instead of portraying slavery as a general phenomenon. It is important to note, however, that the relationship between Skiffington's map and Alice's art is not entirely one of contrast. Taken together, the three works present a series that takes us from the entire planet through a particular county to a single plantation. Alice's art is not in opposition to Skiffington's map; rather, it contextualizes it. Taken alone, Alice's art is limited by dint of its parochial nature, whereas Skiffington's map is inadequate because of its expansive, continental vision. For all its inaccuracies, however, Skiffington's map provides an overarching vision in relation to Alice's local one. They possess much less meaning in isolation than they do when read in dynamic relation with one another. Similarly, historians concerned with particular aspects or localities of slavery also explore grand theories about the institution as a whole in relation to its localized manifestations. Joyner's study of All Saints, for example, considers the relevance of Blassingame's arguments to that region.

Skiffington's outdated map also reminds the reader that our own paradigms for understanding the world may be limited as well. The meanings of the world are never fixed. New narratives, new theories, and new discoveries constantly oblige us to redraw our mental maps and to reconsider the world that we thought we knew, including the world of slavery. Contrary to the unexamined implications of earlier narratives, not only was slavery not a monolithic institution across the South for more than two hundred years, it was not even coherent or consistent in a single county over just a couple of decades. *The Known World* emphasizes that the world of slavery that we believe we know is less clearly mapped than we thought.

The world known to slaveholders and slaves is not a world known to us. We in the twentieth and twenty-first centuries project our own biases and values upon the antebellum South. Jones's novel acknowledges—in Jamesian fashion—the impossibility of recapturing the psychology of an earlier era, but it also purports to show it to us as it was known by slaveholders and slaves. *The Known World* portrays slavery as a far more complex phenomenon than we may have ever conceived—in Manchester County alone. Like this study, then, Jones's novel complicates common assumptions about slavery and its representations in discourse. It dismantles the opposition between black and white, between history and fiction, and it rejects the notion of a single coherent master narrative versus oppositional, authentic countervisions in favor of a complicated chorus of narratives—a cacophonous but beautiful series of calls and responses.

Conclusion

BEYOND BLACK AND WHITE

*T*his study demonstrates that the contemporary novel of slavery has *not* torn down a monolithic version of history that ruled unchallenged for two centuries or more. Nonetheless, novels about slavery continue to perform valuable cultural work, as they always have done. They engage knowledgeably, imaginatively, and accessibly with specific interpretations and theories advanced in the discipline of history. Literary scholarship often suggests that recent historical novels possess radical insight that supposedly dull, dusty, and conservative historiography lacks. It is more the case that the depiction of slavery in fiction essentially parallels discourses in the discipline of history. *Black Thunder* and *The Red Cock Crows* were almost exact contemporaries of, respectively, James Carroll's and Herbert Aptheker's studies of slave rebellion. Even so innovative a work of fiction as *Kindred* portrays the institution of slavery and its effects upon individuals in similar terms to Eugene Genovese's *Roll, Jordan, Roll.*

The real achievement of such fiction has been to bring debates about slavery out of the academy and into the wider cultural arena. Whether or not Abraham Lincoln really called Harriet Beecher Stowe "the little lady who made this big war," the implications of this legend are clear. Stowe took existing arguments about slavery and explored them in a vivid, critical, accessible, and widely circulated form. Similarly, millions in our own time who are not familiar with such historians as Stanley Elkins or John Blassingame have nonetheless considered questions about slave subjectivities, communities, and resistance via the pages of such novels as *The Confessions of Nat*

Turner, Roots, Kindred, and *Beloved.* Contemporary fiction is not in opposition to historiography; it is often its popular transmitter. The simplistic but pervasive notion in literary studies that the discipline of history is—or was until very recently—characterized by a monolithic, hegemonic orthodoxy obscures this plain fact and encourages the view that contemporary novels challenge rather than participate in the discourses of history. American fiction about slavery is not a rigidly polemical or narrowly didactic literature. It is not a genre that was once essentially supportive of "the status quo" and is now fundamentally oppositional and subversive. Instead, the historical novel has always engaged in imaginative dialogue with nonfiction accounts of the past. It thus enables a broad audience to participate in the same interpretive arguments and debates that historians routinely wrestle over.

This is not the only kind of dialogue that characterizes slavery fiction. Novels on the topic not only engage with historiography but also with each other, from the "anti-Tom" novels that responded to Stowe's famous text to *Kindred*'s critical allusions to *Roots.* It is also important to attend to the calls and responses between black and white writers in the cultural conversation about slavery. The emphasis upon fiction by African American authors in current literary scholarship is quite understandable, since writers of color have been responsible for the most notable achievements in American slavery fiction since at least the sixties. In my own pantheon of novels about the institution, *Kindred, Beloved,* and *The Known World* are the most prominent. It is a mistake, however, to neglect the contributions of white writers to the cultural discourse about slavery, or to characterize white-authored novels and histories as essentially antagonistic to the black-authored fiction we find so compelling. Even works produced by white novelists that are commonly criticized for their racism have played the important role of inspiring literary responses. *Flight to Canada* talks back to Harriet Beecher Stowe's representations of American slaves, while *The Wind Done Gone*'s primary raison d'être is its intertextual relationship with *Gone with the Wind.* Furthermore, white-authored texts have often done much more than merely inspire critical countervisions. *The Red Cock Crows* provides a sympathetic portrait of slave rebels, while *Mandingo* bluntly dramatizes the callous exploitation of slavery. The same black critics who resented William Styron's attempts to recreate the character of Nat Turner were impressed by Daniel Panger's fictionalization of the Southampton insurrection in *Ol'*

Prophet Nat. Finally, *Property's* despairing portrait of the psychology of the plantation mistress complicates the optimism of *Dessa Rose's* depiction of a woman slaveholder's growing enlightenment and interracial friendships. In sum, the cultural conversation about slavery is—and always has been— characterized by intertextual, interdisciplinary, and interracial dialogue.

Nonetheless, for all the fundamental continuities in the national discourses concerning slavery, American fiction about the subject also developed in significant and profound ways in the twentieth century—and it continues to develop in the twenty-first. It is not sufficient, however, to simply attribute these developments to the emergence of a body of African American fiction about the institution after the 1960s. Such a view neglects the significance of earlier novels by both black and white writers that engage in sophisticated dialogue with each other as well as with historical studies of slavery. Scholars are right to celebrate and analyze the notable works of such writers as Toni Morrison, Sherley Anne Williams, Octavia Butler, and Charles Johnson, but the almost exclusive emphasis upon contemporary authors tends to eclipse the importance of earlier African American novelists, including Arna Bontemps, Frank Yerby, Margaret Walker, and Harold Courlander, as well as white writers such as Frances Gaither, Mary Johnston, and even Kyle Onstott.

Existing criticism also tends to overstate postmodernism's potential to revolutionize historical fiction. While postmodernism provides valuable strategies for interrogating literary and cultural conventions for representing slavery, its anti-totalizing tendencies and its emphasis upon discourse effectively prohibit novelists from advancing fully developed interpretations about the actual conditions of the institution. Postmodernism deconstructs metanarratives, but only a more traditionalist approach to historical reality allows for the assertion of compelling alternative narratives about the past.

Kindred's pioneering approach was to make an informed, coherent, and persuasive argument about what slavery actually may have been like, while simultaneously drawing critical attention to the ways in which slavery has conventionally been represented in American culture. *Kindred* thus ushered in a contemporary hybrid form of the historical novel that draws upon postmodern literary techniques (such as intertextual parody, blurring of genres, and fictive self-conscious) and marries them to more traditionally realist impulses (such as constructing believable worlds and characters in which readers are invested). This fiction stages a postmodern exploration of history as a discursive field while also making compelling arguments about the nature of slavery and slave identities in reality, thus engaging with and contributing to contemporary historiographical discourses about the past. Kimberly Chabot Davis correctly reads Morrison's *Beloved* as just such a hybrid, arguing that "while the novel exhibits a postmodern skepticism of sweeping historical narratives of 'Truth,' and of Marxist teleological notions of time as diachronic, it also retains an African American and modernist political commitment to the crucial importance of deep cultural memory, of keeping the past alive in order to construct a better future" (242).

This development was an entirely necessary one in historical fiction, for the division between history as past reality and history as discursive field is a false dichotomy. History is necessarily *both* of these things. The past actually existed, even if it is available to us only through discourse. Consequently, literature that approaches history only as a discursive field *or* only as a past reality possesses an incomplete view. Most contemporary historical novels acknowledge that textual discourses refer to an actual if not fully accessible past, and they address both these dimensions of "history."

As we step further into the twenty-first century, literary and cultural representations of slavery appear to be less popular than they once were. *Uncle Tom's Cabin, Gone with the Wind,* and *Roots* were publishing sensations and hugely popular phenomena on stage, film, and TV respectively. However, while the Nobel Prize and Oprah Winfrey may have helped to make Toni Morrison's novels bestsellers, the commercial failure of the movie adaptation of *Beloved* (1998) was matched only by the equally cool popular reception of Spielberg's *Amistad* (1997). Perhaps partly because of such box office disappointments, Spike Lee abandoned plans to film Styron's *The Confessions of Nat Turner,* which had the potential to be an immensely valuable dialogue about American slavery between a black director and a white novelist.[1]

If the general public and popular media seem to have become oblivious to America's peculiar institution, the novel of slavery has arguably never been healthier. By negotiating between the traditional idea of history as past reality and the postmodern emphasis on history as a discursive field—and by modulating between historiographical debates about slavery and literary representations of the institution—the novel of slavery has continued to develop and remains an extremely compelling form. The twenty-first century has already revealed itself to be a fertile and promising era for the novel of American slavery. In addition to *Property* and *The Known World*, there has also been *Lion's Blood* (2002), Steven Barnes's intriguing tale of an alternative past in which the New World was populated by African Muslims and their Irish slaves. The signs suggest that the calls and responses between races, disciplines, and texts on the subject of slavery have barely begun.

APPENDIX

Major Historical Studies, Fiction, Drama, Films, and TV
Presentations since 1918 concerning Slavery in the United States

The following is not intended to be an exhaustively comprehensive survey. So many works have addressed American slavery in one form or another that to catalog them all is neither feasible nor desirable. The purpose of this appendix is to give the reader a clear timeline of the general historical development of the cultural conversation about slavery in a variety of genres. I have elected to date the chronology back beyond *Gone with the Wind* to 1918—the end of World War I and the year that Ulrich Phillips's *American Negro Slavery* was published.

This appendix is least comprehensive in its treatment of historiography. Of the thousands of existing historical studies of slavery, I have limited myself to fewer than one hundred particularly significant and representative works here. The list barely mentions, for example, studies of the slave trade, the Civil War, and abolitionism, and it largely neglects edited collections and volumes of primary source material. For fuller information, I refer the reader to the many useful bibliographies that have been compiled by professional historians: a good starting point is the excellent bibliographical essay in Peter Kolchin's *American Slavery, 1619–1877*.

The primary aim of this chronology is to clarify the extent to which modern American fiction has been concerned with slavery. I hope it will introduce the reader to several neglected works—including some not addressed in this study, such as Frances Gaither's *Follow the Drinking Gourd* and Edmund Fuller's novelistic treatment of the life of Frederick Douglass, *A Star Pointed North*. I have tended to exclude texts that emphasize *only* the experiences of the white ruling class—most obviously the legions of tedious plantation potboilers—as well as some interesting novels on tangentially relevant subjects, such as abolitionism (including several significant books about John Brown).

This appendix also cites a significant number of twentieth-century dramatic works about slavery—an area largely neglected by scholars. The frequent focus of plays upon slave rebellions and resistance—including several works about Nat Turner, Dorothy Heyward's dramatization of the Denmark Vesey conspiracy, an adaptation of the life of Harriet Tubman, and Clifford Mason's *Gabriel*—is particularly notable, intriguing, and worthy of further study.

Natalie Zemon Davis explores several cinematic representations of slavery in *Slaves on Screen* (2000), but a wide-ranging study of the treatment of the institution on film remains to be written. It would be particularly interesting to see scholarly explorations of such neglected and unusual works as *Uncle Tom without a Cabin* (a 1929 comedy short), *Slave Ship*, *Slaves*, and *Manderlay* alongside analysis of such culturally prominent motion pictures as *Gone with the Wind*, *Mandingo*, *Amistad*, and Jonathan Demme's adaptation of *Beloved*.

YEAR	HISTORICAL STUDIES	FICTION	DRAMA, FILM, AND TV
1918	Ulrich B. Phillips, *American Negro Slavery*		*Uncle Tom's Cabin* (dir. J. Searle Dawley)
1919			*Uncle Tom without a Cabin* (dir. Edward F. Cline, Ray Hunt)
1924		Mary Johnston, *The Slave Ship*	
1926		Stark Young, *Heaven Trees*	
1927			*Uncle Tom's Cabin* (dir. Harry A. Pollard) *Topsy and Eva* (dir. Del Lord)
1929	Ulrich B. Phillips, *Life and Labor in the Old South*		
1930			May Miller, *Harriet Tubman*
1934			Randolph Edmunds, *Nat Turner*
1935			Georgia Douglas Johnson, *Frederick Douglass* *So Red the Rose* (dir. King Vidor)
1936		Margaret Mitchell, *Gone with the Wind* Arna Bontemps, *Black Thunder* William Faulkner, *Absalom, Absalom!*	
1937			*Slave Ship* (dir. Tay Garnet)
1938	Joseph C. Carroll, *Slave Insurrections in the United States, 1800–1865*	Allen Tate, *The Fathers*	*Jezebel* (dir. William Wyler)
1939			*Gone with the Wind* (dir. Victor Fleming)

Continued

YEAR	HISTORICAL STUDIES	FICTION	DRAMA, FILM, AND TV
1940		Willa Cather, *Sapphira and the Slave Girl*; Frances Gaither, *Follow the Drinking Gourd*	
1941	Melville J. Herskovits, *The Myth of the Negro Past*		
1942		John Weld, *Sabbath Has No End*; Philip Van Doren Stern, *The Drums of Morning*	
1943	Herbert Aptheker, *American Negro Slave Revolts*		
1944		Frances Gaither, *The Red Cock Crows*	Paul Peters, *Nat Turner*
1946	Frank Tannenbaum, *Slave and Citizen: The Negro in the Americas*	Frank Yerby, *The Foxes of Harrow*; Edmund Fuller, *A Star Pointed North*	
1947	John Hope Franklin, *From Slavery to Freedom*		*The Foxes of Harrow* (dir. John Stahl); Dorothy Heyward, *Set My People Free*
1949	E. Franklin Frazier, *The Negro Family in the United States*	Frances Gaither, *Double Muscadine*	
1956	Kenneth Stampp, *The Peculiar Institution: Slavery in the Ante-Bellum South*	Robert Penn Warren, *Band of Angels*	
1957		Kyle Onstott, *Mandingo*	*Band of Angels* (dir. Raoul Walsh)
1959	Stanley Elkins, *Slavery: A Problem in American Institutional and Intellectual Life*		
1961			Jack Kirkland, *Mandingo* (adaptation)

Year				
1962	Daniel Mannix and Malcolm Cowley, *Black Cargoes: A History of the Atlantic Slave Trade, 1518–1865*		Kyle Onstott, *Drum*	Martin Duberman, *In White America*
1964	John Lofton, *Insurrection in South Carolina: The Turbulent World of Denmark Vesey* Richard C. Wade, "The Vesey Plot: A Reconsideration," *Journal of Southern History* Richard C. Wade, *Slavery in the Cities: The South, 1820–1860*		Kyle Onstott, *Master of Falconhurst*	
1965		Ronald L. Fair, *Many Thousand Gone: An American Fable*	*Onkel Toms Hütte (Uncle Tom's Cabin)* (dir. Géza von Radványi)	
1966	David Brion Davis, *The Problem of Slavery in Western Culture* Herbert Aptheker, *Nat Turner's Slave Rebellion* (written 1937)	Margaret Walker, *Jubilee*		
1967	Eugene Genovese, *The Political Economy of Slavery: Studies in the Economy and Society of the Slave South*	Williams Styron, *The Confessions of Nat Turner* Daniel Panger, *Ol' Prophet Nat* Harold Courlander, *The African*	Amiri Baraka, *Slave Ship*	
1968	Winthrop D. Jordan, *White over Black: American Attitudes toward the Negro, 1550–1812*	John Henrik Clarke, ed., *William Styron's Nat Turner: Ten Black Writers Respond*	Clifford Mason, *Gabriel*	
1969	Eugene Genovese, *The World the Slaveholders Made: Two Essays in Interpretation*	John Oliver Killens, *Slaves* (novelization)	*Slaves* (dir. Herbert Biberman)	
1970	Anne Firor Scott, *The Southern Lady: From Pedestal to Politics, 1830–1930*			

Continued

YEAR	HISTORICAL STUDIES	FICTION	DRAMA, FILM, AND TV
1970	Robert S. Starobin, *Industrial Slavery in the Old South*		
1971	Ann J. Lane, ed., *The Debate over Slavery: Stanley Elkins and His Critics* Carl N. Degler, *Neither Black Nor White: Slavery and Race Relations in Brazil and the United States*	Ernest Gaines, *The Autobiography of Miss Jane Pittman*	
1972	John Blassingame, *The Slave Community: Plantation Life in the Antebellum South* George P. Rawick, *From Sundown to Sunup: The Making of the Black Community* (Vol. 1 of *The American Slave: A Composite Autobiography*) Gerald W. Mullin, *Flight and Rebellion: Slave Resistance in Eighteenth-Century Virginia* John Oliver Killens, *Great Gittin' Up Morning: A Biography of Denmark Vesey*		*Charcoal Black* (dir. Chris Robinson)
1974	Eugene Genovese, *Roll, Jordan Roll: The World the Slaves Made* Robert William Fogel and Stanley L. Engerman, *Time on the Cross: The Economics of American Negro Slavery* Ira Berlin, *Slaves without Masters: The Free Negro in the Antebellum South*		*The Autobiography of Miss Jane Pittman* (TV)

1975	Edmund S. Morgan, *American Slavery, American Freedom: The Ordeal of Colonial Virginia*	*Mandingo* (dir. Richard Fleischer)
	Stephen B. Oates, *The Fires of Jubilee: Nat Turner's Fierce Rebellion*	
	Herbert Gutman, *Slavery and the Numbers Game: A Critique of "Time on the Cross"*	
1976	Herbert Gutman, *The Black Family in Slavery and Freedom, 1750–1925*	Alex Haley, *Roots*
	Leslie H. Owens, *This Species of Property: Slave Life and Culture in the Old South*	Ishmael Reed, *Flight to Canada*
	Paul A. David et al., *Reckoning with Slavery: A Critical Study in the Quantitative History of American Negro Slavery*	*Drum* (dir. Steve Carver)
1977	Lawrence W. Levine, *Black Culture and Black Consciousness: Afro-American Folk Thought from Slavery to Freedom*	*Roots* (TV)
	Nathan Huggins, *Black Odyssey: The Afro-American Ordeal in Slavery*	
1978	Albert Raboteau, *Slave Religion: The "Invisible Institution" in the Antebellum South*	*A Woman Called Moses* (TV)
	Thomas L. Webber, *Deep like the Rivers: Education in the Slave Quarter Community, 1831–1865*	

Continued

YEAR	HISTORICAL STUDIES	FICTION	DRAMA, FILM, AND TV
1979	Eugene Genovese, *From Rebellion to Revolution: Afro-American Slave Revolts in the Making of the Modern World* William Van Deburg, *The Slave Drivers: Black Agricultural Labor Supervisors in the Antebellum South*	Octavia Butler, *Kindred* Barbara Chase-Riboud, *Sally Hemings* Frank Yerby, *A Darkness at Ingraham's Crest*	
1980		Octavia Butler, *Wild Seed*	
1981	Vincent Harding, *There Is a River: The Black Struggle for Freedom in America* James A. Rawley, *The Transatlantic Slave Trade: A History*	David Bradley, *The Chaneysville Incident*	
1982	Orlando Patterson, *Slavery and Social Death: A Comparative Study* James Oakes, *The Ruling Race: A History of American Slaveholders* Catherine Clinton, *The Plantation Mistress: Woman's World in the Old South* Willie Lee Rose, *Slavery and Freedom* (ed. William Freehling)	Charles Johnson, *Oxherding Tale*	*A House Divided: Denmark Vesey's Rebellion* (TV)
1984	Charles Joyner, *Down by the Riverside: A South Carolina Slave Community* John B. Boles, *Black Southerners, 1619–1869*		*Solomon Northup's Odyssey* (TV) *House of Dies Drear* (TV)

Year			
	Michael P. Johnson and James L. Roark, *Black Masters: A Free Family of Color in the Old South*		
	William Van Deburg, *Slavery and Race in American Popular Culture*		
1985	Deborah Gray White, *Ar'n't I a Woman? Female Slaves in the Plantation South*		
1986	August Meier and Elliott Rudwick, *Black History and the Historical Profession, 1915–1980*	Sherley Anne Williams, *Dessa Rose*	
1987	Sterling Stuckey, *Slave Culture: Nationalist Theory and the Foundations of Black America*	Toni Morrison, *Beloved*	*Uncle Tom's Cabin* (TV)
	Mechal Sobel, *The World They Made Together: Black and White Values in Eighteenth-Century Virginia*		
	Peter Kolchin, *Unfree Labor: American Slavery and Russian Serfdom*		
1988	Elizabeth Fox-Genovese, *Within the Plantation Household: Black and White Women of the Old South*		
1989	Peter J. Parish, *Slavery: History and Historians*	Allan Gurganus, *Oldest Living Confederate Widow Tells All*	
		Barbara Chase-Riboud, *Echo of Lions*	
1990	James Oakes, *Slavery and Freedom: An Interpretation of the Old South*	Charles Johnson, *Middle Passage*	Robert Alexander, *I Ain't Yo Uncle: The New Jack Revisionist "Uncle Tom's Cabin"*
1991	Sylvia Frey, *Water from the Rock: Black Resistance in a Revolutionary Age*	J. California Cooper, *Family*	

Continued

YEAR	HISTORICAL STUDIES	FICTION	DRAMA, FILM, AND TV
1991	Melton A. McLaurin, *Celia: A Slave* William S. McFeely, *Frederick Douglass*		
1992	Ann Patton Malone, *Sweet Chariot: Slave Family and Household Structure in Nineteenth-Century Louisiana* Sidney W. Mintz and Richard Price, *The Birth of African-American Culture: An Anthropological Perspective*		
1993	Peter Kolchin, *American Slavery, 1619–1877* Douglas R. Egerton, *Gabriel's Rebellion: The Virginia Slave Conspiracies of 1800 and 1802* Winthrop Jordan, *Tumult and Silence at Second Creek: An Inquiry into a Civil War Slave Conspiracy*	Alex Haley and David Stevens, *Queen*	*Queen* (TV)
1994		Fred D'Aguiar, *The Longest Memory* Barbara Chase-Riboud, *The President's Daughter* Louise Meriwether, *Fragments of the Ark*	*Race to Freedom: The Underground Railroad* (TV) *Oldest Living Confederate Widow Tells All* (TV)
1995		Lorene Cary, *The Price of a Child*	*The Journey of August King* (TV)
1996			*Robert O'Hara, Insurrection: Holding History*
1997	James Sidbury, *Ploughshares into Swords: Race, Rebellion, and Identity in Gabriel's Virginia, 1730–1810*		*Amistad* (dir. Steven Spielberg)

1998	Steven Weisenburger, *Modern Medea: A Family Story of Slavery and Child-Murder from the Old South*	Phyllis Alesia Perry, *Stigmata*	*Beloved* (dir. Jonathan Demme)
	Joanne Pope Melish, *Disowning Slavery: Gradual Emancipation and "Race" in New England, 1780–1860*		
	Edward Ball, *Slaves in the Family*		
1999	Douglas R. Egerton, *He Shall Go Out Free: The Lives of Denmark Vesey*		
	David Robertson, *Denmark Vesey*		
	Edward A. Pearson, ed., *Designs against Charleston: The Trial Record of the Denmark Vesey Slave Conspiracy of 1822*		
	John Hope Franklin and Loren Schweninger, *Runaway Slaves: Rebels on the Plantation*		
	Walter P. Johnson, *Soul by Soul: Life inside the Antebellum Slave Market*		
	John David Smith, *Slavery, Race, and American History: Historical Conflict, Trends, and Method, 1866–1953*		
2001	Michael P. Johnson, "The Making of a Slave Conspiracy: Part 1," *William and Mary Quarterly*	Alice Randall, *The Wind Done Gone*	
2002	Douglas Egerton et al., "The Making of a Slave Conspiracy: Part 2," *William and Mary Quarterly*	Steven Barnes, *Lion's Blood*	

Continued

YEAR	HISTORICAL STUDIES	FICTION	DRAMA, FILM, AND TV
2003	Ira Berlin, *Generations of Captivity: A History of African-American Slaves* David Brion Davis, *Challenging the Boundaries of Slavery* Wilma A. Dunaway, *The African-American Family in Slavery and Emancipation*	Edward P. Jones, *The Known World* Valerie Martin, *Property* Steven Barnes, *Zulu Heart*	*Nat Turner: A Troublesome Property* (dir. Charles Burnett)
2004	Jonathan D. Martin, *Divided Mastery: Slave Hiring in the American South*		
2005	Betty Wood, *Slavery in Colonial America, 1619–1776*	Nancy Rawles, *My Jim*	*Manderlay* (dir. Lars Von Trier)
2006	David Brion Davis, *Inhuman Bondage: The Rise and Fall of Slavery in the New World*		

NOTES

Introduction

1. In terms of the number of texts considered in detail, this is an uncommonly wide-ranging study. Inevitably, however, there are numerous twentieth-century novels about slavery that I do not have sufficient space to discuss in depth—and many that are barely mentioned at all. See the appendix for a broad chronological listing of relevant fiction. Among the best critical works on slavery fiction are William Van Deburg, *Slavery and Race in American Popular Culture* (1984), Ashraf Rushdy, *Neo-slave Narratives* (1999), and Angelyn Mitchell, *The Freedom to Remember* (2002).

2. See, for example, Rushdy's treatment of Styron's *The Confessions of Nat Turner* in *Neo-slave Narratives*.

3. In addition to the critical works by Hutcheon, McHale, A. Mitchell, Rushdy, and Van Deburg addressed in this introduction, other relevant literary scholarship on postmodern and contemporary African American historical fiction includes Robert Holton, *Jarring Witnesses* (1994), Venetria K. Patton, *Women in Chains* (2000), Deborah E. McDowell and Arnold Rampersad, eds., *Slavery and the Literary Imagination* (1989), and Albert E. Stone, *The Return of Nat Turner* (1992).

4. Van Deburg provides brief but useful analyses of Trowbridge's *Cudjo's Cave* (1863) and Sargent's *Peculiar* (1864) (90–91). He critiques black poets Daniel Webster Davis, James David Corrothers, and James Edwin Campbell (98).

5. See Higginson, *Black Rebellion* (1969), which collects the author's *Atlantic Monthly* articles from the 1850s and 1860s on slave rebellions.

6. Peter Parish's *Slavery* (1989) is an excellent survey of the central debates in the historiography of American slavery since the 1950s. Peter Kolchin's *American Slavery, 1619–1877* (1993) is the definitive contemporary synthesis of existing slavery scholarship.

7. See John David Smith, "James Ford Rhodes, Woodrow Wilson, and the Passing of the Amateur Historian of Slavery," in *Slavery, Race, and American History* (1999).

8. See my analysis of Rhodes's passages on slavery in *History of the United States from the Compromise of 1850*, vol. 1 (1893), in chapter 2.

9. See my treatment of Phillips's *American Negro Slavery* (1918) in chapter 1.

10. See William Wells Brown, *The Black Man* (1863), and George Washington Williams, *History of the Negro Race in America, 1619-1880* (1882). Carter Woodson produced several books, including *The Negro in Our History* (1928) and *The Education of the Negro prior to 1861* (1919), and won renown as the "Father of Black History" (Van Deburg 132). W. E. B. Du Bois published several works that deal either directly or peripherally with slavery, including *The Suppression of the African Slave-Trade to the United States of America* (1896), *The Gift of Black Folk* (1924), *John Brown* (1909), and *Black Reconstruction in America* (1935). Both Woodson and Du Bois published critical reviews of Phillips's *American Negro Slavery* when it first appeared (Van Deburg 194).

11. Another crucial study of the period is *Slave Insurrections in the United States, 1800-1865* (1938), by the black historian Joseph C. Carroll.

12. See Albert E. Stone's analysis of the treatment of slavery in history textbooks in *The Return of Nat Turner* (301-5).

13. See Kenneth Stampp, *The Peculiar Institution* (1956), and John Hope Franklin, *From Slavery to Freedom* (1947). E. Franklin Frazier's *The Negro in the United States* (1949) is a more conservative black-authored study of African American history.

14. See John Blassingame, *The Slave Community* (1972), Eugene Genovese, *Roll, Jordan, Roll* (1974), George P. Rawick, *From Sundown to Sunup* (1972), Herbert Gutman, *The Black Family in Slavery and Freedom* (1976), and Lawrence W. Levine, *Black Culture and Black Consciousness* (1977). In an attempt to refute Elkins's arguments about slave personality, historians of the 1970s also took a renewed interest in slave resistance and rebellion. See, for example, Eugene Genovese, *From Rebellion to Revolution* (1979), Stephen B. Oates, *The Fires of Jubilee* (1975), John O. Killens, *Great Gittin' Up Morning* (1972), and Vincent Harding, *There Is a River* (1981).

15. See, for example, Charles Joyner's *Down by the Riverside* (1984), and Ann Patton Malone's *Sweet Chariot* (1992). Chapter 5 contains a brief discussion of Joyner's study.

16. Walter Johnson's *Soul by Soul* (1999) is a powerful study of the antebellum domestic slave trade. Books concerning the experiences of women under slavery include Deborah Gray White, *Ar'n't I a Woman?* (1985), Catherine Clinton, *The Plantation Mistress* (1982), and Elizabeth Fox-Genovese, *Within the Plantation Household* (1988). Two studies of African American slaveholders are Michael P. Johnson and James L. Roark, *Black Masters* (1984), and Larry Koger, *Black Slaveowners* (1985). Recent explorations of slave rebellions include three studies of the Denmark Vesey conspiracy—Douglas R. Egerton, *He Shall Go Out Free* (1999), David Robertson, *Denmark Vesey* (1999), and Edward A. Pearson, *Designs against Charleston* (1999). Two books on Gabriel's 1800 insurrection in Richmond also emerged in the 1990s— Douglas R. Egerton, *Gabriel's Rebellion* (1993), and James Sidbury, *Ploughshares into Swords* (1997). Winthrop Jordan, meanwhile, provides a remarkable reconstruction of a Mississippi slave conspiracy during the Civil War in *Tumult and Silence at Second Creek* (1993), while John Hope Franklin and Loren Schweninger examine fugitives from slavery in *Runaway Slaves* (1999).

1. Designs against Tara

1. For an account of the Mitchell Trust's litigious response to Randall's parody, see Laura Miller, "Mammy's Revenge," and Jay Flemma, "Parody as Fair Use II."

2. Aside from a 1972 paperback, *The Red Cock Crows* has been consistently out of print since its Armed Services edition of World War II. Beyond Van Deburg's small footnote, virtually the only scholar to even have acknowledged its existence is Lynn Veach Sadler in "The Figure of the Black Insurrectionist in Stowe, Bouvé, Bontemps, and Gaither" (1986). *Black Thunder* has fared somewhat better. It remains in print, and recent studies of it include Mary Kemp Davis, "Arna Bontemps' *Black Thunder*: The Creation of an Authoritative Text of 'Gabriel's Defeat'" (1989), and Christine Levecq, "Philosophies of History in Arna Bontemps' *Black Thunder*" (2000). William Faulkner's *Absalom, Absalom!* is, of course, another novel concerned with slavery that was published in 1936 and which presents a very different picture of the planter class from that painted by Mitchell's novel. See James W. Matthews, "The Civil War of 1936: *Gone with the Wind* and *Absalom, Absalom!*" (1967).

3. The film adaptation of *Gone with the Wind* also only individualizes members of the slave elite. Unlike the novel, however, the film briefly acknowledges the existence of the field hand class. One of the very first images in the film's opening titles is of slaves working in the fields under the setting sun. This image romanticizes slavery, of course, but for anyone who has read Mitchell's novel, the brief visibility of field hands in the film is striking.

4. For a different reading of the references to class in *Gone with the Wind*, see Hazel V. Carby's analysis of Mitchell's "fears of a mass democracy" in "Ideologies of Black Folk: The Historical Novel of Slavery" (131).

5. As Robert E. May observes in "*Gone with the Wind* as Southern History: A Reappraisal" (1978), Mitchell's novel sold a million copies within a year of its 1936 publication "and had an instant impact upon various aspects of American life and thought, including fashion, home decorating styles, and the advertising media" (51). The film adaptation, which was released at the end of 1939, "if anything, upstaged the novel. . . . [W]ithin one year twenty-five million Americans had viewed it" (51).

6. Aptheker first published his scholarship as a two-part article entitled "American Negro Slave Revolts" in *Science and Society* in 1937 and 1938, and in a pamphlet entitled "Negro Slave Revolts in the United States, 1526–1860" in 1939 (Aptheker, *American Negro Slave Revolts*, 5). In the introductory note to her fiction, Gaither indicates that *The Red Cock Crows* is loosely based upon "happenings in the summer of 1835 at the now vanished town of Livingston, Mississippi," events that are discussed in *American Negro Slave Revolts* (325–27).

7. There are, however, a couple of significant differences between Aptheker's report of the 1835 Mississippi conspiracy and Gaither's dramatization of it. Aptheker notes that a local slaveholder was implicated in the historical plot and that confessions were elicited from slaves by torture. *The Red Cock Crows* does not suggest that any slaveholders were involved in the insurrection and does not portray even the racist lower-class whites of the Forks as being capable of carrying out torture. In addition, *The Red Cock Crows* also incorporates details from other slave rebellions described by Aptheker into its plot. Gaither's slave rebel leader, General Scofield, shares several qualities in common with Nat Turner. Like Turner, Scofield is liter-

ate and is inspired by heavenly visions (Gaither, *The Red Cock Crows*, 45–46, 62; Aptheker, *American Negro Slave Revolts*, 296).

8. See chapter 2 for an analysis of the depiction of slave subjectivities in *The Confessions of Nat Turner*.

9. Numerous historians in recent years have attended to the ways in which a discourse of racial privilege discouraged lower-class whites from identifying with African Americans in the nineteenth century. See, for example, David Roediger, *The Wages of Whiteness* (1991).

10. For an analysis of how fiction has often equated the situation of white women under patriarchy to the situation of black men in slavery, see chapter 4.

11. See chapters 2 and 3 for detailed examinations of responses by later novelists and historians to Elkins's "Sambo thesis."

12. In chapter 4, I consider in greater detail the simplistic and stereotypical portrayals of the plantation mistress in nineteenth- and twentieth-century fiction.

13. Such works include Octavia Butler's *Kindred* (1979), Sherley Anne Williams's *Dessa Rose* (1986), Toni Morrison's *Beloved* (1987), and J. California Cooper's *Family* (1991). See chapter 3 for discussions of *Kindred* and *Beloved* and chapter 4 for an analysis of *Dessa Rose*.

2. From Tara to Turner

1. For accounts of how African American activists threatened a black boycott of the film adaptation of *The Confessions of Nat Turner* and successfully demanded several concessions from Hollywood before the project was finally abandoned, see Scot French, *The Rebellious Slave* (2004) 253–72, and Kenneth Greenberg, "Nat Turner in Hollywood," *Nat Turner* (2003) 243–49.

2. See William Wells Brown, *Clotel, or The President's Daughter* (1853), Martin Delany, *Blake, or The Huts of America* (1861–1862), and Frederick Douglass, *The Heroic Slave* (1853). Fugitive slave narratives are, of course, available in a variety of editions, but the Library of America's *Slave Narratives* volume, edited by William L. Andrews and Henry Louis Gates Jr., is a particularly good collection.

3. See, for example, John D. Stevens, "The Black Reaction to *Gone with the Wind*" (1973). Stowe's novel, of course, was also the subject of criticism, including a barrage of "Anti-Tom" novels that were designed to defend slavery, including such works as Mary Eastman's *Aunt Phillis's Cabin* (1852).

4. After decades of neglect, scholars are finally discovering Yerby's work. The opening chapter of *The Foxes of Harrow* now appears in Gene Andrew Jarrett's collection, *African American Literature beyond Race* (2006), and Yerby was also the subject of a symposium held in Oakland, California, in May 2006.

5. Another significant white-authored 1950s slavery novel is Robert Penn Warren's *Band of Angels* (1956), in which Amantha Starr, an idealistic plantation belle, discovers at her father's funeral that her mother was a slave—and then is promptly sold into slavery herself.

6. See chapter 5 for an analysis of the problems inherent in the generic categorization "neoslave narrative."

7. Stone observes that the attempt of a slave named Hark to run away to Pennsylvania

in *Confessions* is "ludicrously inept" and "serves as ironic commentary on slave narratives like Frederick Douglass's, in which the flight to freedom is the central action. Hark's escape proves instead an exercise in futility" (Stone 83–84; Styron, *Confessions* 276–86).

8. A number of these essays are collected in Ann J. Lane, ed., *The Debate over Slavery* (1971), a text I address later in this chapter.

9. Certainly, *The Confessions of Nat Turner* sometimes echoes the language of pre–World War II slavery historiography. For example, Styron's depiction of slave labor is highly reminiscent of that of James Ford Rhodes. In the novel, Nat describes watching "a horde of Negroes laboring with hoes. . . . Like animals, glistening with sweat . . . they ply their hoes in unison, chop-chopping beneath the eyes of a black driver. The sight of their dumb toil fills me with a sickening dread" (146). This is uncannily close to the passage from Rhodes's *History of the United States* quoted earlier in this chapter.

10. Styron did not help his case by fulsomely praising *Gone with the Wind* as "a remarkable novel, precisely because this little woman from Atlanta has a fire of an imagination, which captured her and somehow allowed her to breathe some kind of miraculous spirit through and around the rather threadbare facts about antebellum Georgia" (quoted in Stone 14).

11. Rushdy, for example, identifies *Jubilee* as the beginning of contemporary fiction about slavery on the very first page of his study of the neoslave narrative genre—but then does not mention it again. *Jubilee's* integrationist politics, after all, hardly accord with the Black Nationalism that Rushdy identifies as the catalyst for significant modern black-authored slavery novels. Angelyn Mitchell similarly acknowledges *Jubilee's* importance while conceding its limitations, concluding that "the portrayal of the objective conditions of slavery, as in Walker's *Jubilee*, no longer assumes priority for Black female revisionists of slavery" (10–11).

12. See Albert E. Stone, *The Return of Nat Turner* (1992), John B. Duff and Peter M. Mitchell, eds., *The Nat Turner Rebellion* (1971), Ashraf Rushdy, *Neo-slave Narratives* (1999), Scot French, *The Rebellious Slave* (2004), Kenneth S. Greenberg, ed., *Nat Turner* (2003), Mary Kemp Davis, *Nat Turner before the Bar of Judgment* (1999), John Henrik Clarke, ed., *William Styron's Nat Turner* (1968), Seymour Gross and Eileen Bender, "History, Politics, and Literature: The Myth of Nat Turner" (1971), and two articles by Eugene Genovese, "William Styron before the People's Court" (1968), and "William Styron's *The Confessions of Nat Turner*: A Meditation on Evil, Redemption, and History" (2001), as well as Styron's own statements on the controversy, in the 1982 introduction to "This Quiet Dust," "Nat Turner Revisited" (1992), and "More Confessions" (2001).

13. Clarke's choice of exclusively male black critics seems limited, given that there was no shortage of talented black women writers in the late sixties—including several who published critiques of *Confessions*, such as Alice Walker, Poppy Cannon White, and June Meyer (Stone 125, 104–5, 120–21). The addition of such voices would have militated against what now seems a markedly macho tone in some of the volume's essays, such as Killens's observation that the American reading public responded to Styron's novel "[l]ike a whore being brutally ravished and loving every masochistic minute of it" ("Confessions," 34). Criticisms by some of the Ten Black Writers of the scene in Styron's novel in which Nat Turner has a homosexual experience with another slave reveal a tendency toward homophobia that, from the vantage point of today, seems no less offensive than Styron's racial stereotyping (Poussaint 21, 22; Killens, "Confessions," 35).

14. Despite the claims of critics, it is simply not true that the debate over *The Confessions of Nat Turner* breaks down into clear black/white positions. It is just not the case that the "white literary establishment received the novel with virtually unanimous acclaim while [white] historians . . . validated it" (Rushdy, *Neo-slave*, 86). Stone observes that several black writers and historians, including John Hope Franklin, Benjamin Quarles, J. Saunders Redding, and, of course, James Baldwin praised the novel (105). Furthermore, Aptheker, the white historian, published one of the first sustained critiques of Styron's book. I should also emphasize that several contemporary black critics are highly critical of the Clarke collection, notably Henry Louis Gates Jr., whose judgment of the Ten Black Writers is that "Censorship is to art as lynching is to justice, and it's just as disgusting when blacks do it as whites" (quoted in Styron, "More Confessions," 222).

15. See http://www.seriesbooks.com/plantationnovels.htm for titles, descriptions, and images of the lurid covers of the plantation potboilers that were common between 1968 and 1980. Although Kyle Onstott's successors continued to churn out increasingly tasteless and exploitative episodes in the Falconhurst series until well into the 1980s, without any of the qualities that make *Mandingo* so interesting, I am not aware of any significant fiction about U.S. slavery by a white writer until virtually the 1990s. Even then, Allan Gurganus's *Oldest Living Confederate Widow Tells All* (1989) is mostly concerned with the postbellum South, since its heroine-narrator is born in 1885, although the narrative does contain a lengthy episode about the burning of a plantation in the Civil War and its former slaves' reactions to their new freedom. Madison Smartt Bell's *All Souls' Rising* (1995) is concerned with slavery and rebellion in Haiti, rather than the United States. As I argue in chapter 5, it is Valerie Martin's *Property* in 2003 that really marks the possible beginnings of a new interracial dialogue about slavery in American fiction.

16. See Introduction, note 14, for significant works of 1970s slavery historiography. One should note, furthermore, the extent to which historians conducted a constructive interracial dialogue about slave resistance in this period. White writers, for example, produced several significant works on the subject of slave resistance, including Herbert Aptheker's *Nat Turner's Slave Rebellion* (1966), Robert Starobin's collection of documents, *Denmark Vesey* (1970), Gerald Mullin's *Flight and Rebellion* (1972), Stephen B. Oates's *The Fires of Jubilee* (1975), and Eugene Genovese's *From Rebellion to Revolution* (1979). Even Van Deburg acknowledges an "unprecedented level of consensus" between black and white historians in the 1970s (140).

3. You Shall See How a Slave Was Made a *Woman*

1. Styron himself dismissed the TV adaptation of Alex Haley's *Roots* as "dishonest tripe" (quoted in Van Deburg 157). Whatever the artistic limitations of this miniseries, Styron's eagerness to publish such a dismissive opinion about a cultural phenomenon that did a great deal for black cultural pride—after his novel had already caused so much offense to the African American community—says a great deal about the antagonism generated by the controversy surrounding *The Confessions of Nat Turner*.

2. Helen Taylor records that 1.5 million copies of *Roots* were sold in its first eighteen months on the market and that 130 million Americans watched some of the TV adaptation—with the final episode securing three-quarters of the TV audience (48).

3. Courlander had personal motives for his hostility toward *Roots*. Haley was ordered to pay Courlander $650,000 in damages for plagiarizing eighty passages from his novel, *The African* (Taylor 53). Nonetheless, other critics interpret *Roots* in similar terms to Courlander. See, for example, David A. Gerber, "Haley's *Roots* and Our Own: An Inquiry into the Nature of a Popular Phenomenon" (102).

4. For a critique of this aspect of *Roots*—which claims that Haley depicts Kunta as "a primitive being ... too often baffled by non-African things that probably would not have perplexed the average Mandinka of his age and times"—see Courlander, "Kunta" (295, 296).

5. White characters, however, play a larger role in the TV adaptation of *Roots* than in the book. William Van Deburg notes that "executive producer David L. Wolper admitted that he 'wasn't even trying to appeal to blacks.' He knew that his potential audience was ninety percent nonblack so he tried to 'reach the maximum white audience' by casting ... well-known white actors and actresses in roles that barely existed in the original version of Kunta Kinte's story" (156).

6. The Mandinka culture that is portrayed as Kunta's lost Edenic utopia in *Roots* is also shown to be a highly patriarchal society (5, 26, 53–54, 61–62, 91, 97, 107).

7. Rushdy persuasively argues that the true killer of Swille is the enigmatic slave Pompey (*Neo-slave* 106–7).

8. For example, in one of the best scholarly articles on the novel, "Power and Repetition: Philosophies of (Literary) History in Octavia E. Butler's *Kindred*," Christine Levecq shows how Butler's text also signifies upon the fugitive slave narrative genre (542–46).

9. Margaret Walker's *Jubilee* is the only other such work by a black woman before the 1980s, and more than a third of that book is set during Reconstruction.

10. Haley referred to *Roots* as a work of "faction," claiming that "[a]ll the major incidents are true, the details are as accurate as very heavy research can make them, the names and dates are real, but obviously when it comes to dialogue and people's emotions and thoughts, I had to make things up" (quoted in Fishbein 286). One might reasonably question, however, if this in any way distinguishes *Roots* from conventional historical fiction. Those few recent scholars who have considered *Roots* at all quite correctly approach it as a novel (Taylor 47; Courlander, "Kunta" 302).

11. David Bradley's *The Chaneysville Incident* (1981), Sherley Anne Williams's *Dessa Rose* (1986), Fred D'Aguiar's *The Longest Memory* (1994), Phyllis Alesia Perry's *Stigmata* (1998), Alice Randall's *The Wind Done Gone* (2001), Steven Barnes's *Lion's Blood* (2002), Valerie Martin's *Property* (2003), and Edward P. Jones's *The Known World* (2003) are all examples of such approaches. The exceptions—those books that eschew Butler's approach—include the novels of Charles Johnson, *Oxherding Tale* (1982) and *Middle Passage* (1990), which are rather more indebted to the metafictional example of Ishmael Reed.

12. See Caroline Woidat, "Talking Back to Schoolteacher: Morrison's Confrontation with Hawthorne in *Beloved*" (1997); Richard C. Moreland, "'He Wants to Put His Story Next to Hers': Putting Twain's Story Next to Hers in *Beloved*" (1997); and Ashraf Rushdy, "Daughters Signifyin(g) History: The Example of Toni Morrison's *Beloved*" (1992). For a full account of the Margaret Garner story, see Steven Weisenburger's *Modern Medea* (1998).

13. Stanley Crouch observes that Morrison's reference is "to the captured Africans who died coming across the Atlantic. But sixty is ten times six, of course. ... *Beloved*, above all else, is a

blackface holocaust novel" (quoted in Mandel 581, 584). For a full consideration of the debate regarding Morrison's comparison of slavery to the Nazi Holocaust, see Naomi Mandel, "I Made the Ink" (2002).

4. Scarlett and Mammy Done Gone

1. Mary Kemp Davis, for example, argues that, in *Dessa Rose*, Williams "critiques the flawed language and the flawed world-view of the slavocracy, and she substitutes a counter-text in which the slave's voice can be heard" ("Everybody" 556–57). See also McDowell, "Negotiating," Rushdy, *Neo-slave*, and cited works by Goodman, Harrison, Mae Henderson, Holton, Kekeh, King, Mathison-Fife, Angelyn Mitchell, Porter, Schultz, Stone, Trapasso, and Winchell.

2. The first-person perspective of the plantation mistress in *Property* is at least unique to American literature. However, the British writer Caryl Phillips tells much of his novel, *Cambridge* (1991), from the perspective of an English plantation mistress in the West Indies.

3. See chapter 2, note 15.

4. Other fiction in this tradition includes Ernest J. Gaines's *The Autobiography of Miss Jane Pittman* (1971), J. California Cooper's *Family* (1991), Phyllis Alesia Perry's *Stigmata* (1998), and Barbara Chase-Riboud's *The President's Daughter* (1994). In keeping with my aim to avoid thinking of the discourse of slavery before the 1960s as being a monolithic hegemony, however, I should also acknowledge a long and vibrant tradition of black women's fiction about slavery that goes back over a century. Henry Louis Gates even claims, for example, that the period from 1890 to 1910 could be called "The Black Women's Era" in literature (xvi).

5. Of course, one might reasonably argue that *all* of Stowe's characters are types. As Jane Tompkins observes, "every character in the novel, every scene, and every incident comes to be apprehended in terms of every *other* character, scene, and incident" (136). The plantation mistresses in the novel are, however, uncommonly formulaic even by these standards. Marie St. Clare is a one-dimensional villain, without any of the complexity of her husband or even the psychology of a Simon Legree.

6. Unlike 1970s historians and novelists such as Styron, Haley, and Butler, Williams does not seem at all concerned with Elkins's influential thesis. *Dessa Rose* assumes the existence of strong slave communities as a given, and does not really address the question that *Kindred* and *Beloved* explore: how could slavery be a Holocaust and yet not prevent assertive slave identities and active slave communities?

7. Several scholars have explored this aspect of the novel. See Goodman and Winchell in particular, but also Mary Kemp Davis, "Everybody" (545), Mathison-Fife (32), Mae Henderson ("Stories" 287), Stone (375), and Angelyn Mitchell (68).

8. See chapter 1.

9. Manon's constantly stated desire for the death of her husband in *Property* is also highly reminiscent of Chopin's 1894 tale, "The Story of an Hour," in which Louise Mallard responds to news of her husband's demise with "a monstrous joy" as she realizes that she will now be able to "live for herself" (Chopin 214).

10. While making very similar arguments about the racial subtext of *The Awakening*, these critics differ over its significance. Some seek to credit Chopin for an intended "critique of the South . . . that insists on the interdependence of race and gender and class" (Ewell 35). Anna Shannon Elfenbein, for one, asserts that "Chopin clearly sees more than Edna does, for she examines the racial order of Edna's society tongue in cheek" (147). Others simply see Chopin's fiction as replicating white southern orthodoxies about race. Such critics have "been quick to point out that Chopin was, after all, raised in a Missouri household of former slaveholders who sympathized with the Confederate cause, and her husband fought in a paramilitary white supremacist group" (Dyer 139).

11. See chapter 1 and "Jezebel and Mammy: The Mythology of the Female Slave" in White 27–61.

5. Mapping the Unrepresentable

1. Another white-authored novel that has inspired many literary responses is, of course, *Uncle Tom's Cabin*, from the anti-Tom novels of the nineteenth century to postmodern satires, including Ishmael Reed's *Flight to Canada* and Robert Alexander's play *I Ain't Yo' Uncle*.

2. Rushdy emphasizes that his definition of "Neo-slave narrative" differs from Bell's, although he does not satisfactorily explain the nature of the distinction. Since one of the central conventions of the antebellum slave narrative is the escape to freedom, and since a first-person account must necessarily possess oral qualities, it is ultimately unclear in what sense Rushdy's use of the term *neoslave narrative* significantly differs from that of Bell.

3. One novel that Rushdy's study does not discuss actually possesses numerous parallels to the fugitive slave narrative. *Kindred* is a text narrated by an exceptional but enslaved individual who tries to resist the effects of slavery upon her and who eventually escapes. That Dana is a twentieth-century time traveler, however, complicates the relationship of Butler's novel to the genre. See Marc Steinberg, "Inverting History in Octavia Butler's Postmodern Slave Narrative" (2004).

4. Rushdy argues that the black response to *The Confessions of Nat Turner* initiated the neoslave narrative, but one might equally say that Styron's novel is the founding text of the genre, however dubious its portrayal of slave psychology. Ironically, *Confessions* is certainly the first twentieth-century novel of slavery narrated from a rebellious bondsman's viewpoint. As the much-reviled work of a white writer, scholars refuse to categorize Styron's novel as a neoslave narrative. However, if 1968—the year of *William Styron's Nat Turner: Ten Black Writers Respond*—was, as Rushdy claims, "the moment of origin for the Neo-slave narratives," one might reasonably question why the earliest novel that Rushdy categorizes as such was not published for a further eight years (*Neo-slave* 5).

5. See Naomi Mandel, "'I Made the Ink': Identity, Complicity, 60 Million, and More" (2002), for a consideration of debates concerning the comparison of slavery to the Holocaust.

6. One of the first African American works of fiction about slavery—Frederick Douglass's *The Heroic Slave* (1853)—actually concerns a successful slave revolt, in contrast to the later literary convention of the doomed slave rebellion. Kunta Kinte's confused culture-shock per-

spective of slavery in *Roots* is, of course, another notable instance of the use of defamiliarization in 1970s slavery fiction.

7. Fogel and Engerman's renowned, if controversial, "cliometric" study of the economics of slavery, *Time on the Cross* (1974), is particularly dependent upon census information.

Conclusion

1. See Kenneth Greenberg, "Nat Turner in Hollywood," in Greenberg 243–49.

WORKS CITED

Aanerud, Rebecca. "Fictions of Whiteness: Speaking the Names of Whiteness in U.S. Literature." *Displacing Whiteness: Essays in Social and Cultural Criticism.* Ed. Ruth Frankenberg. Durham: Duke UP, 1997. 35–59.

Alexander, Robert. *I Ain't Yo' Uncle: The New Jack Revisionist "Uncle Tom's Cabin."* Woodstock, Ill.: Dramatic Publishing, 1996.

Ammons, Elizabeth. *Conflicting Stories: American Women Writers at the Turn into the Twentieth Century.* New York: Oxford UP, 1991.

Andrews, William L. *To Tell a Free Story: The First Century of Afro-American Autobiography, 1760–1865.* Urbana: U of Illinois P, 1986.

Andrews, William L., and Henry Louis Gates Jr., eds. *Slave Narratives.* New York: Library of America, 2000.

Angelo, Bonnie. "The Pain of Being Black: An Interview with Toni Morrison." *Conversations with Toni Morrison.* Ed. Danille Taylor-Guthrie. Jackson: UP of Mississippi, 1994. 255–61.

Aptheker, Herbert. *American Negro Slave Revolts.* 1943. New York: International Publishers, 1983.

———. *Nat Turner's Slave Rebellion.* New York: Grove, 1966.

Barnes, Steven. *Lion's Blood.* New York: Warner Books, 2002.

Beck, Janet Kemper. "I'll Fly Away: Ishmael Reed Refashions the Slave Narrative and Takes It on a *Flight to Canada.*" Dick 132–39.

Bell, Bernard W. *The Afro-American Novel and Its Tradition.* Amherst: U of Massachusetts P, 1987.

Bell, Madison Smartt. *All Souls' Rising.* New York: Penguin, 1995.

Bennett, Lerone, Jr. "Nat's Last White Man." Clarke 3–16.

Bentley, Nancy. "White Slaves: The Mulatto Hero in Antebellum Fiction." *American Literature* 65.3 (September 1993): 501–22.

Birnbaum, Michele A. "'Alien Hands': Kate Chopin and the Colonization of Race." *American Literature* 66.2 (June 1994): 301–23.

The Birth of a Nation. Dir. D. W. Griffith. Perf. Henry B. Walthall, Mae Marsh, Miriam Cooper, and Lillian Gish. Epoch, 1915.

Blassingame, John. *The Slave Community: Plantation Life in the Antebellum South.* Rev. ed. New York: Oxford UP, 1979.

Bontemps, Arna. *Black Thunder.* 1936. Boston: Beacon, 1968.

Bradley, David. *The Chaneysville Incident.* 1981. New York: Harper and Row, 1990.

Brown, William Wells. *The Black Man: His Antecedents, His Genius, and His Achievements.* 1863. New York: Kraus, 1969.

———. *Clotel, or The President's Daughter.* 1853. *Three Classic African-American Novels.* Ed. William L. Andrews. New York: Penguin, 1990. 71–283.

Butler, Octavia E. *Kindred.* 1979. Boston: Beacon, 1988.

Carby, Hazel. "Ideologies of Black Folk: The Historical Novel of Slavery." McDowell and Rampersad, eds. 125–43.

Carmichael, Jacqueline Miller. *Trumpeting a Fiery Sound: History and Folklore in Margaret Walker's "Jubilee."* Athens: U of Georgia P, 1998.

Carroll, Joseph C. *Slave Insurrections in the United States, 1800–1865.* 1938. New York: Negro Universities P, 1973.

Cather, Willa. *Sapphira and the Slave Girl.* 1940. New York: Vintage, 1968.

Chase-Riboud, Barbara. *The President's Daughter.* New York: Ballantine, 1995.

———. *Sally Hemings.* 1979. New York: Ballantine, 1994.

Cheuse, Alan. "When a Former Slave Becomes Master." *San Francisco Chronicle.* 14 September 2003. http://www.sfgate.com/cgi-bin/article.cgi?f=/chronicle/archive/2003/09/14/RV257493.DTL (accessed 18 July 2007).

Chopin, Kate. *The Awakening, and Selected Stories.* New York: Penguin, 1984.

Chrisman, Robert. "*Roots:* Rebirth of the Slave Mentality." *Black Scholar* 8.7 (May 1977): 41–42.

Clarke, John Henrik, ed. *William Styron's Nat Turner: Ten Black Writers Respond.* Boston: Beacon, 1968.

Clinton, Catherine. *The Plantation Mistress: Woman's World in the Old South.* New York: Pantheon, 1982.

Condé, Mary. "Some African-American Fictional Responses to *Gone with the Wind.*" *Yearbook of English Studies* 26 (1996): 208–17.

Cooper, J. California. *Family.* New York: Anchor, 1992.

Courlander, Harold. *The African.* 1967. New York: Holt, 1993.

———. "Kunta Kinte's Struggle to Be African." *Phylon* 47.4 (1986): 294–302.

Crossley, Robert. Introduction. Butler ix–xxvii.

D'Aguiar, Fred. *The Longest Memory.* New York: Avon, 1996.

Davis, Kimberly Chabot. "'Postmodern Blackness': Toni Morrison's *Beloved* and the End of History." *Twentieth Century Literature* 44.2 (Summer 1998): 242–60.

Davis, Mary Kemp. "Arna Bontemps' *Black Thunder*: The Creation of an Authoritative Text of 'Gabriel's Defeat.'" *Black American Literature Forum* 23.1 (Spring 1989): 17–36.

———. "Everybody Knows Her Name: The Recovery of the Past in Sherley Anne Williams's *Dessa Rose*." *Callaloo* 40 (Summer 1989): 544–58.

———. *Nat Turner before the Bar of Judgment: Fictional Treatments of the Southampton Slave Insurrection.* Baton Rouge: Louisiana State UP, 1999.

Davis, Matthew R. "'Strange, history. Complicated, too': Ishmael Reed's Use of African- American History in *Flight to Canada*." *Mississippi Quarterly* 49.4 (Fall 1996): 743–53.

Davis, Natalie Zemon. *Slaves on Screen: Film and Historical Vision.* Cambridge, Mass.: Harvard UP, 2000.

Delany, Martin R. *Blake, or The Huts of America.* 1861–1862. Boston: Beacon, 1970.

Dick, Bruce Allen, ed. *The Critical Response to Ishmael Reed.* Westport, Conn.: Greenwood, 1999.

Douglass, Frederick. *The Heroic Slave.* 1853. *Three Classic African-American Novels.* Ed. William L. Andrews. New York: Penguin, 1990. 23–69.

———. *Narrative of the Life of Frederick Douglass, an American Slave, Written by Himself.* 1845. Ed. William L. Andrews and William S. McFeely. New York: Norton, 1997.

Du Bois, W. E. B. *Black Reconstruction in America.* 1935. New York: Atheneum, 1969.

———. *The Gift of Black Folk: The Negroes in the Making of America.* 1924. New York: AMS, 1971.

———. *John Brown.* 1909. Millwood, N.Y.: Kraus-Thompson, 1962.

———. *The Souls of Black Folk.* 1903. New York: Penguin, 1996.

———. *The Suppression of the African Slave-Trade to the United States of America.* 1896. New York: Schocken Books, 1969.

Duff, John B., and Peter M. Mitchell, eds. *The Nat Turner Rebellion: The Historical Event and the Modern Controversy.* New York: Harper and Row, 1971.

Dyer, Joyce. "Reading *The Awakening* with Toni Morrison." *Southern Literary Journal* 35.1 (Fall 2002): 138–54.

Eastman, Mary H. *Aunt Phillis's Cabin.* Philadelphia: Lippincott, Grambo, 1852.

Egerton, Douglas R. "Forgetting Denmark Vesey; or, Oliver Stone Meets Richard Wade." *William and Mary Quarterly* 59.1 (January 2002): 143–52.

———. *Gabriel's Rebellion: The Virginia Slave Conspiracies of 1800 and 1802.* Chapel Hill: U of North Carolina P, 1993.

―――. *He Shall Go Out Free: The Lives of Denmark Vesey*. Madison: Madison House, 1999.

Elfenbein, Anna Shannon. *Women on the Color Line: Evolving Stereotypes and the Writings of George Washington Cable, Grace King, Kate Chopin*. Charlottesville: UP of Virginia, 1989.

Elias, Amy J. *Sublime Desire: History and Post-1960s Fiction*. Baltimore: Johns Hopkins UP, 2001.

Elkins, Stanley. *Slavery: A Problem in American Institutional and Intellectual Life*. 2nd ed. Chicago: U of Chicago P, 1968.

―――. "Slavery and Ideology." Lane 325–78.

Ewell, Barbara. "Unlinking Race and Gender: *The Awakening* as a Southern Novel." *Southern Quarterly* 37.3–4 (Spring/Summer 1999): 30–37.

Faulkner, William. *Absalom, Absalom!* 1936. London: Penguin, 1971.

Fiedler, Leslie. *The Inadvertent Epic: From "Uncle Tom's Cabin" to "Roots."* New York: Simon and Schuster, 1979.

Fishbein, Leslie. "*Roots*: Docudrama and the Interpretation of History." *Why Docudrama?* Ed. Alan Rosenthal. Carbondale: Southern Illinois UP, 1999. 271–95.

Flemma, Jay. "Parody as Fair Use II: The Wind Done Got Away with It." http://www.alanbergman.com/parody.doc (accessed 18 July 2007).

Fogel, Robert William, and Stanley L. Engerman. *Time on the Cross: The Economics of American Negro Slavery*. New York: Norton, 1989.

Fox-Genovese, Elizabeth. *Within the Plantation Household: Black and White Women of the Old South*. Chapel Hill: U of North Carolina P, 1988.

Franklin, John Hope. *From Slavery to Freedom*. 1947. 7th ed. New York: McGraw-Hill, 1994.

Franklin, John Hope, and Loren Schweninger. *Runaway Slaves: Rebels on the Plantation*. New York: Oxford UP, 1999.

Frazier, E. Franklin. *The Negro in the United States*. New York: Macmillan, 1949.

French, Scot. *The Rebellious Slave: The Image of Nat Turner in the American Mind*. Boston: Houghton Mifflin, 2004.

Friedlander, Saul. "Probing the Limits of Representation." Jenkins 387–91.

Gaines, Ernest J. *The Autobiography of Miss Jane Pittman*. New York: Bantam, 1972.

Gaither, Frances. *Double Muscadine*. New York: Macmillan, 1949.

―――. *The Red Cock Crows*. New York: Macmillan, 1944.

Gates, Henry Louis, Jr. "Foreword: In Her Own Write." Harper vii–xxvi.

Genovese, Eugene. *From Rebellion to Revolution: Afro-American Slave Revolts in the Making of the Modern World*. Baton Rouge: Louisiana State UP, 1979.

―――. *Roll, Jordan, Roll: The World the Slaves Made*. New York: Vintage, 1976.

―――. "William Styron before the People's Court." *Red and Black: Marxian Ex-*

plorations in Southern and Afro-American History. New York: Pantheon Books, 1972. 200–217.

———. "William Styron's *The Confessions of Nat Turner*: A Meditation on Evil, Redemption, and History." *Novel History: Historians and Novelists Confront America's Past (and Each Other)*. Ed. Mark C. Carnes. New York: Simon and Schuster, 2001. 209–20.

Gerber, David A. "Haley's *Roots* and Our Own: An Inquiry into the Nature of a Popular Phenomenon." *Journal of Ethnic Studies* 5.3 (Fall 1977): 87–111.

Gone with the Wind. Dir. Victor Fleming. Perf. Vivien Leigh, Clark Gable, Olivia de Havilland, Leslie Howard, Hattie McDaniel, and Butterfly McQueen. MGM, 1939.

Goodman, Susan. "Competing Histories: William Styron's *The Confessions of Nat Turner* and Sherley Ann Williams's *Dessa Rose*." *The World Is Our Home: Society and Culture in Contemporary Southern Writing*. Ed. Jeffrey J. Folks and Nancy Summers Folks. Lexington: UP of Kentucky, 2000. 12–28.

Goss, Fred. "Gay with the Wind." *The Advocate*. 11 September 2001. http://articles .findarticles.com/p/articles/mi_m1589/is_2001_Sept_11/ai_78265990 (accessed 4 February 2004).

Govan, Sandra Y. "Homage to Tradition: Octavia Butler Renovates the Historical Novel." *MELUS* 13.1/2 (Spring/Summer 1986): 79–96.

Greenberg, Kenneth S., ed. *Nat Turner: A Slave Rebellion in History and Memory*. Oxford: Oxford UP, 2003.

Gross, Seymour L., and Eileen Bender. "History, Politics, and Literature: The Myth of Nat Turner." *American Quarterly* 23.4 (October 1971): 487–518.

Gurganus, Allan. *Oldest Living Confederate Widow Tells All*. New York: Knopf, 1989.

Gutman, Herbert. *The Black Family in Slavery and Freedom*. New York: Vintage, 1977.

Gwin, Minrose C. *Black and White Women of the Old South: The Peculiar Sisterhood in American Literature*. Knoxville: U of Tennessee P, 1985.

Hairston, Loyle. "William Styron's Nat Turner—Rogue Nigger." Clarke 66–72.

Haley, Alex. *Roots*. Garden City, N.Y.: Doubleday, 1976.

Harding, Vincent. *There Is a River: The Black Struggle for Freedom in America*. New York: Vintage, 1983.

———. "You've Taken My Nat and Gone." Clarke 23–33.

Harper, Frances E. W. *Iola Leroy, or Shadows Uplifted*. 1892. New York: Oxford UP, 1988.

Harris, Norman. "The Gods Must Be Angry: *Flight to Canada* as Political History." *Modern Fiction Studies* 34.1 (Spring 1988): 111–23.

Harrison, Suzan. "Mastering Narratives: Rhetorics of Race in *The Confessions of Nat Turner*, *Dessa Rose* and *Celia, a Slave*." *Southern Quarterly* 35.3 (Spring 1997): 13–28.

Henderson, Mae G. "The Stories of O(Dessa): Stories of Complicity and Resistance." *Female Subjects in Black and White: Race, Psychoanalysis, Feminism*. Ed.

Elizabeth Abel, Barbara Christian, and Helene Moglen. Berkeley: U of California P, 1997. 285–304.

———. "(W)riting *The Work* and Working the Rites." *Black American Literature Forum* 23.4 (Winter 1989): 631–60.

Higginson, Thomas Wentworth. *Black Rebellion.* 1969. New York: Da Capo, 1998.

Holton, Robert. *Jarring Witnesses: Modern Fiction and the Representation of History.* New York: Harvester Wheatsheaf, 1994.

Horne, Philip, ed. *Henry James: A Life in Letters.* New York: Putnam, 2000.

Hutcheon, Linda. *A Poetics of Postmodernism: History, Theory, Fiction.* New York: Routledge, 1988.

———. *The Politics of Postmodernism.* London: Routledge, 1989.

Jacobs, Harriet. *Incidents in the Life of a Slave Girl.* 1861. New York: Signet, 2000.

James, Henry. *The Sense of the Past.* 1917. New York: Adamant Media Corporation, 2000.

Jarrett, Gene Andrew, ed. *African American Literature beyond Race: An Alternative Reader.* New York: New York UP, 2006.

Jenkins, Keith, ed. *The Postmodern History Reader.* London: Routledge, 1998.

Johnson, Charles. *Middle Passage.* New York: Plume, 1991.

———. *Oxherding Tale.* 1982. New York: Plume, 1995.

Johnson, Michael P. "Denmark Vesey and His Co-Conspirators." *William and Mary Quarterly* 58.4 (October 2001): 913–76.

Johnson, Michael P., and James L. Roark. *Black Masters: A Free Family of Color in the Old South.* New York: Norton, 1984.

Johnson, Walter. *Soul by Soul: Life inside the Antebellum Slave Market.* Cambridge, Mass.: Harvard UP, 1999.

Johnston, Mary. *The Slave Ship.* Boston: Little, Brown, 1924.

Jones, Edward P. *The Known World.* New York: Amistad, 2003.

Jordan, Winthrop D. *Tumult and Silence at Second Creek: An Inquiry into a Civil War Slave Conspiracy.* Rev. ed. Baton Rouge: Louisiana State UP, 1995.

Joyner, Charles. *Down by the Riverside: A South Carolina Slave Community.* Urbana: U of Illinois P, 1985.

———. "Styron's Choice: A Meditation on History, Literature, and Moral Imperatives." Greenberg 179–213.

Kaiser, Ernest. "The Failure of William Styron." Clarke 50–65.

Kekeh, Andrée-Anne. "Sherley Anne Williams's *Dessa Rose*: History and the Disruptive Power of Memory." *History and Memory in African-American Culture.* Ed. Geneviève Fabre and Robert O'Meally. New York: Oxford UP, 1994. 219–27.

Kellner, Hans. "'Never Again' Is Now." Jenkins 397–412.

Killens, John O. "The Confessions of Willie Styron." Clarke 23–33.

———. *Great Gittin' Up Morning.* Garden City, N.Y.: Doubleday, 1972.

———. ed. *The Trial Record of Denmark Vesey*. Boston: Beacon, 1970.

King, Nicole R. "Meditations and Mediations: Issues of History and Fiction in *Dessa Rose*." *Soundings* 76.2–3 (Summer/Fall 1993): 351–68.

Koger, Larry. *Black Slaveowners: Free Black Slave Masters in South Carolina, 1790–1860*. Jefferson, N.C.: McFarland, 1985.

Kolchin, Peter. *American Slavery, 1619–1877*. New York: Hill and Wang, 1994.

Lane, Ann J., ed. *The Debate over Slavery: Stanley Elkins and His Critics*. Urbana: U of Illinois P, 1971.

Levecq, Christine. "Philosophies of History in Arna Bontemps' *Black Thunder*." *Obsidian III* 1.2 (Fall–Winter 2000): 111–30.

———. "Power and Repetition: Philosophies of (Literary) History in Octavia E. Butler's *Kindred*." *Contemporary Literature* 41.3 (Fall 2000): 525–53.

Levine, Lawrence W. *Black Culture and Black Consciousness: Afro-American Folk Thought from Slavery to Freedom*. New York: Oxford UP, 1977.

Malone, Ann Patton. *Sweet Chariot: Slave Family and Household Structure in Nineteenth-Century Louisiana*. Chapel Hill: U of North Carolina P, 1992.

Mandel, Naomi. "'I Made the Ink': Identity, Complicity, 60 Million, and More." *Modern Fiction Studies* 48.3 (Fall 2002): 582–613.

Marcus, Greil. "From the Shadows." Dick 126–31.

Martin, Valerie. *Property*. New York: Talese/Doubleday, 2003.

Mason, Clifford. *Gabriel*. *Black Drama Anthology*. Ed. Woodie King and Ron Milner. New York: Signet, 1972. 167–227.

Mathison-Fife, Jane. "*Dessa Rose*: A Critique of the Received History of Slavery." *Kentucky Philological Review* 8 (1993): 29–33.

Matthews, James W. "The Civil War of 1936: *Gone with the Wind* and *Absalom, Absalom!*" *Georgia Review* 21 (Winter 1967): 462–69.

May, Robert E. "*Gone with the Wind* as Southern History: A Reappraisal." *Southern Quarterly* 17.1 (Fall 1978): 51–64.

McDowell, Deborah E. "In the First Place: Making Frederick Douglass and the Afro-American Narrative Tradition." Douglass, *Narrative* 172–83.

———. "Negotiating between Tenses: Witnessing Slavery after Freedom—*Dessa Rose*." McDowell and Rampersad, eds., 144–63.

McDowell, Deborah E., and Arnold Rampersad, eds. *Slavery and the Literary Imagination*. Baltimore: Johns Hopkins UP, 1989.

McHale, Brian. *Postmodernist Fiction*. New York: Methuen, 1987.

McKible, Adam. "'These Are the Facts of the Darky's History': Thinking History and Reading Names in Four African American Texts." *African American Review* 28.2 (Summer 1994): 223–35.

Mellard, James M. "This Unquiet Dust: The Problem of History in Styron's *The Confessions of Nat Turner*." *Mississippi Quarterly* 36.4 (Fall 1983): 525–43.

Miller, Laura. "Mammy's Revenge." *Salon.* 2 May 2001. http://archive.salon.com/ books/feature/2001/05/02/wind/index.html (accessed 18 July 2007).

Mitchell, Angelyn. *The Freedom to Remember: Narrative, Slavery, and Gender in Contemporary Black Women's Fiction.* New Brunswick, N.J.: Rutgers UP, 2002.

Mitchell, Margaret. *Gone with the Wind.* New York: Macmillan, 1936.

Moreland, Richard C. "'He Wants to Put His Story Next to Hers': Putting Twain's Story Next to Hers in *Beloved.*" *Toni Morrison: Critical and Theoretical Approaches.* Ed. Nancy J. Peterson. Baltimore: Johns Hopkins UP, 1997. 155–79.

Morrison, Toni. *Beloved.* 1987. New York: Vintage, 2004.

———. *Playing in the Dark: Whiteness and the Literary Imagination.* New York: Vintage, 1993.

———. "Unspeakable Things Unspoken: The Afro-American Presence in American Literature." *Modern Critical Views: Toni Morrison.* Ed. Harold Bloom. New York: Chelsea House Publishers, 1990. 201–30.

Mullin, Gerald W. *Flight and Rebellion: Slave Resistance in Eighteenth-Century Virginia.* London: Oxford UP, 1972.

The Negro Family: The Case for National Action. Washington, D.C.: Office of Policy Planning and Research, U.S. Department of Labor, 1965.

Oates, Stephen B. *The Fires of Jubilee: Nat Turner's Fierce Rebellion.* 1975. New York: HarperCollins, 1990.

Onstott, Kyle. *Drum.* London: Pan, 1965.

———. *Mandingo.* London: Pan, 1961.

"Orange Broadband Prize for Fiction: Interview with Valerie Martin." http://www .orangeprize.co.uk/opf/author_interview.php4?bookid=137 (accessed 18 July 2007).

Panger, Daniel. *Ol' Prophet Nat.* Greenwich, Conn.: Fawcett, 1967.

Parish, Peter J. *Slavery: History and Historians.* New York: Harper and Row, 1989.

Patton, Venetria K. *Women in Chains: The Legacy of Slavery in Black Women's Fiction.* New York: State U of New York P, 2000.

Pearson, Edward A., ed. *Designs against Charleston: The Trial Record of the Denmark Vesey Slave Conspiracy of 1822.* Chapel Hill: U of North Carolina P, 1999.

Perez-Torres, Rafael. "Knitting and Knotting the Narrative Thread: *Beloved* as Postmodern Novel." *Toni Morrison: Critical and Theoretical Approaches.* Ed. Nancy J. Peterson. Baltimore: Johns Hopkins UP, 1997. 91–109.

Perry, John C. *Myths and Realities of American Slavery: The True History of Slavery in America.* Shippensburg, Pa.: Burd Street, 2002.

Perry, Phyllis Alesia. *Stigmata.* New York: Hyperion, 1998.

Phillips, Caryl. *Cambridge.* New York: Vintage, 1993.

Phillips, U. B. *American Negro Slavery.* 1918. Baton Rouge: Louisiana State UP, 1966.

Pinderhughes, Charles A. "Questions of Content and Process in the Perception of Slavery." Lane 102–8.

Porter, Nancy. "Women's Interracial Friendships and Visions of Community in *Meridian, The Salt Eaters, Civil Wars,* and *Dessa Rose.*" *Tradition and the Talents of Women.* Ed. Florence Howe. Urbana: U of Illinois P, 1991. 251–67.

Poussaint, Alvin F. "The Confessions of Nat Turner and the Dilemma of William Styron." Clarke 17–22.

Randall, Alice. *The Wind Done Gone.* Boston: Mariner, 2002.

Rawick, George P. *From Sundown to Sunup: The Making of the Black Community.* Westport, Conn.: Greenwood, 1972.

Reed, Ishmael. *Flight to Canada.* 1976. New York: Scribner, 1998.

Rhodes, James Ford. *History of the United States from the Compromise of 1850.* Vol. 1. New York: Harper and Brothers, 1893.

Robertson, David. *Denmark Vesey.* New York: Knopf, 1999.

Roediger, David. *The Wages of Whiteness.* London: Verso, 1991.

Roots. By Alex Haley. Dir. Marvin Chomsky, David Greene, Gilbert Moses, and John Erman. Perf. LeVar Burton, John Amos, Leslie Uggams, Georg Stanford Brown, and Louis Gossett Jr. 7 episodes. ABC, 23–30 Jan. 1977.

Rowell, Charles H. "An Interview with Octavia E. Butler." *Callaloo* 20.1 (1997): 47–66.

Rushdy, Ashraf. "Daughters Signifyin(g) History: The Example of Toni Morrison's *Beloved.*" *Toni Morrison.* Ed. Linden Peach. London: Macmillan, 1998. 140–53.

———. *Neo-slave Narratives: Studies in the Social Logic of a Literary Form.* New York: Oxford UP, 1999.

Sadler, Lynn Veach. "The Figure of the Black Insurrectionist in Stowe, Bouvé, Bontemps, and Gaither: The Universality of the Need for Freedom." *MAWA Review* 2.1 (June 1986): 21–24.

Sargent, Epes. *Peculiar: A Tale of the Great Transition.* New York: Carleton, 1864.

Schultz, Elizabeth. "And the Children May Know Their Names." *Callaloo* 35 (Spring 1988): 371–77.

Scott, Anne Firor. *The Southern Lady: From Pedestal to Politics, 1830–1930.* Chicago: U of Chicago P, 1970.

See, Carolyn. "Scarlett Fever." *Washington Post* 24 June 2001: BW03.

Shklovsky, Victor. "Art as Technique." 1917. *Modern Criticism and Theory: A Reader.* Ed. David Lodge. London: Longman, 1988. 15–30.

Sidbury, James. *Ploughshares into Swords: Race, Rebellion, and Identity in Gabriel's Virginia, 1730–1810.* New York: Cambridge UP, 1997.

Skaggs, Merrill Maguire. "*Roots:* A New Black Myth." *Southern Quarterly* 17.1 (Fall 1978): 42–50.

Smith, John David. *Slavery, Race, and American History: Historical Conflicts, Trends, and Method, 1866–1953.* Armonk, N.Y.: Sharpe, 1999.

Spillers, Hortense J. "Changing the Letter: The Yokes and Jokes of Discourse; or, Mrs. Stowe, Mr. Reed." *Slavery and the Literary Imagination*. McDowell and Rampersad, eds., 25–61.

Stampp, Kenneth M. *The Peculiar Institution: Slavery in the Ante-Bellum South*. New York: Vintage, 1956.

Starobin, Robert S., ed. *Denmark Vesey: The Slave Conspiracy of 1822*. Englewood Cliffs, N.J: Prentice-Hall, 1970.

Steinberg, Marc. "Inverting History in Octavia Butler's Postmodern Slave Narrative." *African American Review* 38.3 (Fall 2004): 467–76.

Stevens, John D. "The Black Reaction to *Gone with the Wind*." *Journal of Popular Film* 2 (1973): 366–71.

Stone, Albert E. *The Return of Nat Turner: History, Literature, and Cultural Politics in Sixties America*. Athens: U of Georgia P, 1992.

Stowe, Harriet Beecher. *Dred: A Tale of the Great Dismal Swamp*. 1856. Edinburgh: Edinburgh UP, 1999.

———. *Uncle Tom's Cabin*. 1852. London: Penguin, 1986.

Styron, William. *The Confessions of Nat Turner*. New York: Random House, 1967.

———. "More Confessions." *Novel History: Historians and Novelists Confront America's Past (and Each Other)*. Ed. Mark C. Carnes. New York: Simon and Schuster, 2001. 220–25.

———. "Nat Turner Revisited." *American Heritage* 43.6 (October 1992): 64–73.

———. "South: Introduction." *This Quiet Dust, and Other Writings*. New York: Random House, 1982. 3–8.

———. "This Quiet Dust." *This Quiet Dust, and Other Writings*. New York: Random House, 1972. 9–30.

Taylor, Helen. "'The Griot from Tennessee': The Saga of Alex Haley's *Roots*." *Critical Quarterly* 37.2 (Summer 1995): 46–62.

Tompkins, Jane. *Sensational Designs: The Cultural Work of American Fiction, 1790–1860*. New York: Oxford UP, 1985.

Trapasso, Ann E. "Returning to the Site of Violence: The Restructuring of Slavery's Legacy in Sherley Anne Williams's *Dessa Rose*." *Violence, Silence, and Anger: Women's Writing as Transgression*. Ed. Deirdre Lashgari. Charlottesville: UP of Virginia, 1995. 219–30.

Trowbridge, John Townsend. *Cudjo's Cave*. Boston: Lothrop, Lee and Shepard, 1863.

Van Deburg, William. *Slavery and Race in American Popular Culture*. Madison: U of Wisconsin P, 1984.

Walker, Margaret. "How I Wrote *Jubilee*." 1972. *How I Wrote "Jubilee," and Other Essays on Life and Literature*. Ed. Maryemma Graham. New York: Feminist P at the City U of New York, 1990. 50–65.

———. *Jubilee*. 1966. Boston: Mariner, 1999.

Warren, Robert Penn. *Band of Angels*. London: Eyre and Spottiswoode, 1956.

Washington, Elsie B. "Talk with Toni Morrison." *Conversations with Toni Morrison*. Ed. Danille Taylor-Guthrie. Jackson: UP of Mississippi, 1994. 234–38.

Weisenburger, Steven. *Modern Medea: A Family Story of Slavery and Child-Murder from the Old South*. New York: Hill and Wang, 1999.

Welter, Barbara. "The Cult of True Womanhood." *American Quarterly* 18 (1966): 151–74.

Werner, Craig. *A Change Is Gonna Come: Music, Race and the Soul of America*. New York: Plume, 1999.

White, Deborah Gray. *Ar'n't I a Woman? Female Slaves in the Plantation South*. 1985. Rev. ed. New York: Norton, 1999.

Williams, George Washington. *History of the Negro Race in America, 1619–1880*. New York: Putnam, 1882.

Williams, John A. "The Manipulation of History and of Fact: An Ex-Southerner's Apologist Tract for Slavery and the Life of Nat Turner; or, William Styron's Faked Confessions." Clarke 45–49.

Williams, Sherley Anne. *Dessa Rose*. 1986. New York: Quill, 1999.

Winchell, Donna Haisty. "Cries of Outrage: Three Novelists' Use of History." *Mississippi Quarterly*. 9.4 (Fall 1996): 727–41.

Woidat, Caroline M. "Talking Back to Schoolteacher: Morrison's Confrontation with Hawthorne in *Beloved*." *Toni Morrison: Critical and Theoretical Approaches*. Ed. Nancy J. Peterson. Baltimore: Johns Hopkins UP, 1997. 181–200.

Wolper, David L., and Quincy Troupe. *The Inside Story of T.V.'s "Roots."* New York: Warner Books, 1978.

Woodson, Carter G. *The Education of the Negro prior to 1861*. 1919. New York: Arnos, 1968.

———. *The Negro in Our History*. Washington D.C.: Associated Publishers, 1928.

Yardley, Jonathan. Review of *The Known World* by Edward P. Jones. *Washington Post* 21 August 2003. http://www.washingtonpost.com/ac2/wp-dyn?pagename=article &node=&contentId=A29251-2003Aug21 (accessed 18 July 2007).

Yerby, Frank. *A Darkness at Ingraham's Crest*. London: Granada, 1981.

———. *The Foxes of Harrow*. 1946. London: New English Library, 1970.

INDEX